Work, Welfare and Taxation

Work, Welfare and Taxation

A Study of Labour Supply Incentives in the UK

MICHAEL BEENSTOCK
and Associates

City University Business School

London
ALLEN & UNWIN
Boston   Sydney

Allen & Unwin (Publishers) Ltd,
40 Museum Street, London WC1A 1LU, UK

Allen & Unwin (Publishers) Ltd,
Park Lane, Hemel Hempstead, Herts HP2 4TE, UK

Allen & Unwin, Inc.,
8 Winchester Place, Winchester, Mass. 01890, USA

Allen & Unwin (Australia) Ltd,
8 Napier Street, North Sydney, NSW 2060, Australia

First published in 1987

British Library Cataloguing in Publication Data

Beenstock, Michael
    Work, welfare and taxation: a study of
    labour supply incentives in the UK.
1. Incentives in industry – Great
Britain 2. Social security – Great
Britain 3. Taxation – Great Britain
306'.36   HF5549.5.I5
ISBN 0-04-331104-0
ISBN 0-04-331105-9 Pbk

Library of Congress Cataloging in Publication Data

Beenstock, Michael, 1946–
    Work, welfare, and taxation.
Bibliography: p.
Includes index.
1. Labor supply – Great Britain. 2. Social security –
Great Britain. 3. Taxation – Great Britain. I. Title.
II. Title: Labour supply incentives in the UK.
HD5765.A6B43 1986   331.12'5'0941   86-7407
ISBN 0-04-331104-0 (alk. paper)
ISBN 0-04-331105-9 (pbk.: alk. paper)

Set in 10 on 12 point Garamond by Columns, Caversham, Reading and
printed in Great Britain by Billing and Sons, London and Worcester

Contents

vii

Preface

The contents of this book form part of a research programme that I have been directing at the City University Business School since 1981. The programme is concerned with the Economics of the Welfare State and in this volume we focus our attention upon the way in which the tax system and the system of welfare benefits affect labour supply incentives. In another volume, *Insurance for Unemployment*, Valerie Brasse and I consider how unemployment insurance might be funded as insurance proper, that is, on the same basis as property insurance or funded pensions. Other publications in the series have related to pensions.

The various chapters in the book have been authored as indicated but it will become apparent that this is not an edited collection of papers concerned with a similar theme. Instead each chapter is related and forms part of a common research plan which I have devised. In this respect I assume general responsibility for the overall contents but not the details, and specific responsibility for the chapters with which I am directly associated.

In Chapter 1 I set out the mechanics of household budget lines which describe the relationship between hours worked and net disposable income after all taxes and welfare benefits have been taken into consideration. These budget lines or constraints embody the set of labour supply incentives because rational individuals are likely to trade off the amount of work they do against net disposable income in deciding how much to work or whether they want to work at all.

I argue that in addition to its traditional application to short-term labour supply decisions the budget line concept may be extended to dynamic labour supply decisions, for example, the amount of labour supplied over a tax year, or the amount supplied over the life cycle. The latter produces a theoretical basis for analysing retirement decisions which forms an integral part of the labour supply decision.

Chapter 1 sets the scene for the remaining chapters. In Chapter 2 Don Egginton illustrates how the tax-benefit system influences household budget lines for a broad category of households. While his analysis refers to 1983 his results are symptomatic and typical of present arrangements. He begins by considering single people and then goes on to consider the budget lines of married people and single parent families. By changing assumptions about wage rates, housing costs, tenure type and the number of children he illustrates the complex interactions between the tax system and the broad range of welfare benefits that currently exist. This is a lengthy and at times heavy-going chapter which reflects the intricacy of the subject matter and the complexity of the system.

Whereas Chapter 2 examines the system in depth as it existed in the early 1980s, in Chapter 3 Don Egginton takes a broader historical view on how budget lines have evolved during the postwar period. He also includes data on replacement ratios dating back to 1920. This longitudinal study is designed to place the contemporary analysis, which forms our primary material, into historical perspective.

Chapter 4 is our first empirical exercise, in which Don Egginton examines the 1978 and 1981 Family Expenditure Surveys to see if labour supply incentives at the household level actually influence labour supply decisions. We wish to thank the ESRC Archive at the University of Essex for providing us with the FES tapes and the Department of Employment for granting permission to use them. Both in respect of hours worked and in respect of whether or not to work at all there seemed to be no obvious support for the thesis that labour supply incentives, as we have measured them, influence household labour supply decisions.

In Chapter 5 Alan Dalziel and I, using the same data but applying econometric techniques, examined the issue in greater detail. Using linear probability and logit analyses we could only find weak support for the thesis that the unemployed are influenced by labour supply disincentives. Accordingly our results are consistent with other microeconometric investigations of labour supply in the UK which suggest that unemployment is not greatly influenced by the tax-benefit system.

The labour supply incentives facing pensioners in the UK are investigated by Peter Warburton in Chapter 6. There are two aspects to this. First, when should one retire? Secondly, how much work, if any, should one wish to do during retirement? Answers to these questions are not independent. This chapter describes static and dynamic budget lines facing pensioners.

For the most part the book is descriptive rather than prescriptive. We seek to describe labour supply incentives as they exist as well as their effects without putting forward, here, any proposals of our own for reforming the tax-benefit system. However, in Chapter 7 Michael Parker and I explain the budget line implications and associated labour supply incentives of the new social security system advocated by the government in June 1985. Our approach parallels that in Chapter 2. We consider various cases to illustrate the workings of the new system which we compare and contrast with the present system.

Finally, in Chapter 8 I bring together the material as a whole.

The research programme as a whole has been funded by the Institute for Economic Affairs. My colleagues and I would particularly like to thank Lord Harris and Arthur Seldon for their support in this venture.

Michael Beenstock
January 1986

1

Budget Lines and Labour Supply Incentives

Michael Beenstock

I
Introduction

Main Objectives

The 1980s have witnessed a renewed interest in the economics of social security and work incentives. In the UK, for example, policy recommendations have been coming thick and fast and the government in 1984 launched a series of major reviews of social security arrangements culminating in its Green Paper published in June 1985. Not since Beveridge's time has the issue attracted so much attention. Within weeks of each other separate proposals for reform have been proposed by Atkinson (1984), Dilnot, Kay and Morris (1984) and Minford (1984). These have been usefully reviewed by Parker (1984).

In this book we try to step back from the frontiers of the policy debate with two major objectives in mind. First, we seek to help the uninitiated understand what the whole problem is about in the first place. To achieve this we show in detail how various taxes and benefits affect work incentives in the UK. In doing so, we focus on the concept of the *budget line* which shows the relationship between net income and effort. The concept of the budget line is introduced in most texts on employment. However, this is usually done in a simplified way. At the other end of the spectrum proponents of reform have calculated complex budget lines which are often difficult to understand. What seems to be missing is a text which explains how complex budget lines are constructed from their elementary counterparts. We believe that such a text will be useful to economists, social administrators and policy makers.

We therefore try to identify the effects of divers taxes and social security benefits upon budget lines. In this chapter we set out the various building blocks for constructing budget lines and we hope that by the time we finish the reader will be familiar with the ways in which the taxes and benefits listed in Table 1.1 affect budget lines and thus work incentives.

While our first objective is essentially pedagogic and descriptive our second main objective is more analytical and difficult. The premises of most reformists are that

(1) the interplay of taxes and benefits has eroded work incentives in the UK, and

(2) these disincentives have reduced the amount of effort supplied by the UK workforce.

If (1) were true but (2) were false attitudes to reform might be different. It is therefore important to ask whether the budget lines and work incentives facing individual families actually affect work decisions. Macroeconomic evidence adduced, for example, by Minford *et al.* (1983), suggests that the tax-benefit system has indeed adversely affected labour supply in the UK. However, this is contested, for example, by Layard and Nickell (1985). Our concern is therefore to look at the microeconomic evidence – that is, at the level of the individual or family rather than across

Table 1.1 Types of Taxes and Benefits

Taxes	*Social security benefits*
Tax thresholds	Supplementary Benefit
Standard rate of tax	Unemployment Benefit
National Insurance contributions	Child Benefit
	Housing Benefit
	Rate Relief
	Family Income Supplement
	Pensions

the economy as a whole. So our second objective is to see if the tax-benefit system actually influences the amount of effort supplied by individuals.

The Chapters Ahead

As stated, the remainder of this chapter sets out the conceptual building blocks that are used in constructing realistic budget lines. An added complication arises in the case of people who are contemplating retirement: should they carry on working or should they retire now? We therefore consider the building blocks for this case too.

In Chapter 2 we apply the concepts set out in Chapter 1 and construct budget lines for various family types. For a given tax-benefit system we show how budget lines are sensitive to wage rates, housing costs, number of children, and so on. Thus, incentives may vary independently of the tax-benefit system. Numerous family cases are examined and we hope that the diversity of choice will give the reader some idea of how incentives vary across families. This exercise is carried out in terms of the tax-benefit system as of 1983.

In Chapter 3 we consider how budget lines have evolved since the early 1960s. The object of this exercise is to see how changes in taxes and benefits over time have jointly influenced work incentives. Ideally, we wanted to extend the analysis further back in time but this was impossible to do comprehensively because the necessary information could not be accurately assembled. Indeed, even for the recent past such as the 1960s it is difficult to infer how Housing Benefits were administered. To avoid the proliferation of cases our historical analysis is illustrated with respect to a married couple with 2 children.

In Chapter 4 we begin the empirical analysis related to our second main objective. From Chapter 2 we already know which family types face greater work disincentives. Is it the case therefore that these families are more work-shy? Our data source is the 1978 Family Expenditure Survey (FES) which provides the necessary information for constructing household budget lines and also reports the work status of the individuals in the approximately 7,000 households surveyed. We look at the distributions of unemployment and hours worked for different household types in order to ascertain the answer to the work-shy question. This overview of the data does not suggest any obvious affirmative answers, that is, it is not self-evident that disincentives induce work-shy behaviour.

In Chapter 5 we attempt to answer the same question but with more refined statistical techniques. We develop a methodology for parameterizing budget lines and for each family we test various hypotheses of labour supply dependence upon budget lines. Here too, the results do not support the work-shy hypothesis either with respect to the 1978 FES or the 1981 FES.

Do these negative results imply that labour market incentives do not matter? We do not think this is the appropriate conclusion primarily because our data base did not appear as reliable as we had hoped. There were too many inconsistencies in the data for comfort. For example, there were unemployed individuals who were reportedly consuming well enough but who were not receiving any income whatsoever! Were they in the 'black economy' or were they holding back information? We shall never know. In many other cases too, it was difficult to understand how people were making ends meet. Thus, our negative results may simply reflect data deficiencies.

This is a pity because affirmative results could have been used to help design a more efficient tax-benefit system. Had we successfully estimated a model of household labour supply we could have used it to liberate people from the ravages of the poverty trap. Proposals for dealing with the poverty trap usually turn out to be very expensive to the Exchequer. Alternatively, if the reforms are to be revenue neutral they usually imply either low zero income support levels or high marginal tax rates for people on relatively low incomes, see, for example, Barr (1975). However, these proposals usually make no allowance for the very disincentive effects that they are designed to remedy and ignore the beneficial effects to the Exchequer that would be implied if people were liberated from poverty. For example, if it were the case that the 3.2 million or so unemployed were only in this state because of the poverty trap, the abolition of the poverty trap would turn 3.2 million people into contributors to the Exchequer from public expenditure burdens. These dynamic benefits are what reform is all about yet they are usually assumed to be zero. This is like assuming there is no problem in the first place.

Whereas the study as a whole is concerned with incentives to work, in Chapter 6 we digress slightly by considering retirement incentives. Retirement decisions and labour supply decisions have much in common and so we think our digression is relevant. We examine the effects of the basic state pension scheme in which the individual is rewarded for postponing retirement to between the ages of 65 and 70. We also consider occupational pension arrangements based on final salary principles. In both cases the individual has to calculate the costs and benefits of postponing retirement and we try to expose the trade-offs implied by such decisions.

In Chapter 7 we consider the proposed reforms of the UK social security system that were published in the Green Paper in June 1985. To some degree these reforms fundamentally change the nature of the social security system and we thought it might be useful to indicate how budget lines and labour supply incentives are likely to be affected. We also compare and contrast the proposed system with the existing system.

Finally, in Chapter 8, the main findings of our research are brought together and conclusions recorded.

II
Budget Line Theory

The Basic Model

The simplest of budget lines is illustrated in Fig. 1.1, where the vertical axis measures income and the horizontal axis measures leisure time. If the individual does no work at all he devotes all his time to leisure which on Fig. 1.1 is represented by the distance *OA*. If the unit of time is a day then *OA* equals 24 hours. If instead he only devotes *OQ* of the day (or time period) to leisure he must be devoting *QA* of the day to work.

In Fig. 1.1 we assume that the individual only gains income through work and that he pays no taxes and receives no state benefits. If he devotes all his time to leisure his income must be zero. Thus, at *A* income is zero. If he spends *AQ* of his time at work his income is equal to *OY*, and if he spends all his time at work (*AO*) his income will be *OB*. The schedule *AB* tells us the

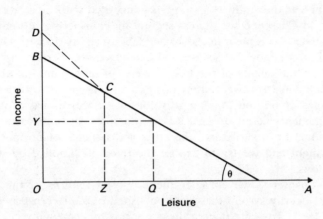

Fig. 1.1 The budget line

relationship between effort and income faced by the individual and is henceforth referred to as the *budget line*.

The slope of the budget line (θ) reflects the individual's wage rate. People on higher rates of pay will have steeper budget lines (i.e. θ will be larger) because their income must be higher for a given amount of time spent at work. If wage rates are constant the budget line must be linear as in the case of *AB*. If instead the individual begins to earn overtime rates after, say, he has worked for *AZ* of time the budget line will no longer be linear and will be kinked at *C*. In this case the budget line will be *ACD*, that is, the marginal return to effort supplied increases after *C*.

Taxation

Let us return to the linear budget line in Fig. 1.1 and consider what happens when we allow for the existence of direct taxation. We must take account of both tax allowances and marginal rates of tax. The government allows us to earn a certain amount (*OS* on Fig. 1.2) without paying any tax at all. This tax allowance depends upon marital status. Thus, along the *AT* segment of *AB* no taxes are paid and gross and net income after tax are the same. If the individual spends more than *AQ* of his time at work his income will exceed the tax allowance and his taxable income is defined as his actual income minus his allowances. The taxable income is

6

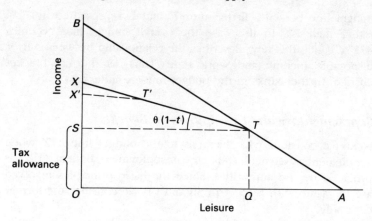

Fig. 1.2 Taxation and the budget line

taxed at the marginal rate of tax (t). For example, if the rate of income tax is 30% the individual retains 70p of every extra pound earned above his allowances and gives the balance of 30p to the Inland Revenue.

This implies that the budget line beyond T is no longer represented by TB since this refers to gross income whereas the individual is concerned with his net income. In fact, the budget line over this range becomes TX since the vertical distance between TB and TX is paid in tax. For example, if the individual spends all his time at work his gross income is OB, he pays XB in direct taxes, so his net income is OX. Therefore, $XB/SB = t$.

As long as the tax rate does not vary with income the segment TX will be linear and its slope will be equal to $(1-t)$. Therefore, if the tax rate is higher TX will be flatter because for a given extra amount of effort the individual's net income rises more slowly. On this basis, his total budget line is represented by ATX rather than AB, the kink at T reflecting the point where tax allowances are used up. For people on higher rates of pay this kink will be further to the right since AB is steeper. The opposite will apply for people on lower rates of pay.

In practice, tax rates are not constant. Richer people face higher tax rates because the tax system is progressive. For example, on Fig. 1.2 we assume that at T' the marginal rate of tax is raised. Since more marginal income is now lost in taxes the

7

budget line becomes flatter after T' and is represented by $T'X'$ rather than TX. In this case the overall budget line becomes $ATT'X'$ since this now describes the relationship between net or disposable income and work time. Thus, as the tax bracket changes further kinks in the budget line are induced.

Supplementary and Unemployment Benefits

Next we consider what happens to the budget line ATX when Supplementary Benefit (SB) or Unemployment Benefit (UB) is provided by the authorities. Since the basic principles involved are the same with respect to SB and UB we consider the former case only.

If a person is in receipt of no income at all he and his family receive SB. The level of SB depends on marital status, number of children and housing costs. It also depends upon whether the claimant has been receiving SB for more than a year and whether he is not seeking employment. In the latter case the scale rates are higher according to long-term SB rates. On Fig. 1.3 the level of SB is represented by AH, that is, if the individual does no work at all and receives no income he is provided with AH of benefits. Notice that the level of SB is assumed to be higher than the tax allowance

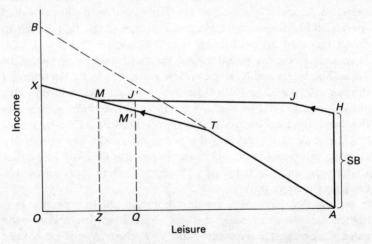

Fig. 1.3 Supplementary Benefit and the budget line

as is fairly typical. However, taxation does not matter here because SB is related to after-tax income. This is because the principle of SB is to provide a basic living standard irrespective of tax deductions, costs of getting to work, and so on. The individual is also allowed to earn a certain small amount (the disregard) without forgoing any SB. On Fig. 1.3 this is represented by the segment *HJ*. Since the disregard is calculated after tax and since Fig. 1.3 assumes that SB exceeds the tax allowance the slope of *HJ* must equal $(1-t)$, that is, *HJ* and *TX* are parallel. If instead *AH* were less than the tax allowance the slope of *HJ* would be the same as the slope of *AT*.

Once the disregards are used up SB is reduced penny for penny with *net* income. This implies that at the given rates of pay that have been assumed the individual can spend more time at work without increasing his net income. Thus, if he spends *AZ* of his time at work his net income is *ZM* which is equal to the SB level plus the disregard. So if he works more than *AZ* he no longer receives SB. Therefore, the next segment of his budget line is *JM* which is perfectly flat. Once he is no longer in receipt of SB his budget line reverts to what is left of *ATX*, that is, *MX*. In this way his overall budget line has become *AHJMX* from *ATX*.

The reader may check that the length of *JM* rises with the level of SB and the rate of tax but falls with the level of tax allowances and the wage rate. As we shall see, *JM* is a major adverse factor in labour supply incentives.

SB cannot be claimed by people in full-time work, which is defined as exceeding 29 hours per week. Therefore, the discussion so far has assumed that *AZ* is less than 29 hours a week. What happens if instead *AQ* is 29 hours per week? In this case only *JJ'* of *JM* is applicable since SB can only be received up to *AQ* of work time. Thereafter, the only source of income is what he earns himself after tax which is represented by *MX*. Thus, he makes himself worse off by working any amount of time between *Q* and *Z*. Taking these factors into consideration his budget line assumes the rather grotesque form of *AHJJ'M'X*. This situation is more likely to occur with families which have high SB entitlements and low rates of pay.

Family Income Supplement (FIS)

FIS is designed to support families *with children* where the head of household works more than 29 hours per week. Therefore FIS takes over where SB leaves off. If the family has no children then Fig. 1.3 applies. In this section we consider how FIS affects the budget line in Fig. 1.3.

Whereas SB is calculated on a net income basis, FIS is calculated on a gross income basis, although Housing Benefit (see below) is netted out. The level of FIS depends on the number of children and claimants receive half the difference between the prescribed income levels and their gross incomes. For example, if the prescribed income level is £90 per week and the claimant's gross income is £70 per week, the weekly FIS payment will be £10. This amount tends to zero as gross income rises to £90 per week. The effects of this are illustrated on Fig. 1.4 where $AHJJ'M'X$ and ATB replicate their counterparts in Fig. 1.3. The prescribed income level according to FIS is represented by OK.

If the individual works more than AN his gross income will be greater than OK and he will not be entitled to FIS. If he only works AQ his gross income is QF which is less than the prescribed income and so his FIS entitlement is $0.5 (OK - QF) = FD$. The shaded area represents the FIS benefit received; it is at a maximum at AQ and it goes to zero as AN of time is worked. On this basis

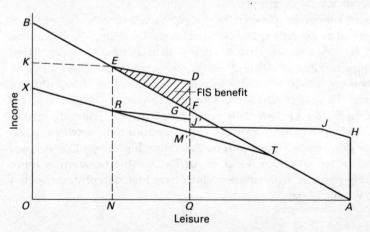

Fig. 1.4 Family Income Supplement and the budget line

10

the gross income schedule is *AFDEB* rather than *AB*. This is because, unlike SB, FIS counts as gross income.

On Fig. 1.4 we assume that the net income associated with the gross income of *QD* is equal to *QG*. This implies that as the family comes off SB its net income jumps upwards from *QJ'*. This need not be the case and sometimes the opposite can occur, that is, *G* lies below *J'* rather than above it. Since the tax rate is constant and the withdrawal rate of FIS is also constant the segment of the budget line between *Q* and *N* must be linear, which implies that it is equal to *GR*. On this basis the overall budget line becomes *AHJJ'GRX*, and FIS has the effect of inducing a bulge in the budget line over the work time range *QN*.

Child Benefit

Child Benefit is received by all families according to the number of children they have. It is provided irrespective of income and it is not subject to tax. It is excluded from FIS but not from SB. This is because SB already reflects the number of children in the family and because the implied Child Benefit rate in SB is more generous than the basic Child Benefit rate.

The effects of Child Benefit on the budget line are illustrated on Fig. 1.5 where *AHJJ'GRX* replicates its counterpart from Fig. 1.4. The level of Child Benefit is represented by *XX'* and the child allowance in SB is represented by *HH'>XX'*.

To calculate the new budget line we must add *XX'* to *GRX* and

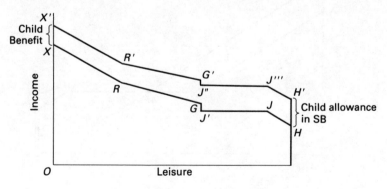

Fig. 1.5 Child Benefit and the budget line

11

HH' to $AHJJ'$. The net effect of this is to generate $AH'J''J'G'R'X'$. Notice how the gap GJ' has been narrowed to $G'J''$.

Raising Child Benefit simply raises $G'R'X'$ and increases $G'J''$. However, for families not entitled to FIS the effects are rather different as may be seen in Fig. 1.6 where $AH'J''MX'$ is the budget line, reflecting the consideration in Fig. 1.5, apart, of course, from FIS. If Child Benefit is raised by $X'X''$ the new budget line becomes $AH'J'''M'X'$. The horizontal element has shortened by MM' implying that people find it pays to come off SB at fewer hours of work.

Housing Benefit (HB)

Housing Benefit consists of rate relief and rent rebates or allowances. HB is not available for people on SB because the latter already includes a housing allowance. In calculating HB each family is ascribed a Needs Allowance which depends on marital status and the number of children. If gross income (including Child Benefit and FIS) minus a disregard (currently £17 per week) is equal to the Needs Allowance, HB equals 60% of rent and rates. If eligible gross income is greater than the Needs Allowance, HB is reduced on a proportionate basis. The rate of tapering in the latter case is slightly lower than the rate of expansion in the former. Also, these effects are more pronounced for rent than for rates.

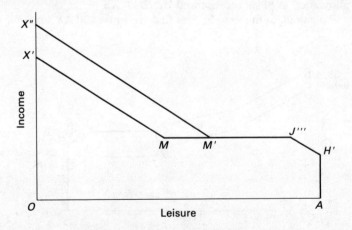

Fig. 1.6   Effects of raising Child Benefit

12

The effects of HB are illustrated on Fig. 1.7 where *AB* is the underlying gross income relationship as before, that is, abstracting for the moment from the complications of FIS and CB. The Needs Allowance is indicated by the broken line and *B'L* is the eligible gross income schedule where *BB'* is the disregard. At *E* eligible gross income is equal to the Needs Allowance and the HB associated with this is NP. The shaded area indicates the amount of HB paid. It tapers to zero as gross income exceeds the Needs Allowance and it rises as gross income falls below the Needs Allowance. Adding HB to gross income induces a new gross income schedule which is AB plus the shaded area. Since HB is subject to tax, the new budget line is *AHJJ'SS'RWX*. The segments *AHJJ'S* and *WX* are unchanged. The kink at *S* reflects the commencement of HB, the kink at *R* reflects the switch to tapering and the kink at *W* reflects the termination of HB. The overall effect of HB is to both augment and flatten the budget line beyond *Q* in place of *AHJJ'SWX*.

Overview

We hope our piecemeal approach to the construction of budget lines has been helpful. In the next chapter, we examine the budget lines for specific families and in doing so consider all the

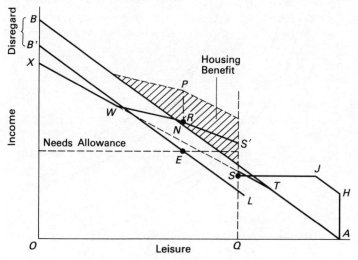

Fig. 1.7 Housing Benefit and budget line

taxes and benefits simultaneously. The interplay of all these benefits and taxes is notoriously complicated and one cannot help feeling that if a claimant is intelligent enough to see his way through all the rules and regulations he should at the very least be gainfully employed as an international tax consultant or something equally labyrinthine! In the meanwhile, the building blocks contained in Figs. 1.1 to 1.7 will help the reader to understand the budget line cases discussed in the next chapter.

III
Labour Supply

Utility Analysis

In this section we consider the implications of budget lines for labour supply decisions. The conventional premiss, for example, Brown (1980), is that individuals gain utility from income but disutility from work (utility from leisure) as indicated on Fig. 1.8. The preference map may be influenced by various parameters. If for example there are many children in the family the marginal utility of income is likely to be higher than otherwise because

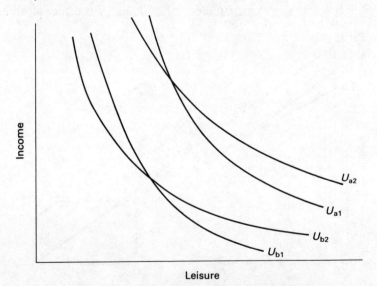

Fig. 1.8 Trade-off between income and leisure

14

there are more mouths to feed. This will tend to flatten the trade-off between income and leisure as in case A on Fig. 1.8. Alternatively, if older people attach higher premiums to leisure the trade-off will steepen as in case B. Therefore the underlying utility function is likely to depend on age, the number of children, and so on.

The budget lines describe the set of choices between income and leisure that decision units face. The indifference curves describe the preferences of units in terms of income and leisure. We put the two together in Fig. 1.9, where the budget line is represented by *AHJX* and the indifference maps refer to cases A and B of Fig. 1.8. In case A utility is maximized at *x* and the individual wishes to supply *AZ* of his time in the labour market. In case B utility is maximized at *H* and the individual does not wish to work at all; he prefers unemployment. In the nature of things the optimal solution cannot be along *HJ*; it must either be at *H* or along *JX*. This implies that the greater is *HJ* the larger will be the number of people who prefer to be unemployed.

So far we have assumed that labour supply is freely determined and that people can choose how long they work. If, however, individual A is required to work 'full-time' his level of utility will decline from U_{a1} at *x* to U_{a2} at *y*. Faced with such a constraint on his behaviour, A will prefer to be unemployed since he is better off at *H* than at *y*. We may deduce from this that the restriction of choice to full-time work tends to raise the incidence of 'voluntary'

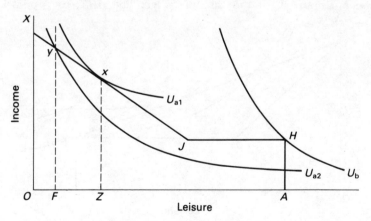

Fig. 1.9 The labour supply decision

unemployment. A further implication of Fig. 1.9 is that as the slope of *JX* steepens the incidence of unemployment is likely to decline – people who are indifferent between work and unemployment will be tempted out of unemployment if *JX* steepens.

Thus, the incidence of unemployment rises as

(1) *AH* or the level of Supplementary Benefit rises,
(2) the horizontal section of the budget line *HJ* increases,
(3) the marginal post-tax wage rate in work falls, i.e., as the slope of *JX* falls, and as
(4) restrictions on the choice of work increase.

Replacement Ratios

Fig. 1.9 reminds us that the incidence of unemployment, in so far as it is influenced by the tax-benefit system, depends upon all the parameters of the budget line and not simply the replacement ratio. The latter is defined as the ratio of net income out of work relative to net income in work. If by the latter we mean 'full-time' work, the replacement ratio in Fig. 1.9 is equal to *AH/Fy*. But it is clearly possible for given replacement ratios to be associated with different unemployment incidences. This is illustrated in Fig. 1.10, where two budget lines are represented, *AHX* and *AHJX*. Since *AO* represents 'full-time' employment, the replacement ratios of both budget lines are identically equal to *AH/OX*. In the case of budget line *AHJX*, utility is maximized at *H* and the individual prefers to be unemployed. In the case of budget line *AHX*, the optimal

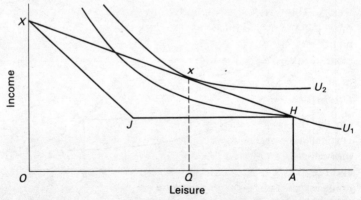

Fig. 1.10 Labour supply ambiguity and the replacement ratio

16

solution is at x and the individual wishes to supply AQ of effort.

Further complications arise when employment is restricted to 'full-time' work. Nevertheless, Fig. 1.10 makes the minimal case against exclusive reliance on replacement ratios as an index of labour supply incentives. Nevertheless, this has become a familiar preoccupation, for example, Nickell (1979) and Atkinson *et al.* (1982).

IV
Dynamic Analysis

Thus far we have been rather vague about our time dimensions. Is the unit of time days, years or what? The answer would not really matter if the tax and benefit assessment period was only a day in length, or if individuals matched their optimization horizons with the assessment periods. In practice, the tax period is a fiscal year in length, while benefits are reviewed at different periods. For example, tax allowances refer to the fiscal year as a whole, therefore a person contemplating employment in, say, January, is likely to face a tax-free budget line. Maybe the optimal decision is only to work part of the fiscal year with alternating periods of employment and unemployment.

Similarly, various benefits are only assessed at fairly long time intervals. For example, FIS benefits are assessed on the basis of average income during the previous 5 weeks (or 2 months if claimants are paid monthly) and are not reassessed for another 52 weeks. This creates the technical opportunity of impoverishing oneself for 5 weeks in order to claim FIS and then to go on to higher pay for the next 47 weeks – and so on. In this section we examine these dynamic incentive structures.

Unemployment

On Fig. 1.11 the distance OA measures one fiscal year, while the vertical axis measures income over the same fiscal year. If the individual is employed for the entire year he spends AO at work and receives a gross wage income of OB. Provided his wage rate is constant, the schedule AB tells us what his wage income would be if he only worked part of the year. The wage rate is reflected by θ;

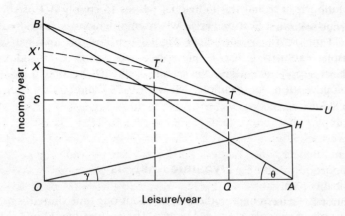

Fig. 1.11 Budget lines over the fiscal year

the greater the wage rate, the higher is θ and the steeper is the *AB* schedule.

If the individual is unemployed for the whole year, that is, if *OA* of his time is spent out of work, we assume that his Unemployment Benefit amounts to *AH*. If the Unemployment Benefit rate is constant, we may read off the *OH* schedule the amount of Unemployment Benefit he receives if he is unemployed for only part of the year. The Unemployment Benefit rate is represented by γ; the higher is γ, the greater is the Unemployment Benefit rate and the steeper is the *OH* schedule.

To find out the individual's gross income over the fiscal year, it is necessary to sum the *OH* and *AB* schedules which give rise to the *HB* schedule. This schedule tells us the gross income from wages and Unemployment Benefit for different proportions of the year spent in unemployment. As in Fig. 1.2, *OS* represents the tax threshold so that, if *AQ* of the year is spent in employment, the individual is not liable to tax. Thereafter, the individual is liable to tax and the net budget line falls below the gross budget line as in Fig. 1.2. Thus, *BX* is the tax liability if the individual spends the entire year in employment. His overall net budget line is therefore *AHTX*.

The outward kink in the budget line at *T* creates an artificial incentive to spend *OQ* of the year unemployed. This is because indifference curves between income and leisure as represented by

18

U (see Fig. 1.8) will have an excessive tendency to generate corner solutions at T. Of course, this will not apply to everybody, but Fig. 1.11 illustrates how the incentive comes about. Such people will use up their tax allowances while spending the balance of the year unemployed. When the next fiscal year begins, they go back to work and repeat the merry-go-round; and so on. No doubt workers take into consideration other factors too, for example, the implications for their work record and so on. Nevertheless, the analysis implies that lower rates of Unemployment Benefit and higher tax thresholds would reduce the proportion of the fiscal year spent in unemployment. It is most probably partly to offset this incentive that Unemployment Benefit cannot be claimed for the first 4 weeks of unemployment.

In Fig. 1.11 it is assumed that Unemployment Benefit is taxable. This accords with the practice established in 1982. If Unemployment Benefit is not liable to tax, the budget line becomes $AHTX'$, that is, the kink moves in a north-westerly direction. The effect of this on unemployment incentives is ambiguous – the income effect (represented by XX') is likely to raise unemployment incentives but the substitution effect is likely to have the opposite effect.

Playing FIS

The level of FIS received by a family is equal to half the difference between the prescribed income level ($\bar{W}$) and the assessment income (W). The latter is assessed over a 5-week period. Thus,

$$FIS = 0.5(\bar{W}-W)$$

At the beginning of this 5-week period, the present value of these benefits is equal to

$$0.5(\bar{W}-W)\delta_1$$

where

$$\delta_1 = \sum_{i=5}^{57} \left(\frac{1}{1+r} \right)^i$$

and r is the rate of interest. If W^* is the normal income of the

19

family, the present value of the income loss from playing the FIS system is

$$(W^* - W)\,\delta_2$$

where

$$\delta_2 = \sum_{i=0}^{4}\left(\frac{1}{1+r}\right)^i$$

Therefore, the net gain from playing FIS is

$$V = 0.5(\bar{W} - W)\delta_1 - (W^* - W)\delta_2$$

Does it pay to lower income below W^* for the 5-week period, and if so, by how much? The problem is therefore to maximize V with respect to W. The nature of the solution may be illustrated by an example. Take the case of a family which is currently earning £140 per week and whose prescribed income is £90, that is, W^* = 140 and $\bar{W}$ = 90, i.e. it pays the family to become totally impoverished over the 5-week assessment period and for every £1 that W falls V rises by £21.04. It is plain that only the very well-off could not afford to play FIS, that is, where

$$W^* = 0.5W\delta_1/\delta_2 = \text{£468.69 per week.}$$

Thus, for most of us it is worth playing FIS but no doubt we have other considerations in mind apart from cash at any price. Nevertheless, the analysis suggests that there is an incentive to go on to low pay for short spells.

V
Pensioners

The tax treatment of pensioners is more generous in that the age allowance gives them a higher tax threshold. Occupational pension income is taxed alongside other income; however, the state pension is withdrawn if other income exceeds a certain limit. How, therefore, do work incentives differ between pensioners and non-pensioners? It is rather odd that incentives should depend arbitrarily upon age and below we explore the basic differences between pensioners' and non-pensioners' budget lines.

A related matter concerns the incentive to become a pensioner in the first place. In other words, when is it optimal for an individual to retire? The basic issue here is that the postponement of retirement can lead to a higher pension in due course both under the state scheme and an occupational pension scheme. On the other hand, if one postpones too long, retirement may be cut short by death if indeed one lives that long in the first place. There is an inevitable trade-off between financial security in retirement and the amount of time enjoyed in retirement.

Incentives in Retirement

We consider first the relative incentives facing pensioners and non-pensioners. On Fig. 1.12 *AB* reflects the basic wage rate as in Fig. 1.1 while *OS* is the tax allowance for non-pensioners and *OS'* is the more generous tax allowance for pensioners. *AH* is the basic income support level for non-pensioners, hence the non-pensioners' budget line is *AHJX*. This follows the basic analysis already discussed in relation to Fig. 1.3.

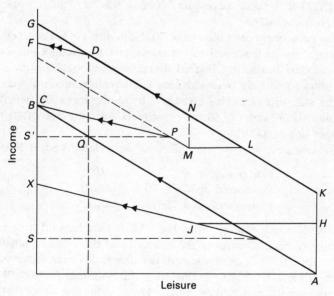

Fig. 1.12 Age and the budget line

21

The pension is assumed to be *AK*. If income from employment were not subject to tax and if pension benefits were not affected by earnings the pensioners' budget line would be *AKG*. However, none of these conditions apply, although for pensioners over the age of 70 the state pension is not affected by earnings. For state pensioners aged 65–70 there is an earnings disregard so that they can earn up to a certain amount without affecting their pension. On Fig. 1.12 this is represented by the segment *KL* which has the same slope as *AB*. After this disregard has been exhausted the state pension is then reduced by 50p for each pound earned. Since this applies over a small income range, we ignore it in Fig. 1.12 and proceed directly to the next segment. Along this segment the pension is reduced by one pound for every pound earned. This characteristic gives rise to a horizontal segment in the budget line which is represented by *LM*. The distance *LM* is determined by the fact that *MN* = *AK*, that is, earnings net of the disregard are equal to the pension; therefore at *M* the pension is zero. Since *M* is below the pensioners' tax threshold subsequent earnings are not subject to tax. However, at *P* this threshold is reached and tax is paid. This is reflected in the segment *PC* which has the same slope as *TX*. The overall pensioners' (aged 65–70) budget line is therefore *AKLMPC*.

For pensioners over the age of 70 the pension is not affected by earnings, nor is it subject to tax. Thus, at *L* the budget line does not become horizontal. Instead it carries on along *KG* until at *D* tax allowances have been exhausted. Thereafter, income is taxed at the standard rate. This gives rise to the segment *DF* which is parallel to *PC* and *TX*. So for pensioners over the age of 70 the budget line is *AKDF*.

In summary, we have the following age-related budget lines:

Non-pensioners	*AHJX*
Pensioners aged 65–70	*AKLMPC*
Pensioners aged 70+	*AKDF*

A complication omitted from Fig. 1.12 is that beyond a certain income the age allowances are reduced and these are eliminated. Once they have been eliminated, tax thresholds have fallen back to their basic level. This implies that the segments *PC* and *DF* in reality contain two further convex kinks – the first occurs when the age allowance is reduced and the second occurs when it has been eliminated completely. The effect of these kinks is to flatten the budget line and thus to erode labour supply incentives.

Incentives to Retirement

As discussed in more detail in Chapter 6 state pensioners can increase their pension by postponing retirement up to the age of 70. Occupational pensioners face similar incentives because their pension depends on the number of years of service. Consider the case of a 65-year-old man with a life expectancy of 78 years. On Fig. 1.13 we plot the present values of his earnings from work and his pension if he retires at different ages. If he retires now (i.e. aged 65) the present value of his pension is given by A while the present value of his earnings (assuming for simplicity that he does not work) is zero. If instead he works until he dies, i.e. until 78, the present value of his pension is zero while the present value of his earnings is represented by B.

If he retires between the ages of 65 and 78, the present value of his earnings may be read off schedule c. Note that the discount factor implies that c is concave to the horizontal. If the pension does not vary with the age of retirement, the present value of the pension may be read off schedule a. The discount factor implies that this schedule is convex to the horizontal. If he delays

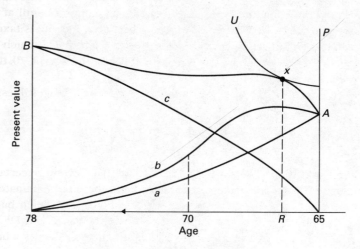

Fig. 1.13 The retirement decision

retirement we assume that up to the age of 70 his pension is raised. This gives rise to schedule *b* which may be non-monotonic depending upon by how much pensions are escalated. Adding together schedules *b* and *c* gives rise to the overall dynamic budget line *AB*. The bulge in this schedule in the vicinity of *x* reflects the escalation of pensions through postponement of retirement.

As discussed at greater length in Chapter 6 we may draw indifference curves between present values on the one hand and retirement age on the other. On Fig. 1.13 *U* is such an indifference schedule. It reflects the fact that utility varies directly with time spent in retirement. However, the indifference schedules become steeper with age and approaching death. Somebody near to death will have a high preference for leisure over income.

On Fig. 1.13 utility maximization suggests that the individual will retire when he is 65+*R* years old. However, for many of us there is a corner solution at *A* and so we retire when we are 65. An interesting complication arises from the fact that as we get older life expectancy changes so that re-optimizing at the age of 66 will not necessarily imply that it is best to retire at 65+*R* years. This is considered further in Chapter 6.

2

Case Studies of Labour Supply Incentives and Budget Lines

Don M. Egginton

In this chapter we describe the components of the tax and social security system which we have modelled in order to estimate budget constraints of the type oulined in Chapter 1. In the second section of this chapter we analyse the budget constraints under varying assumptions about wage rates, family composition, housing costs, housing tenure and housing cost distribution. This section has two aims: first to demonstrate how the various components of the social security system influence an individual's budget constraint, and secondly, to build up a general knowledge about the shape of the budget constraints which will be used in Chapter 4 to analyse the distribution of hours worked in the 1978 and 1981 Family Expenditure Surveys, and for the econometric analysis of participation behaviour presented in Chapter 5.

Throughout this chapter the budget constraints relate to the year from November 1982. Subsequent changes in the social security system have had little effect on the general shape of the budget constraints up to the time of writing (July 1985), although the level of disposable income will have been changed by successive upratings.

I
Modelling the Social Security
and Tax Systems

Past Efforts

The model of the social security and tax systems is simply a set of equations and identities which are then used to calculate the entitlement and amount of benefit due, given a set of assumptions for wage rates and so on. The model used in this book is by no means the first model of the social security and tax systems, although the aims of the other models appear to be different from the model presented here. In 1974 Michael Adler and David Du Feu built a model with the aim of assessing the feasibility of using computerized models to encourage the take up of benefits.[1] Work of this form has been continued by Harrigan *et al.* (1977), by Nigel Gilbert at the University of Surrey and by the Cardiff Citizens Advice Bureau. Computerization of entitlement decisions from the DHSS standpoint is also being seriously investigated.[2]

A second set of initiatives consists of models to calculate a range of replacement ratios which is, broadly speaking, the ratio of disposable income when unemployed to disposable income when in work. The calculated replacement ratios may then be used in models of unemployment duration and the incentive to work. Such models may use either pooled cross-section and time series data such as the Family Expenditure Surveys, notable attempts being Morris and Dilnot (1984) and Atkinson *et al.* (1984) or replacement ratios derived from hypothetical families based on average attributes for use in time series analysis. Examples of the latter are Minford *et al.* (1983) and Holden and Peel (1978).

A third strand is the modelling of the social security system in order to evaluate implicit marginal tax rates and especially the 'poverty trap' using both hypothetical and actual data. Examples of these are the DHSS Tax-Benefit model tables, Bradshaw (1980), and Dilnot *et al.* (1984).

The tax-benefit model used in this study has many similar features to the above models. For example, in this chapter hypothetical data will be used but in later chapters the data will be read from the Family Expenditure Survey. The model can be used to calculate both replacement ratios and marginal tax rates. The main difference between the present model and other models of the social security system is that our model evaluates net income over a range of working hours, whereas for example the DHSS model evaluates net income for a given level of earnings irrespective of the number of hours worked. These dimensions are important because, as noted in Chapter 1, labour supply incentives depend intrinsically on the relationship between net income and the amount of time that is supplied at work.

In this chapter at each hour of work per week between zero and 40 the model calculates total disposable income, Y. This is defined as

$$Y = W.\ H - T - NI - C + CB + FIS + RER + RAR + UB + SB$$

where

W	= Gross wage rate	T	= Income Tax
H	= Hours of work	NI	= Employees' National Insurance contributions
FIS	= Family Income Supplement	C	= Travel costs
UB	= Unemployment Benefit	CB	= Child Benefit
SB	= Supplementary Benefit	RER	= Rent Rebates
		RAR	= Rate Rebates

An understanding of the model therefore requires an understanding of the tax-benefit system and it is to this which we now turn.

An Outline of the Social Security and Tax System

In this section we outline the salient features of the social security system in so far as they are relevant to the building of the model. We will deal with each component of the system in turn.

INCOME TAX

Income Tax (T) is paid on earned income above the tax threshold. For all the budget constraints calculated in this study the marginal rate of tax is the basic rate, 30%. The level of tax threshold depends upon the individual or family circumstances. Everyone who works is entitled to a personal allowance of £1,565 from April 1982. If the individual is married the husband receives an additional married man's allowance of £880. The wife is given a single person's allowance on her own earnings and any of her earnings above the single person's allowance is added to her husband's income and is taxed at the rate relevant to the husband. Married couples have the option of selecting separate taxation of earnings but a reduction in tax payments will only result if the husband and wife originally paid a substantial amount of tax in the higher tax brackets and because of this we ignore the possibility of independent tax liabilities for married couples. Single parents also receive the additional married man's allowance. The model also incorporates the tax allowance on mortgage interest payments, but no other allowances are modelled.[3]

NATIONAL INSURANCE

National Insurance contributions (NI) depend on whether the employer has chosen to contract out of the state pension scheme. If the employer had contracted into the scheme the employee pays 8.75% of earnings in National Insurance contributions, if earnings are above the lower earnings limit (LEL) of £29.50 per week. If earnings were above the upper earnings limit of £220.00 per week, the employee simply paid NI contributions of 8.75% of the upper earnings limit. Below the LEL no contributions are paid.

If the employer has contracted out of the state pension scheme the employee pays 8.75% of earnings up to LEL as National Insurance contributions. If earnings are between the upper and lower earnings limits, the employee pays 8.75% of the lower earnings limit plus 6.25% of the difference between the employee's earnings and the lower earnings limit. If earnings are above the upper earnings limit National Insurance contributions are 8.75% of the lower limit plus 6.25% of the difference between the upper and lower earnings limit. Since October 1985 the upper earnings limit has been abolished for employer contributions while contribution rates have been graduated for people on lower wage rates.

The model does not have the capacity to evaluate class 2 and 4 National Insurance contributions and so analysis of the budget constraints is confined to non-self-employed individuals. Furthermore, the model does not allow for married women who have previously opted to pay lower National Insurance contributions.

As this option is being phased out this last point is not a significant weakness of the model.

CHILD BENEFIT

Child Benefit (CB) is payable weekly to each family with eligible children regardless of the number of hours worked or the level of earnings. Child Benefit will alter the shape of the budget constraint because it counts as income for the purpose of calculating SB and Housing Benefits. Child Benefit is paid to the wife but is included in the husband's budget constraint because it can be regarded as unearned income. The model also evaluates the addition to Child Benefit payable to single parent families. The model assumes that Child Benefit can be allocated to the budget constraint as a simple average of the weekly payments. We also assume that the family does not accumulate arrears of Child Benefit (up to one year is possible) in order to collect it when the family is not receiving Supplementary Benefit (when it would be implicitly taxed at 100%).

FAMILY INCOME SUPPLEMENT

The Family Income Supplement (FIS) is also directed at families with children where the head of the household is in 'full-time' work. Full-time work is defined as more than 30 hours per week for a married man, and 24 hours per week for a single parent. It is important to note that because the husband is defined as being the head of the household wives cannot claim FIS if they work more than 30 hours per week, but their husbands work less than 30 hours.

FIS is calculated as half the difference between the family's gross income and the prescribed income level which depends upon the number of children in the family. Gross household income is defined as being average gross income from all sources averaged over the last 5 weeks or, if paid monthly the last 2 months. Income includes earnings and income from savings but excludes Child Benefit and the extra one parent benefit together with a number of other benefits, of which the model only takes account of rent and rate rebates/allowances.

The prescribed income levels are determined by the number of children in the family. As of November 1982 a family with one child had a prescribed income of £82.50 and this is increased by

£9 for every extra child. There is a maximum amount payable on FIS of £21 for a one-child family which is increased by £2 for every extra child and the model takes this into account.

FIS has some important features. First entitlement to FIS gives access to other benefits, such as free dental treatment and glasses, free prescriptions and free school meals. This feature is known as passporting. The model only allocates a value to free school meals, of £2.50 p.w., since the values of other passported benefits are difficult to calculate because take-up is dependent upon the health of the family. Secondly, FIS is awarded for 52 weeks irrespective of the family circumstances for the rest of the year. The model does not take this into account so the budget lines have to be interpreted as being static, in that no account of families receiving FIS and then changing their hours of work is allowed for.

RENT AND RATE REBATES
The model evaluates one other set of benefits which are payable to families even if the head of the family is in 'full-time' work; these are the rent (RER) and rate (RAR) rebates and allowances. Broadly speaking, rent rebates are payable to families living in council tenancies, while rent allowances are payable to private tenants. For our purposes we do not distinguish between the two classes of benefits which we will call rent and rate rebates.

Rent and rate rebates are calculated with reference to the family's gross weekly income, the needs allowance and the rent and rates payable on the family's housing. The definition of weekly income is not the same as for FIS and is defined as including Child Benefits, FIS and National Insurance benefits. Certain items of earnings are partly disregarded for the calculations of gross weekly income, but for the purposes of the model these were confined to £18 of the applicant's earnings and £5 of their partner's earnings. These earnings disregards can be swapped between partners to maximize the rent and rate rebates. The model ignores all other disregards. The amount of needs allowance depends upon the size of the household. A single person was allocated a value of £41, a married couple and a single person with one child £61, and each extra child £11.40. The rent is the average weekly rent calculated over the year for unfurnished accommodation but the local authority will deduct an amount it believes to be for furniture and, if applicable, board.

30

The local authority then uses a set of functions in order to calculate the rent and rate rebates. If the family's income equals the needs allowance the rent and rate rebates are 60% of the family's rent and rates. If income is more than the needs allowance the rent allowance is 60% of the rent minus 17% of the difference between the family's income and the needs allowance. If income is less than the needs allowance the rent rebate is 60% of the rent plus 25% of the difference between the needs allowance and the family's income. The rate rebates are calculated in a similar manner to rent rebates but the earnings tapers or implicit marginal tax rates are 6% if income is more than the needs allowance and 8% if income is less than the needs allowance. We also assume that local authorities do not use their discretionary powers so the maximum amounts payable are £35 in Greater London and £30 elsewhere for rent, and £9 in Greater London and £5.50 elsewhere for rates.

From April 1983 this system was altered for some households: specifically pensioners who will have higher earnings tapers if their income is below their needs allowance, and lower earnings tapers if it is above. The model set-up for November 1982 does not distinguish between pensioners and non-pensioners for the purposes of calculating rent and rate rebates.

It should be emphasized that the rent and rate rebate system is not as clear-cut as we present it in the model. First, the local authority may decide that the family's residence is above the needs of the family: in this case the authority will estimate a reasonable rent and base the rent and rate rebates on this amount. A similar procedure will be initiated if the authority believes the rent to be too high. It is assumed throughout this study that neither of the above conditions prevail and it is also assumed that the council does not use its discretionary powers to increase the Housing Benefits above the government's scheme.

SUPPLEMENTARY BENEFITS

Supplementary Benefit (SB) payments are calculated as being the difference between the family's resources and its requirements. A family's resources comprise both capital and income. In general, if the family has capital worth over £2,500 the family is ineligible to receive Supplementary Benefit. However, as the value of capital excludes the value of the house the family occupies and as this makes up a large proportion of many families' wealth, it is assumed no families are disqualified from receiving SB because of their holdings of capital. Further, because income from capital below £2,500 is also ignored, it seems appropriate to ignore capital as a source of income as well.

Income for the purposes of Supplementary Benefit is defined as earnings minus work expenses, of which the model includes tax payments, National Insurance payments and travel expenses. Amounts of £4 of any earnings and £4 of the spouse's earnings are also disregarded. If the worker is a single parent then a further disregard of half of any earnings between £4 and £20 also applies. If the individual's earnings are derived from full-time work (in general more than 30 hours per week) then they are not entitled to SB no matter how low their earnings are. Unemployment Benefit, FIS, Child Benefit, and extra one-parent Child Benefit are all counted in full as income and these are taken into account by the model. But all other forms of income and benefits are ignored.

A family's requirements come under three headings: normal requirements, housing requirements and additional requirements. The latter, which includes allowances for home helps, special diet and fares to hospital, will not be dealt with by the model in order to keep the discussion in general terms. We have included the age allowance in our calculations as this has an objective criterion to determine eligibility. This raises SB requirements by £1.90 if the household contains a person over 70 or under 5 years of age. Normal requirements are determined by the family's circumstances and are designed to meet living expenses excluding housing costs. The model excludes 'joint householders' and non-householders from consideration, again to maintain generality, so that the model determines the requirements at the husband and wife rate of £41.70 p.w. or at the individual householder rate (by which is meant that the individual lives on their own) of £25.70 p.w. Added to this are allowances for children who are under 16 or still at school and these allowances depend upon the ages of the children. The model also allows an extra £1.90 weekly heating addition if the household contains a child under the age of 5.

The model also has the option of assigning long-term Supplementary Benefits to single parent families and to men over the age of 60. In order to qualify the individual must have been

32

unemployed for the previous year and to have signed off the unemployment register. As long-term Supplementary Benefits exceed the alternative of short-term Supplementary Benefit it is assumed that individuals who are eligible will claim.

The housing requirement of the family is calculated for the purposes of the model as the rates, rent and mortgage interest payments, but not capital repayments, which the family is liable for per week. It is assumed that the DHSS does not use its discretionary power to reduce payments in respect of rent or mortgage because it regards these payments as excessive. Implicitly we are assuming that the rent level has been set by a rent tribunal, or the house is council-owned or the family has become eligible for SB within the last 6 months.

UNEMPLOYMENT BENEFIT

The last benefit which the model evaluates is Unemployment Benefit. Eligibility to this benefit is determined by the individual's National Insurance contribution record. In order to receive Unemployment Benefit two conditions need to be satisfied.

First, the individual must have paid Class 1 contributions, in any one contributing year, producing an earnings factor of at least 25 times that year's lower earnings limit. The earnings factor, for Class 1 contributions, is defined as being equal to the earnings on which the contribution was paid. This condition must always be met if the individual is to receive any Unemployment Benefit.

Secondly, the individual must have paid or been credited with, in the last contribution year which ended before the claim for Unemployment Benefit, Class 1 contributions producing an earnings factor of at least 50 times that year's lower earnings limit.

If these conditions have been met in full the individual will receive Unemployment Benefit of £25 plus an increase of £15.45 for the spouse and £0.30 for each dependent child. If the individual only has an earnings factor of 37½ times the lower earnings limit under the second condition for Unemployment Benefit the increase for dependents will be paid at 75% of the full amount. If the earnings factor is above 25 times the lower earnings limit, but below 37½ times, the Unemployment Benefit will be paid at 50% of the full amount.

Although Unemployment Benefit is not means tested the allowance made to a wife will be reduced if she is earning more

33

than £45 p.w. The reduction is at a rate of 50% for the first £4 and then pound for pound until the wife's allowance is exhausted. The wife's earnings do not affect the level of Unemployment Benefit paid to the husband, so that the maximum amount lost if the wife works would be £15.45 p.w.

The model assumes that the individual has been unemployed longer than the waiting period of 3 days, during which time no benefit can be received, but shorter than a year, after which time Unemployment Benefit cannot be claimed. We implicitly assume that the individual has no linked unemployment spells. We also assume that the individual is not disqualified from receiving Unemployment Benefit because dismissal was due to misconduct, or the individual left his last job voluntarily and without due cause, or the benefit officer decides that the claimant has no intention of working. These restrictions mean that budget constraints have to be interpreted as being relevant to a person already unemployed and not to a person having a full-time job. If a person who has a full-time job decided to become unemployed in order to take up the benefit, he or she would be disqualified from reciving Unemployment Benefit for a maximum of 6 weeks. Furthermore, the individual's Supplementary Benefit would be reduced by up to 40% (but not the housing allowance or the increase for dependants), for the period of disqualification. A reduction of 20% will be made in certain circumstances. Consequently if the model is used for individuals who already have a job it will overestimate disposable income when the individual is unemployed.

The Model

The model uses the set of rules described to calculate total disposable income for each hour of work per week, between 0 and 40, once it is given information about the family type: i.e. married or single, number of children, wage rates, and housing costs. For some families, there will be a choice between different sets of social security benefits, for example, between Supplementary Benefit and rent or rate rebates. This is known as the 'better-off' problem. The model assumes that the family will always pick the set of benefits which maximizes total disposable income.

A number of objections can be raised about modelling the budget lines facing the unemployed in this manner. First, we model only eight benefits whereas there are over sixty ways of receiving money from the state. Therefore, the model may be described as a severe abstraction from reality and its ability to cast light on a highly complex system put into doubt. In response to this criticism we would argue that the benefits we model are the major features of the social security system. In May 1980, 593,000 people were receiving Unemployment Benefit and 2,850,000 individuals were receiving Supplementary Benefit, while 81,000 families were receiving FIS at the end of 1979. Furthermore, some of the benefits, for example, Sickness Benefit and Maternity Benefit may imply that the individual is temporarily unavailable for work and hence modelling the work–leisure decision is inappropriate.

Secondly, the degree of information required in order to calculate the budget constraint may make it inappropriate to assume that individuals have full knowledge of even the limited benefits discussed above. Critics would point out that take-up rates are usually below 100%. For example, for the unemployed the Child Poverty Action Group (1982) estimates that take-up of Housing Benefits and free school meals were only 18% and 35% respectively while for the general population these figures were 46% and 80% respectively. For Supplementary Benefit, take-up was 70% in 1979 and for FIS 50%.

Consequently, it can be argued that the model overestimates total disposable income which is likely to be received by a selection of families. While it is likely that the model will overestimate total disposable income, it can be argued that looking at the number of non-claimants overstates the seriousness of the problem for the purposes of calculating budget constraints. A large number of the non-claimants do realize that they could claim extra benefits but that the 'costs' of claiming outweigh the benefits from doing so. Hence, low take-up rates may overestimate the degree of ignorance in the population about the social security system.

One suggested way around this problem may be to weight each benefit by its take-up rate. We do not pursue this approach because the budget constraints so constructed would be highly unlikely to reflect reality whereas, it is hoped, the model will do so, at least for those who make full use of the system.

Further criticisms can also be made of the assumptions regarding the efficiency of the social security system. The budget constraints are calculated on the basis that the individual will have his or her benefits immediately altered to correspond to their new circumstances. The analysis therefore ignores any delays in processing of claims and as such is extremely unrealistic. Unlike the DHSS Tax-Benefit model tables, which assume that FIS remains payable for the first 6 months of unemployment, we assume that there is no continuation of benefits from one point on the budget constraint to another.

The Assumptions

The model allows budget lines to be calculated for different assumptions about family type, housing costs, housing tenure, past work history and travel expenses. For the purposes of this study we will analyse budget constraints for different assumptions about the first three variables.

ASSUMPTIONS ON FAMILY COMPOSITION
The family types we shall deal with are:

> single man
> married couple, no children, wife not working
> married couple, 2 children, wife not working
> married couple, 4 children, wife not working
> single parent family, 2 children
> married couple, both partners working

In 1982, 12% of households in Great Britain were single persons or lone parents with independent children, 35% were married couples without dependent children. Married couples with children accounted for 29% of households and single parent families 4%.[4] Of married couples with children, 43½% of families had 2 children and 4% had 4 children.[5] Consequently, the four family types outlined above account for nearly 65% of all households in Great Britain.

The children's ages are assumed to be 4 and 6 in the 2-child families and 4, 6, 11 and 16 in the 4-child families. These choices of ages are made for no other reason than that they correspond to the assumptions used in the DHSS Tax-Benefit model tables.[6]

However, once it is accepted that by assumption each family with children has a child 4 years old, the assumption that the wife does not work can be rationalized by noting that in 1980–2, 73% of married mothers with youngest dependent child aged between 0 and 4 years did not work, compared with 41% of married mothers with youngest dependent child aged 5–9 and 30% with a youngest child aged 10 or over. However, the effect of joint assumptions of family composition and children's ages must be noted. In 1981 there were 3.3 million children aged under 4, but there were nearly 6 million married couples with children and 916,000 single parent families with children and, assuming that no family has more than one child aged 4 or under, at least 52% of married couple families and single parent families cannot contain a child aged 4 or under. Consequently, the joint assumptions of children's ages and family composition reduce the coverage of the whole population by our representative cases from roughly 65% to 51%. Furthermore, we have ignored the effect of the assumption of the wife's employment status on the coverage of our representative cases. However, we hope it is clear from this simple example, that as more assumptions are added our representative cases will portray a smaller and smaller fraction of the whole population. Indeed, we do not believe it is possible to pick a representative case. Such a view is supported by Atkinson *et al.* (1983), who calculate from the FES sample that the DHSS model tables only cover 4% of the population. The aim of this chapter is not to claim exhaustive cover of a large proportion of the population, but rather to show the workings of the social security and tax system in so far as they affect labour supply incentives.

Three further points about the family types need to be noted. First, as 89% of all single parent families are headed by women, we have assumed that the single parent family is likewise headed.[7] Second, while 55% in 1980–2 of all single parent families had only one child, we have assumed 2 children in order to facilitate comparisons between the budget constraints.[8] Thirdly, we assume that the families are either in the process of buying their own homes, that is, they are owner-occupiers, or they rent their accommodation from the local authority. These accounted for 59% and 29% respectively of all UK dwellings in 1982.[9]

ASSUMPTIONS ON WAGE RATES

In order to demonstrate the effect of differing wage rates on the budget constraint we have chosen three gross hourly wage rates of £2.17, £3.28 and £5.88. In 1982, 10% of the male full-time working population aged 21 and over earned less than this amount per hour and 10% more.[10] These wage rates reflect both manual and non-manual workers, include overtime pay but exclude those whose pay was affected by absence. We assume that wages are invariant to the number of hours worked and hence we ignore the effect of overtime hours in this exposition.[11] At these wage rates roughly 40% of females earned less and 3% more per hour in 1982. In fact, 10% of full-time working women earned less than £1.60 per hour, but as we wish to compare budget constraints controlling for wage rates, this low wage rate will be ignored. We further assume that the individual has a complete contribution record so that they qualify in full for National Insurance benefits.

ASSUMPTIONS ON HOUSING COSTS

The families are assumed either to rent their accommodation or are assumed to be in the process of buying their own accommodation. We assume that rents and mortgages are £18 p.w. and rates are £4.92 p.w. Separate sensitivity analyses are carried out on both rent and rates between the value of 60% of their average values and 140%. Although analysis of the 1978 and 1981 FES tapes showed that both the mortgage and rates paid by mortgagors tended to be higher than in the rented sector, no attempt has been made to make housing costs consistent with the family type or to make rent and mortgages consistent with rates, because during the course of this chapter we wish to vary these factors while holding the other factors constant.

The housing costs assumed in this study can be compared to those used in the November 1982 issue of the DHSS Tax-Benefit model tables. That model makes rate and rents dependent upon the number of rooms required by the family for sleeping purposes and is based on average council house rent. Their figures range from £11.90 p.w. to £14.20 p.w. for rent and £5.50 p.w. to £6.40 p.w. for rates. The comparable range of figures in this study are £10.80 to £25.20 p.w. for rent and £2.95 to £6.89 p.w. for rates.

ASSUMPTIONS ON TRAVEL TO WORK

The travel costs of £1.20 per 8 hours of work (£6.00 for a forty hour week) compare to a DHSS assumption of £5.50 per week.[12] The DHSS's model and our own model will have similar assumptions for a number of simulations, but it is hoped that by varying the assumptions used we will weaken the criticism that models of this type crucially depend upon the assumptions used.

II

Budget Line Case Study

Glossary of Terms

The following terms are frequently used in the case studies to describe the budget constraint and are illustrated in Fig. 2.1.

The *Choice Set of Hours* is defined as the range of hours from which the rational individual would choose to work. Since this rational individual would not endure marginal rates of tax of 100% or more, the choice set is limited to upward sloping segments of the budget line as indicated in Fig. 2.1.

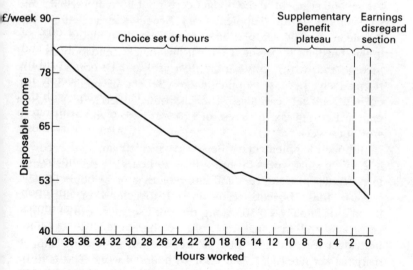

Fig. 2.1 The budget constraint of a single man on average wages with average rent and rates

39

The *Supplementary Benefit Plateau* is defined as the range of hours over which the withdrawal of Supplementary Benefit generates 100% marginal tax rates, thereby flattening the budget line as indicated in Fig. 2.1. The SB plateau and the choice set hours are mutually exclusive by definition.

The *Poverty Trap* includes the SB plateau because of the 100% marginal tax rates along it. However, 100% marginal tax rates may also occur under other circumstances.

Single Men

We begin by analysing the budget constraints of single men. Figure 2.1 is the budget constraint of an unemployed man who would expect to receive average manual earnings and pays average rent and rates. The budget constraint can be divided into three segments for expositional purposes. At zero hours of work the individual receives Unemployment Benefit and Supplementary Benefit. As he begins to work part-time his income increases as he is allowed to keep all his net earnings up to the earnings disregard. In under 2 hours this disregard has been 'used up' and the individual has any extra earnings taxed at 100%. Consequently, the second segment of the budget constraint is completely flat and we will call it the 'Supplementary Benefit plateau'. Along this Supplementary Benefit plateau the individual is insulated from the initial burden of paying National Insurance contributions and Income Tax, which come into effect at 9 and 10 hours of work respectively, because Supplementary Benefit payments are calculated on net earnings. The individual therefore avoids a marginal rate of tax in excess of 100% at both 9 and 10 hours of work per week.

Although Supplementary Benefit payments cannot be received if the individual works for more than 29 hours a week, this single man decides to claim rent and rate rebates after 13 hours of work because these benefits result in a higher level of disposable income of initially £0.30. Along the third segment of the budget constraint the marginal rate of tax therefore falls. After the individual leaves the SB plateau, he faces an underlying implicit marginal tax rate of 71.75% until 18 hours of work. This is made up of the income tax at 30%, National Insurance at 8.75%, rent rebate at 25.0% and rate rebate at 8.0%. Between 18 and 32 hours the tax rate is 61.75% because of the reduction in the income tapers on Housing Benefits once the individual's income (minus disregard) is above the needs allowance. After 32 hours the marginal tax rate falls again to 65.75% as rate rebates are withdrawn. Finally, after 38 hours of work the marginal tax rate is 38.75% when rent rebates are withdrawn. The kinks after 16, 24, and 32 hours of work are caused by extra travel costs of £1.20 (as a new day's work is started), and this gives a marginal rate of deductions close to 100%. The individual was protected from the effect of increases in travel costs along the SB plateau because his Supplementary Benefit was increased to compensate.

A single man earning average wages with average housing costs will be better off in terms of income by working rather than remaining unemployed. How many hours the individual would choose to work, given the opportunity, will of course depend upon his relative preferencs for leisure and income. However, applying the indifference curve analysis from Chapter 1, we would expect the individual's preferred hours of work to be at any point other than on the SB plateau. The hours from which an individual would consider working we have termed the 'choice set of hours'. What will happen to the budget constraint, and hence the choice set for labour supply, as we change the assumptions about the individual's circumstances? First we change the individual's hourly wage rate holding his housing costs constant.

THE EFFECT OF WAGES ON THE BUDGET CONSTRAINT
OF SINGLE MEN
From Fig. 2.2 it can be seen that the budget line may be substantially changed as the wage rate is altered. In each of the three cases, average wages, high and low wages, the level of disposable income on the SB plateau and at zero hours are equivalent at £52.62 and £48.62 p.w. This is because these levels are determined by the individual's family type and housing costs which, of course, are held constant.

If the individual's wage rate is assumed to be 140% of the average wage rate the SB plateau is shortened to lie between 1 and 6 hours, whereas with an average wage the plateau lies between 2 and 13 hours. The reduction of the plateau is the result of two offsetting factors: the fall in the number of hours of work required to use up the earnings disregard, which marginally

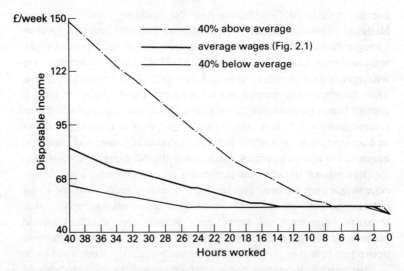

Fig. 2.2 The budget constraints of a single man with average rent and rates but different wage rates

lengthens the plateau, and a reduction of the number of hours of work required before net earnings plus rent and rate rebates exceed the level of income on the SB plateau. The latter effect dominates the former and so there is a reduction in the length of the SB plateau. Furthermore, the higher wage rate ensures that the individual does not face marginal deduction rates in excess of 100% when travel costs increase at 16, 24 and 32 hours of work. The choice set for a single man on a higher wage rate is therefore larger by 6 hours than on the average wage rate.

Conversely, if the wage rate is assumed to be only 60% of the average, the choice set is significantly diminished by 9 hours in comparison with the average wage case. At this wage rate the SB plateau is extended to 22 hours per week.

Additional points worthy of consideration are as follows. First, the single man on low wages is dependent upon income support over the full range of hours and at 40 hours Housing Benefits of £7.41 are receivable. These benefits account for 11.63% of the individual's disposable income. Consequently, even at 40 hours of work per week the implicit marginal tax rate is 61.75%. This compares with a marginal tax rate of only 30% for the high wage earner, because his earnings exceed the upper earnings limit on National Insurance contributions after 39 hours of work per week.

Secondly, for the low wage individual, increases in travel costs reduce income between 32 and 33 hours of work, even when the individual is above the needs allowance on Housing Benefits. Travelling expenses are therefore likely to play a proportionately greater part in determining the shape of the budget constraint the lower the level of wages. Although, at the wage rates encountered in these three cases, after 2 hours' work the loss of disposable income, even at the lowest wage rate, is recovered.

Thirdly, although the choice set of hours declines with wages, *ceteris paribus*, in none of the three cases was the choice set of hours restricted to those hours on the earnings disregard section. It would be quite consistent with the postulated income–leisure preferences for any of these individuals to work more than 23 hours per week.

The reader should not gain the impression that lower wage rates always imply a smaller choice set of hours regardless of other circumstances. This will be demonstrated later in the chapter.

THE EFFECT OF HOUSING COSTS ON THE BUDGET CONSTRAINT OF SINGLE MEN

Having varied wage rates to observe their effect on the budget constraint we now turn to housing costs. The individual is again assumed to receive the average wage rate and live in rented accommodation. The budget constraints for the single man when housing costs vary between 60% and 140% of the average case are depicted in Fig. 2.3.

The first noticeable difference in comparison to the budget constraints in Fig. 2.2 is that the SB plateau and zero hours of work no longer exhibit the same level of disposable income between the cases. This is because the differences in housing costs are transferred directly into the level of SB being received at both zero hours and along the SB plateau. The high and low housing cost budget constraints lie £9.17 above and £9.17 below the average housing cost budget constraint.

The second effect of differing housing costs is on the choice set of hours. As housing costs increase, the choice set of hours declines from 29 to 27 at average housing costs and at the highest

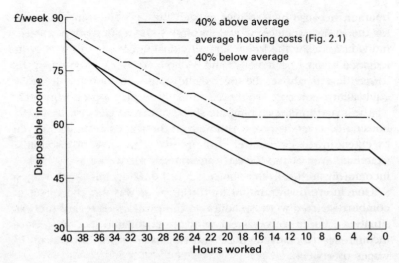

Fig. 2.3 Budget constraints of single men with average wages but different housing costs

housing costs to 22 hours per week. This is because, although the SB plateau matches the increase in housing costs, rent and rate rebates at a given level of income can only match, at most, 60% of the rise in housing costs. If the individual originally had the same level of disposable income by accepting SB or Housing Benefits he will be better off by keeping SB when his housing costs are higher. Consequently, higher housing costs extend the SB plateau in Fig. 2.3 from a low of 11 hours to 18 hours with high housing costs, and reduce the choice set of hours.

Thirdly, higher housing costs mean that at greater levels of working hours Housing Benefits are being received and in consequence 'high' implicit marginal tax rates will operate on the budget constraints for longer periods than with lower housing costs. This results in an average marginal tax rate between the end of the SB plateau and 40 hours of work of 66.1% for the high housing cost individual and 58.1% for the low cost individual. The implicit marginal rate of tax for average housing costs is 65.3%. The payment of Housing Benefit, in this case rent rebate, even at 40 hours of work, to the high housing cost individual implies that his disposable income is in excess of other individuals for all hours of work. The exhaustion of Housing Benefits after 29 hours for the low cost and 37 hours of work for the high housing cost individual imply that after 37 hours the budget constraints are identical. This is simply because after 37 hours their shape is being determined by the level of net earnings which are equivalent by design.

The main result of this conceptual experiment is that higher housing costs in the rented sector reduce the choice set of hours by extending the SB plateau. However, in none of the three cases examined was a choice of full-time work inconsistent with our income–leisure utility postulates.

One interesting question which may be asked is whether a combination of low wages and high housing costs can produce a situation where full-time working is inconsistent with the income–leisure postulates. In short, the answer is no, even with wages of only £2.18 per hour and housing costs of £32.09 per week. The choice set still comprises all the hours above 29 hours per week (ignoring the kink caused by travel costs at 33 hours per week). It should be pointed out that by working 40 hours the individual only raises his disposable income by £7.40 above the SB plateau. The single man in rented accommodation over this range of earnings and housing costs always has the option of working full-time in order to make himself better off.

THE EFFECT OF TENURE TYPE ON THE BUDGET CONSTRAINTS OF SINGLE MEN

We now change the tenure type to a mortgage and examine how this affects the budget constraint. There are two factors which imply that the budget constraints of a mortgagor will differ from those of a similar person who rents. These are the income tax relief on mortgage interest payments and the lack of an equivalent benefit to rent rebate for mortgagors.

The extra tax allowance will, *ceteris paribus*, increase the choice set of hours because, at the wage rate we are analysing, the individual begins paying tax before he has left the SB plateau. The increase in net pay would encourage the individual to stop claiming SB at a lower level of hours and thus increase his choice set of hours. However, it should be noted that there may be a discontinuity in this process as increases in wages push the individual into higher tax bands. Furthermore, the increase in the choice set is also limited by the £25,000 mortgage ceiling (in November 1982) and the associated maximum interest payments which attract tax relief. This sets an overall maximum increase in the choice set to 6.6 hours for individuals in the lowest wage rate class. For the cases we have analysed the maximum increase in the choice set is 3.5 hours.

The increase in the choice set caused by tax relief is offset by the lack of a 'mortgage rebate'. As the individual can only receive rate rebate on leaving the SB plateau, this will tend to extend the number of hours over which the individual claims SB. This extension of the SB plateau reduces the choice set. The degree of extension relative to an individual in rented accommodation depends upon how much the individual would have received in rent rebates, had he been paying rent, and the implicit marginal tax rate, which in turn depends upon the level of housing costs and the wage rate. The higher the level of mortgage and the higher the implicit marginal tax rates the greater the extension of the SB plateau and the greater the reduction in the choice set. A high mortgage and high rates will tend to reduce the choice set both directly and indirectly, by raising the average implicit marginal tax rate more than would a lower level of housing costs, *ceteris paribus*. A high wage rate, which has a lower average implicit marginal tax rate, once the individual has left the SB plateau, will tend to reduce the choice set by less than a low wage rate in comparison to similar renters.

The factors underlying the tax effect and lack of mortgage rebate act in opposite directions. Therefore, as we change wage rates or housing costs, the two effects will partially cancel each other out. Table 2.1 presents the net effect in the choice set of hours for various wage rates and mortgage and rent levels.

The change in tenure type to mortgaged accommodation reduces the choice set of hours by up to 8 hours compared with the comparable individual in the rented sector. It can be seen that across housing costs there is not a continuous change in the choice set, but in all cases the change to a mortgage reduces the choice set of hours. The maximum increase in the choice set rises with the level of mortgage and falls as wage rates increase. The maximum increase in the choice set may not, however, be achieved. This is because the number of hours between the end of the SB plateau and the point at which income tax starts to be paid

Table 2.1 Net Effect on the Choice Set of Hours Comparing a Single Mortgagor with Renters

Hourly wage rate £	Rent or mortgage £ p.w.		
	10.8	18.0	25.2
2.18	−7	−8	−7
3.28	−4	−6	−4
5.88	−2	−4	−3

Note: minus sign indicates that mortgagors have the smaller choice set of hours and longer SB plateaux.

may be less than the maximum number of hours and any hours after the end of the SB plateau are already included in the choice set. The higher the level of housing costs and the lower the wage rate, the greater is the number of hours between the commencement of paying income tax and the end of the SB plateau. Both the maximum and actual increase will tend to move together, which implies that a high mortgage and low wage rates will still lead to larger reductions in the choice set.

Figure 2.4 illustrates two comparisons of rented against mortgaged accommodation. These are the average wage and housing cost cases and the low wage, high housing cost cases. In both pairs it can be seen that the level of disposable income at zero hours and along the initial stages of the SB plateau are exactly the same with the high housing cost pair £9.17 above the average housing cost pair.

In the average cost comparison the renting individual loses his SB after 13 hours, but the mortgagor loses his after 19 hours. This 6-hour extension of the SB plateau accounts for the 6-hour reduction in the choice set for a mortgagor. The mortgagor, once he leaves the SB plateau, has a lower implicit tax rate and so his disposable income increases at a faster rate than the renter's. Consequently, the mortgagor's disposable income exceeds that of the renter after 27 hours and, after 38 hours, when the renter's rent rebate is exhausted, income exceeds the renter's by £5.40 which is maintained up to 40 hours per week.

For the high cost comparison, there are a number of differences. First, both individuals leave SB at the same point, 29 hours. The difference is that the renter does not suffer a loss of

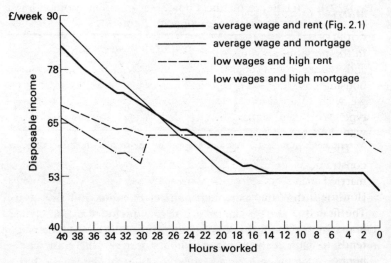

Fig. 2.4 Budget constraints of single men under different housing costs, wages and tenure

disposable income because Housing Benefit replaces some of the lost SB, whereas the mortgagor does. Indeed, had SB not ceased by the 30 hours rule, the mortgagor would claim them until 37 hours of work, as it is only after working this number of hours that his disposable income increases above the SB plateau. It is this implicit extension of the SB plateau by 7 hours which reduces the choice set of hours. The loss of £6.34 by the mortgagor as he works an extra hour at the end of the SB plateau represents over 10% of his disposable income and is equivalent to a marginal tax rate of 291%. Alternatively, the renter increases his disposable income by £0.28, which implies a marginal tax of 86.9%.

Additionally, although the mortgagor has a lower implicit tax rate after 30 hours of work, his disposable income, unlike the previous comparison, never exceeds that of the renter, over the level of hours analysed here.

Finally, it should be remembered that the conclusions reached for renters on high wages and low housing cost regarding the contraction in the SB plateau applies equally to individuals in mortgaged accommodation. Moreover the conclusions reached here are equally applicable to female workers.

Married Couples

COUPLES WITH NO CHILDREN

In the previous sections we have varied wage rates, housing costs and tenure type keeping family type and the distribution of housing costs constant. In this section and the following sections we wish to analyse the sensitivity of budget lines to household type. We begin with a married couple and we assume that the wife does not work.

There are three factors which will change the budget constraint as compared to that of a single man. These are the married man's tax allowance, the increased needs allowance for Housing Benefits, and the increase in the SB normal requirements. The first two of these effects tend to increase the choice set of hours by reducing the length of the SB plateau, while the latter tends to increase the SB plateau and reduce the choice set of hours.

Initially, let us consider the effect of holding family type constant and varying separately wages, housing costs and tenure type. As the transition of family type to a married couple has not changed any of the building blocks of the budget constraints it should not surprise the reader to discover that all the conclusions made about the single man also apply to the married couple. As wages rise, *ceteris paribus*, the choice set of hours increases from 9 hours at low wages to 30 hours at high wages in rented accommodation and from 1 hour at low wages to 27 at high wages for a mortgagor. As housing costs increase, the choice set falls from 23 to 18 hours and from 19 to 12 hours for renters and mortgagors, at low and high costs respectively. Finally, mortgagors have smaller choice sets than their corresponding renters. These differences range between 2 and 8 hours. They correspond to the low pay, high housing cost comparison, and the average housing cost, low pay comparisons. A full comparison can be made by the interested reader from the summary table at the end of the chapter.

We can now compare the budget constraints of single and married persons to analyse the differences caused by changing the family type. In each of the budget constraints hitherto calculated the choice set of hours is smaller for the married man in comparison to that available to the single man. The differences in the choice set range from a maximum of 9 hours to a minimum of 3 hours. The reason for this is that the introduction of the married man's allowance and the increased needs allowance for Housing Benefits are worth at most £11.55 while the rise in the SB needs allowance is worth £16 p.w. Even at the highest wage rate this difference can reduce the choice set by nearly 1¼ hours for a married couple. Indeed, it is the wage rate which is the main cause of the differences in the choice set, with high wages implying small differences and vice versa.

The result of the higher normal requirement payments is that the SB plateau lies above the corresponding plateau for the single person and is extended into a higher range of working hours, and it is this extension (or implicit extension) which reduces the available choice set. While the extension of the SB plateau reduces the dependence on Housing Benefit at low levels of hours worked, the increased needs allowance extends the number of hours over which Housing Benefits can be claimed for given income. The net effect of these two factors determines whether the average implicit marginal tax rate beyond the SB plateau is greater for the married couple or for the single person. In all of the rented accommodation cases the needs allowance effect outweighs the SB effect, and so the average implicit tax rate, beyond the SB plateau, is higher for the married person as compared to the single person.

In passing, it can be noted that the rise in the level of the SB plateau relative to disposable income beyond the plateau has increased the occurrences of marginal rates of tax in excess of 100% for married couples. Whereas for the examined budget constraints of single people only one occurrence was found, for married couples there were four. These families all have low wages and either high or average housing costs. In the case of the high mortgage cost family leaving SB involves a marginal tax rate of 817%. Even after 40 hours of work disposable income has not risen sufficiently to exceed the SB plateau. Consequently, for a married couple on low wages with a high mortgage the available choice set of hours is confined to the earnings disregard section, 3 hours, and in practice the individual, if he had normal income–leisure preferences, would probably be unemployed.

In summary, the budget constraints of married people behave in a similar manner to those of single people. Increases in wage rates and reductions in housing costs increase the choice set of hours. Those living in rented accommodation have larger choice sets, *ceteris paribus*, than mortgagors. Finally, single persons have larger choice sets than their married couple counterparts.

MARRIED COUPLES WITH CHILDREN

While the change of household type from single to married status involved no new principles, the introduction of children involves three new elements. These are Child Benefit (CB), Family Income Supplement (FIS) and free school meals. In this section we propose to analyse the effects CB and FIS have on the budget constraints both within a given family type and across family types. In order to do this we will analyse the budget constraints of married couples with 2 and 4 children.

From the point of view of work incentives CB appears quite promising because it is paid irrespective of the earnings and hours of the male parent, but it counts in full as income which is subtracted from SB payments. This feature will tend to increase the relative disposable income of those who do not claim SB. However, CB counts in full as income for the purposes of Housing Benefit. This feature will partially offset the improved relative position of those claiming Housing Benefit by up to 33% of Child Benefit. The exact figure depends upon the relationship between the family's income and the needs allowance.

FIS is not payable below 30 hours of work to a married man with children (or below 24 hours to a single parent family). Consequently, FIS will also tend to increase the level of income at higher hours of work relative to the SB plateau. The receipt of FIS will again reduce the level of Housing Benefit by up to 33% because it counts as income for the purposes of calculating rent and rate rebates. The reduction in Housing Benefit, due to FIS and Child Benefit counting as income, will be offset by the rise in the needs allowance which is dependent upon the number of children in the family.

These features tend to raise the level of disposable income at higher hours relative to the SB plateau. However, their interaction, as we shall see later, may be such that they actually reduce the choice set of hours.

Offsetting the relative rise in disposable income is the increase in the normal requirements for SB which elongate the SB plateau.

Free school meals which are payable if the family receives either
SB or FIS tends to raise the level of disposable income relative to
the hours at which FIS is not payable. As free school meals are
withdrawn in a lump sum when FIS is exhausted, they can
introduce implicit marginal rates of tax in excess of 100%.

We begin our formal analysis by considering the effect these
factors have on the comparative budget constraints of a married
couple and a married couple with children. The results are
summarized in Table 2.2.

Initially, consider the effect children have upon the length of
the SB plateau. For the 2-child family Child Benefit plus the
change in Housing Benefit fall short of the change in normal
requirements by £5.92, and for the 4-child family by £23.35
assuming income is below the Housing Benefit needs allowance.
These are equivalent to an extension of 9.6 and 38 hours in the SB
plateau, at the lowest wage rate for the 2- and 4-child family
respectively. The figure may be an underestimate if the maximum
level of Housing Benefit is reached.

Families with children therefore have extended SB plateaux
compared to their childless counterparts and this reduces the
choice set of hours. Moreover, the more children the family has,
the more elongated is the SB plateau. A similar situation exists for
those families with mortgages. The comparable families with
mortgages would have their SB plateaux extended by 7.5 and 24.9
hours for the 2- and 4-child families respectively.

With such large possible extensions to the SB plateau,

Table 2.2 The Relationship between Benefits and Children
(£ p.w.)

Number of children	Child Benefit	FIS payable at 30 hours on low wage rate	Change in Housing Benefit		Change in normal requirements including age allowance and free school meals
			at 30 hrs.	below 30 hrs.	
2	11.70	13.13	−0.67	3.66	21.28
4	23.40	22.13	0.02	7.33	54.08

especially for the 4-child families, it should not surprise the reader
to see in Table 2.3 that in the 14 cases analysed 10 of the 4-child
families had SB plateaux of the maximum of 29 hours. This
compares with 7 and 4 cases for the 2-child families and childless
married couples respectively. It can be seen that across family
types, the length of the SB plateau increases, where it is not
already at a maximum, as the family progresses from no children
to 4 children. Furthermore, it can also be seen that within family
types higher housing costs extend the SB plateau, *ceteris paribus*,
and higher wages reduce the SB plateau for both 2- and 4-child
families. In this the 2- and 4-child families exhibit the same
features in the SB plateau as the single and childless married
couple. The 2-child family also has the same features in the SB
plateau as single and childless couples in that mortgage payers
have longer SB plateaux than renters. This is not the case in the 4-
child family, nor is it true in the example constructed in Table 2.2
at high wage rates.

From Table 2.3 it can be seen that at average housing costs the
renting family's SB plateau is 2 hours longer than the correspond-

Table 2.3 The Number of Hours of Work per Week After Which
the SB Plateau Terminates for Three Family Types

Tenure type	Total housing costs £	Hourly wage rate £ p.h.	Family type (hours)		
			childless	2 children	4 children
Rented	22.92	3.28	19	27	29
Rented	22.92	2.18	29	29	29
Rented	22.92	5.88	10	13	23
Rented	13.75	3.28	17	22	29
Rented	32.09	3.28	23	29	29
Rented	32.09	2.18	29	29	29
Rented	13.75	5.88	10	12	20
Mortgage	22.92	3.28	25	29	29
Mortgage	22.92	2.18	29	29	29
Mortgage	22.92	5.88	13	16	21
Mortgage	13.75	3.28	21	27	29
Mortgage	32.09	3.28	28	29	29
Mortgage	32.09	2.18	29	29	29
Mortgage	13.75	5.88	11	13	19

ing mortgagor's and at low housing costs it is 1 hour longer. At the high wage rate SB is exhausted between, in our examples, 19 and 23 hours. This is because the high level of wages reduces Housing Benefit below the level of SB plus free school meals so that it is never worth leaving SB voluntarily. Those families who pay mortgages receive a mortgage interest tax allowance and consequently their net income from work is higher at this range of hours than that of the corresponding renter. Consequently, the SB plateau of mortgagors is shorter because they will be better off by leaving SB at lower hours of work. There are four cases in Table 2.3 of 4-child families in which the SB plateau terminates before 29 hours of work. In one of these cases, the average rent case, the change from SB to Housing Benefit at 23 hours involves a fortuitous increase in disposable income and for this family this represents the beginning of the choice set of hours. For the other three cases the loss of SB involves a loss, albeit slight, of disposable income of between £0.88 for the low rent, 4-child family, and £3.82 for the low mortgage, 4-child family. Consequently, for these three cases the choice set of hours is determined by the implicit SB plateau, that is, the number of hours at which disposable income exceeds disposable income on the SB plateau, even though SB is no longer being paid. These extra hours reduce the choice set by 2, 1 and 2 hours so that the choice set begins at 22, 22 and 21 hours for the low rent, average mortgage and low mortgage 4-child families respectively. The choice set of hours is therefore larger by 1 hour for mortgage-paying families as compared to the equivalent rent-paying family at the high wage rate for 4-child families. This is the reverse of what was found for single and married people.

A similar set of arguments also applies to the 2-child family on low housing costs at the high wage rate but in this case the choice set is only made equivalent between the mortgage and rent-paying families. At high and average wages the choice set of hours is determined by the SB plateau or its implicit extension.

However, for the 4-child families on low or average wages and the 2-child family on low wages their budget constraints are crucially affected by their entitlement to FIS. It can be seen from Table 2.3 that these families all leave SB after the maximum number of hours possible, i.e. 29, and at 30 hours they become eligible for FIS. From Table 2.2 it can be seen that FIS is worth

£13.13 for the 2-child and £22.13 for the 4-child family on the lowest wage rate. This means that for the 2-child family at 30 hours they will be £4.76 better off compared to the SB plateau than the corresponding married couple, as FIS entitles the family to free school meals. The 4-child family will be £2.90 worse off relative to the SB plateau than the childless couple. Previously at 29 hours Table 2.2 indicated that a 2-child family could be £5.92 worse off and a 4-child family £23.35 worse off than the corresponding childless married couple relative to the SB plateau. FIS reduces, and in the case of 2-child renting families eliminates the disposable income reduction upon leaving the SB plateau at 30 hours of work.

It can also be seen from Table 2.2 that FIS reduces the level of Housing Benefit entitlement because FIS counts as income for the purposes of calculating Housing Benefit. It is this interaction between benefits which stops those in the rented sector from increasing their choice set of hours and from increasing their disposable income through FIS. This is because both FIS and Housing Benefit are calculated on gross income. Consequently, for every extra £1 earned, Income Tax takes £0.30, National Insurance £0.0875, FIS is reduced by £0.50 and Housing Benefit by between £0.165 and £0.115, depending upon the relationship of income to the needs allowance. This gives a fall in disposable income of £0.0525 and £0.0025 for each £1 earned.

For the mortgagor the situation is slightly better, because of the absence of a 'mortgage rebate' with marginal tax rates of 92.75% and 91.75%. These high marginal tax rates continue until the entitlement to FIS is exhausted. The 2-child family on low wages and the 4-child family with average or lower wages in the rented sector therefore face quite different budget constraints to single or childless married couples in similar circumstances. Indeed, for all intents and purposes these families have choice sets restricted to the earnings disregard section of the budget constraint because an individual would not choose a point, using our postulates and given a free choice of hours, which corresponded to an implicit marginal rate of tax in excess of 100%.

In Fig. 2.5 we illustrate these features using a 2-child family on low wages and average housing costs in both rented and mortgaged accommodation. Both families have the same budget constraint until 29 hours, after which their budget constraints

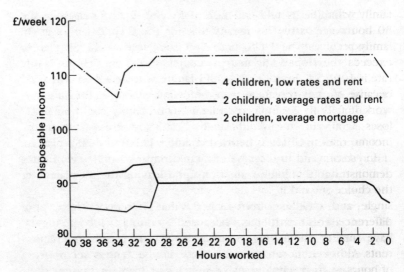

Fig. 2.5 Budget constraints of married couples on average wages

diverge. The renting family gains £13.13 in FIS plus £17.62 in Housing Benefit and this raises their disposable income by £3.70 above the SB plateau. In contrast, the mortgage family only receives £3.89 in rate rebate and this, together with the same amount of FIS, means that at 30 hours disposable income has fallen £4.63 below the SB plateau.

In both cases FIS is still being paid (£2.25) at 40 hours of work and therefore the interaction between the tax and social security systems imposes high marginal tax rates. For the renting family these are 105.25% and for the mortgage family 92.75%. These tax rates are further compounded by the extra travel costs involved at 32 hours per week which cause a fall in income of £1.04 for the mortgagor and £1.32 for the renter. The net results of these tax rates are that the income of the mortgagor has only risen by £0.37 and the renter's income has fallen by £2.35 between 30 and 40 hours of work. The choice set of hours for the mortgagor is therefore confined to the earnings disregard segment, while that of the renter includes the disregard segment and the hours between 29 and 30 hours where disposable income rises due to FIS.

Figure 2.5 also illustrates the budget constraint of a 4-child family which earns average wages and pays low rent and rates. At 30 hours disposable income falls by £1.77 to £111.76 and the family receives £5.58 FIS and £7.63 Housing Benefit. As income exceeds the Housing Benefit needs allowance the marginal tax rate is 100.25%. Between 32 and 33 hours disposable income falls because of extra travelling costs and between 33 and 34 hours of work it falls by £4.88 because FIS is exhausted and the family loses £5.63 in free school meals. After 34 hours disposable income rises until at 40 hours it is £0.33 below the SB plateau.

In summary, the analysis of married couples has again demonstrated that higher wages and lower housing costs increase the choice set and in this the 2- and 4-child families are similar to single and childless married persons. There is, though, one difference. This is that high wage earners with mortgages need not have smaller choice sets than the corresponding family which rents. Although more children imply a reduction in the choice set of hours, such differences may be unnoticeable over the range of hours zero to 40. This is because in fourteen comparisons which were made for the 2-child family, the choice set was empty in four and for the 4-child family this had risen to nine out of fourteen comparisons. It is tempting to conclude that the state has misaligned the various components of income support and the misalignment increases with the number of children. Finally, let us remember that in the 'poverty trap' high implicit marginal tax rates occur in the rented sector and these make it possible for an individual to receive a level of disposable income in excess of the level on SB. However, the benefits may well interact to exclude all but the first hour at which FIS is received from the choice set of hours.

Single Parents

The social security arrangements underlying the budget constraint of single parents is a combination of those underlying single people and those of a married couple with a similar number of children. Single parent families receive the same personal tax allowance as married couples except for the working wives' allowance. They receive the same Unemployment Benefit as single people and SB normal requirements (plus the addition for each child) but the needs allowance for Housing Benefit is the same as a married couple's. The prescribed income for FIS is not dependent upon family type, only upon the number of children.

There are, however, three differences in social security arrangements from either single or married couples with children. First, eligibility for FIS is achieved after 24 hours, not 30 hours of work, as in the case of 2-parent families. Secondly, single parent families not only have the first £4 of earnings disregarded, but also half of earnings between £4 and £20 for the purposes of calculating SB. Finally, single parent families also receive an extra one parent benefit of £3.65 in Child Benefit.

The earlier eligibility to FIS and the increase in Child Benefit will tend to reduce the length of the SB plateau relative to those of a married couple with 2 children. The SB plateau is at a lower level than that of a married couple because the single parent receives the normal requirements of a single person plus children requirements, and this would also tend to shorten the SB plateau. This last feature is partially offset by the increase in the earnings disregard of £8 so that the net SB plateau is only £8 lower for a single parent family than the corresponding married couple with children. We would therefore expect the end point of the SB plateau to be at a lower level of hours than the corresponding married couple with children.

We have already noted that the SB plateau is shorter for a single parent family than for the comparable married couple with children even though they share some of the underlying social security arrangements. The next question is: how does the ending of the SB plateau compare with a similar single person with whom single parents also share some social security arrangements? The answer is: it depends upon the interaction of wage rates and housing costs. If these result in an ending of the SB plateau before 24 hours of work, then single parent families will tend to have longer SB plateaux. On the other hand, if the single person's SB plateau ends after 24 hours then there is the possibility that a single parent family's SB plateau will terminate before the single person's.

These points are illustrated in Table 2.4. Below 24 hours of work, the single parent received £15.35 in Child Benefit plus £8.92 in Housing Benefit more than the comparable single person. However, extra SB payments for children, the heating allowance and the higher earnings disregard, total £29.28. It follows that

Table 2.4 Single Parent Benefits (£ p.w.)

Child Benefit	*FIS payable at 24 hrs. of work at low wage rate*	*Change in Housing Benefit at 24 hours*	*below 24 hrs.*	*Change in normal require-ments plus earnings disregard, age allowance & free school meals*
15.35	19.65	2.44	8.92	29.28

Housing Benefit and Child Benefit are £5.01 below the SB plateau compared to the same level of hours for a single person. At the lowest wage rate this is equivalent to roughly 8.2 hours of work.

At 24 hours of work the situation changes because the single parent family is now eligible for FIS which, together with Housing and Child Benefit, amount to £37.44, exceeding the increment to the SB plateau by £10.04. This will tend to reduce the length of the SB plateau of the single parent family relative to the single person. The increase in disposable income of £10.04 does not necessarily ensure that the single parent family leaves the SB plateau or its implicit level before the single person if FIS and Housing Benefit are not preferred to SB at 24 hours of work. This is because of the poverty trap, marginal tax rates in excess of 100% reduce disposable income and the gap between the SB plateau or its implicit level, and disposable income available from FIS and Housing Benefit increases. Hence, when FIS is exhausted, the difference in income between the SB plateau and actual disposable income will be larger for the single parent family compared to the single person and the single person will eliminate this difference at a lower level of hours. In this case, even though the SB plateau is longer than 24 hours, the single person achieves a level of disposable income in excess of the SB plateau before the single parent family and in this case because FIS is also exhausted, the single person has a larger choice set of hours (ignoring for the moment the earnings disregard section).

If the families are mortgagors, the above arguments have to be modified. If the level of hours at which the single person leaves the SB plateau is less than 24 hours, then as before, the single person's SB plateau is shorter. As with the rented case, if at all hours the single parent family's receipt of FIS pushes it above the SB plateau, then the single parent has a shorter SB plateau, compared with the single person. If at 24 hours FIS and Housing Benefit would not raise the single person's disposable income above the SB plateau, then the relative lengths of the plateaux depend upon the actual wage rate and housing costs for families with mortgages.

Figure 2.6 compares a single parent family on low wages and with a high mortgage and rates with a similar single man. In both cases the households choose to stay on SB until they are forced off after 29 hours. At 30 hours the single parent's income is £1.19 below the SB plateau and the single man's is £6.34 below. After 32 hours the single parent has disposable income in excess of the SB plateau, but the single person has to work 37 hours before this is achieved. Even though FIS does not cause the single parent disposable income to exceed the SB plateau at 24 hours of work the single parent has a larger choice set than the comparable single person. Of the thirteen other comparisons made, in only one other case, that of high rent and rates and low wages, did the single parent leave the SB plateau before the single person.

Returning to Fig. 2.6, if mortgage interest had been £1 more (£26.20 p.w.) then the single parent family would have risen above the implicit SB level after 38 hours of work and the single

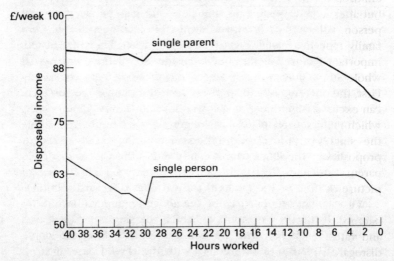

Fig. 2.6 Budget constraint of a single parent family with 2 children and a single person on low wages and high mortgage

person after 37 hours of work. A small change in the level of housing cost is able to reverse the ordering of the single person and single parent families with respect to leaving the SB plateau.

To recapitulate, the comparison of single parent families against single persons who rent indicates that if the single person leaves the SB plateau before 24 hours of work are completed, then the single person leaves the SB plateau first. This is true if the families have mortgages. If the single parent family fails to raise its disposable income above the SB plateau at 24 hours of work then again the single person will leave the SB plateau first. This does not apply to the comparison of single people and single parent families with mortgages. In this latter case, whether the single person or the single parent family attains an income in excess of the SB plateau depends upon the level of wages and housing costs. High housing costs or low wages will tend to increase the probability of the single person leaving the SB plateau first. If the single parent family does not achieve income in excess of the SB level, when FIS is exhausted, then both in the renter and mortgagor cases the single person will surpass the SB income level first.

In terms of leaving the SB plateau, single parent families with 2 children usually leave before their married couple counterparts but after, with the exception noted above, the comparable single person. Although the level of hours at which the comparable family types leave the SB plateau, or its implicit extension, is an important feature of the budget constraints, it does not tell the whole story of comparable choice sets. This is for two reasons. First, the poverty trap, which can affect those in the rented sector, can exclude from the choice set all the hours, except the first, for which FIS is received. Secondly, the greater earnings disregard for the single parent family makes part-time working a realistic proposition. Therefore, the level of hours at which the single parent family leaves the SB plateau does not give a complete picture of the choice of hours open to it.

We can illustrate this point by Fig. 2.7, which shows a single parent family with 2 children on average wages and average rent and rates. The first point of interest is the extended earnings disregard of 7 hours compared to a disregard of 2 hours for a similar single person or married couple with children. At 7 hours the SB plateau is established at £81.89 and extends until 15 hours

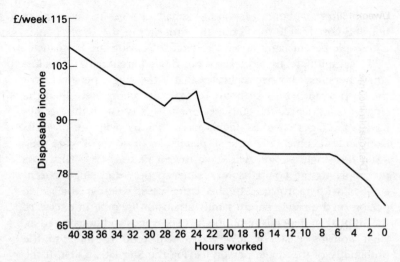

Fig. 2.7 Budget constraint of a single parent with 2 children on average wages and average rent and rates

of work after which Housing Benefit provides greater disposable income. At 24 hours of work the single parent claims FIS and disposable income increases by £7.10 between 23 and 24 hours worked. After 24 hours the poverty trap reduces disposable income and although FIS is exhausted at 27 hours disposable income does not exceed that 24 hours, which is £96.53 until 31 hours are worked. Even though the level of disposable income between 24 and 31 hours exceeds that available from SB, these hours of work do not form part of the choice set because they are dominated by the level of income at 24 hours of work. Consequently, the point at which SB is no longer claimed does not give an accurate description of the choice set because it ignores the 7 hours on the earnings disregard and the 7 hours excluded by the poverty trap. Alternatively, a single person on average wages and average rent and rates would leave the SB plateau after 13 hours and a married couple with 2 children at 27 hours. This is consistent with our previous discussion.

SENSITIVITY ANALYSIS
Having analysed single parent families in comparison to other family types we now turn our attention to the effects of changing

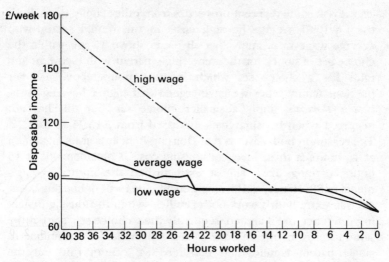

Fig. 2.8 Budget constraints of single parent families with 2 children with average mortgage and rates

wage rates and housing costs upon the budget constraint of a single parent with 2 children.

Higher wage rates, *ceteris paribus*, tend to increase the choice set of hours for renters but not necessarily for mortgagors. This is illustrated in Fig. 2.8, where single parent families with 2 children and an average mortgage are analysed at different wage rates. The single parent on high wages leaves the SB plateau after 12 hours of work. In the case of the low and average wage rate cases they both leave the SB plateau after 23 hours of work in order to claim FIS. As there is no poverty trap for mortgagors all the hours, ignoring those following travel cost increases, are in the choice set of hours. However, the single parent with a low wage rate has a larger earnings disregard of 11 hours compared with only 7 hours for the average wage rate single parent. As a result, the lower wage rate parent has the larger choice set of hours, albeit that this extra choice is confined to part-time working. This effect would not occur if single parents were not allowed to claim FIS until 30 hours of work. If this were the case, the single parent on low wages would remain on SB until 29 hours, whereas the average wage earner would still leave after 23 hours.

Comparing across housing costs, the single parent family cases also reveal some different properties from other family types. Both the low and average housing costs in the rented sector with average wage rates imply that all hours above 15 are within the choice set of hours, for the same single parent with high rent and rates has a choice set which includes hours above 19. For previous family types we have argued that higher housing costs, *ceteris paribus*, imply a smaller choice set, but this has not occurred when housing costs increased from £13.75 to £22.92. The reason in both cases is that Housing Benefit is at its maximum at 15 hours at these levels of housing costs. Coincidentally, at 15 hours, earnings have almost extinguished the normal requirements of SB. Hence, as Housing Benefit covers all of housing costs, after an extra hour's work both families switch to Housing Benefit in preference to SB and consequently their choice sets start at the same level of hours. Of course, this explanation is not unique to single parent families and therefore we cannot rule out the possibility of it occurring for other family types. However, for other family types the probability of different housing costs resulting in the same choice is lower. This is because the ratio of SB normal requirements to the needs allowance for Housing Benefit are lower for the 2-child single parent family than for any of the other family types analysed. The lower this ratio, roughly speaking, the greater the percentage of housing costs which are covered by Housing Benefit once SB is no longer claimed. Consequently, 2-child single parent families are more likely to have all their housing costs covered when they leave the SB plateau, and this is what causes the coincidence of choice sets even with different levels of housing costs.

Neither do single parent families who have mortgages have a consistent fall in the choice set of hours as housing costs increase. This is due to the families' claiming FIS which raises the level of disposable income above the SB plateau at 24 hours of work. This occurs for both the high and average cost families, whereas the low housing cost single parent family leaves the SB plateau after 20 hours of work, which is consistent with our previous findings. Had FIS not been available at 24 hours of work then the choice set of hours would have been larger for the single parent family on average housing costs, as was found for previous family types.

We now compare across tenure types, holding wages and housing costs constant. In this the single parent family follows the general trend of other family types in that single parents who rent have a larger choice set than their counterparts in mortgaged accommodation. The difference in the choice set is between 3 hours for the high wage, low housing cost case, and 8 hours for the average wage and housing cost case. There are two exceptions, out of seven comparisons, to this pattern. Both of these are for the low wage comparisons and occur because after 24 hours of work the poverty trap operates on the families which rent. This eliminates in these examples all the hours above 24 from the choice set so that single parents who rent have smaller choice sets than comparable mortgagors.

SUMMARY

To sum up our analysis we argued that in terms of the termination of the SB plateau the single parent family with 2 children usually lies between the single person and the married couple with 2 children. In the case of renting, this result depends upon whether or not FIS at 24 hours pushes disposable income above the SB plateau. In the case of the single parent family with a mortgage, the result depended upon not only whether FIS pushed disposable income above the SB plateau but, if it does not, by how much it fails to do so. We then argued that, while the SB plateau was an important part of the budget constraint, the existence of the extended earnings disregard and the poverty trap made comparisons of choice sets across family types difficult.

The comparisons across wage rates, housing costs and tenure types had features which implied that the choice set increased with higher wages, lower housing costs and with rented rather than mortgage accommodation. However, in our examples there were a number of instances where this did not occur either because of the ability of single parents to claim FIS at 24 hours of work or the low ratio of the SB normal requirements to the needs allowance. The budget constraints of a single parent family are therefore very complex and it is not true that the general principles which we have drawn from the previous family types hold for the single parent family at least over the range of variables covered by this analysis.

THE 'BETTER-OFF' PROBLEM

Before we leave the single parent family, let us examine the budget constraint of the single parent family with a high mortgage and rates and average wages to illustrate the 'better-off' problem. The 'better-off' problem refers to a property of the system which allows the individual a choice of benefits – in our case SB or Housing Benefit plus FIS. The problem arises because an incorrect choice can leave the person worse off than if they had chosen the alternative. In our example the individual chooses FIS and rate rebate at 24 hours of work because his level of disposable income exceeds that which he would have received from SB by £3.01. As he works an extra hour, travel costs increase by £1.20. This offsets his extra wages and leaves him worse off by £0.96, but this still exceeds the SB payments he would receive, so he continues claiming FIS and rate rebate. Assuming that the mortgage was, say, £2.50 higher than at 24 hours the individual would still claim FIS and rate rebate, although he would now be only £0.51 better off. As he works an extra hour, his income falls due to the extra travelling costs, but now his income is below the SB plateau by £0.45 and he should claim SB rather than FIS and rate rebates in order to maximize disposable income. This is, of course, an extreme case, but it does highlight the point that the 'better-off' problem can be very complex.

Working Spouses

Married couples when both partners work, are frequently ignored by modellers of the social security system, for example in the DHSS model tables. However, working wives made up a significant proportion of all workers in 1982. For expositional purposes we assume that the wife has gross earnings of £99 p.w. This figure represents average gross wages, including overtime, of all female workers who were unaffected by sickness, from the New Earnings Survey in April 1982. We further assume that her earnings are unaffected by her husband's labour supply decision, so that we can ignore any second round effects on the budget constraint.

The introduction of a wife's earnings has two effects on the budget constraint. First, her income reduces and, at £99 p.w., eliminates SB payments from the budget constraint. Secondly, the wife's income reduces or eliminates the Unemployment Benefit paid in respect of the husband. Consequently, when the husband is unemployed he receives basic Unemployment Benefit plus rent and rate rebate depending upon the level of housing costs. At 1 hour of work, the family loses basic Unemployment Benefit of £25.00 and as a result disposable income falls because the increase in Housing Benefit does not fully compensate. It is the number of hours after which this fall in income is recovered that determines the choice set of hours. The hours with disposable income below that at zero hours are equivalent to an implicit SB plateau in that they do not enter the choice set of hours.

The length of this implicit plateau is determined by wage rates and tenure type. A higher wage rate, *ceteris paribus*, results in a shorter implicit plateau and consequently a larger choice set of hours. This is true for both tenure types. Using our examples, the choice set starts at 8 hours of work for a high wage case and 22 hours for a low wage individual, both with average mortgages.

Across tenure types, mortgagors will usually have the larger choice set. This is the reverse of our findings for previous family types, the reason for this is that when the husband works 1 hour the family loses £25 in UB, but in the case of the renting couple this is partly offset by an increase in rent rebates. The renting couple therefore have a smaller gap in disposable income than their counterparts in mortgaged accommodation. However, the renting couple face a higher implicit tax rate of 61.75% compared to an implicit tax rate of 44.75% for the couple with a mortgage. The couple with a mortgage close their larger gap in disposable income at a faster rate than the renting couple. At some level of hours the disposable income available to both couples will be equivalent. Does this occur before or after the renting family's disposable income has exceeded its level at zero hours? If it does occur at a lower level of hours than required to exceed the implicit plateau, then the couple with a mortgage have the larger choice set. The reverse is the case if disposable income equivalence occurs after exceeding the plateau.

In the case of the couples on average housing costs and wage rates, which is illustrated in Fig. 2.9, the disposable income of the renters exceeds that of mortgagors by £3.69, relative to their respective levels at zero hours. The different implicit tax rates imply that after 6.6 hours this variation will be made up. However, at 1 hour of work the income gap is £18.91 and, at the given wage rate and tax rate this requires 15 extra hours of work to close the gap. Therefore, the income of the two couples becomes

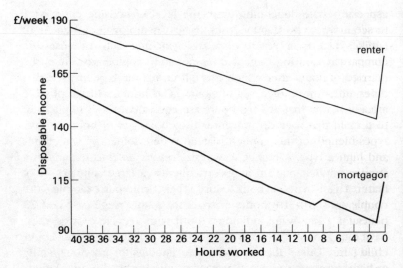

Fig. 2.9 Budget constraints of married couples when both partners work on average wages and housing costs

equivalent before the renting couple's income exceeds their implicit plateau and the mortgagor couple then has the larger choice set of hours. Similar conclusions can be reached for high housing costs on average wages where the choice set is 4 hours larger for the mortgagor couple. At low housing costs it is possible that the joint earnings of wife and husband and his Unemployment Benefit are sufficient to eliminate Housing Benefit at both zero hours and at the beginning of the choice set. If the wife's earnings are sufficient to utilize all of the tax allowance on mortgage interest payments then the choice set will be equivalent across tenure type. This situation occurs for both the average and high wage households in our examples.

It is worth pointing out that as the gross wages of the wife increase so that no Housing Benefit is received at any level of hours then the choice sets will become equivalent between tenure types, providing the wife's earnings are sufficient to exhaust the tax relief on mortgage interest payments. This is because disposable income of the mortgagor always exceeds that of the renting couple by the same amount. Alternatively, as the wife's income falls, the SB plateau will be re-established and the choice sets will tend towards those where the wife does not earn, that is renters have the larger choice set, *ceteris paribus*.

If we analyse the effect of changing housing costs, holding tenure type constant, we also find changes from the results where the wife does not work. If the wife's earnings are high enough to extinguish both SB payments and Housing Benefit, then, *ceteris paribus*, the choice set of hours is invariant to the level of housing costs. This is simply because the budget constraint, and hence the choice set, is being determined by other factors such as the wage rate and tenure type. Indeed, provided that Housing Benefit is not received at zero hours and at the level of hours the choice set begins, the choice set is independent of housing cost even if Housing Benefit is received. If Housing Benefit is received at zero hours but not at the level of hours at the end of the implicit plateau, an increase in housing costs reduces the choice set of hours.

Although the above points apply equally to married couples with mortgages, they are not likely to be of great practical significance because the the value of rate rebates are relatively small. In fact, a comparison of high, average and low mortgages with average wages revealed that in all three cases the choice set of hours began at 14 hours of work, even though there is a difference of £18.34 in housing costs between the high and low cost cases.

We can also compare the budget constraints of the childless married couples when the wife works against when she does not. In each of our standard fourteen cases working couples had larger choice sets than their counterparts. This is because the wife's earnings make the family ineligible for SB, in which case the implicit plateau is determined by the single person's Unemployment Benefit (£25.00) rather than by the SB normal (£41.70) and housing requirements. Hence the income gap to be covered by the 2-worker couple is smaller and they cover this gap before their counterparts. This effect will be most apparent at higher housing costs for when only the husband works the couple receives all the extra housing costs in SB, whereas working couples receive only 60% of the increase in Housing Benefit. Hence, when housing costs are high the gap which the husband has to cover is relatively large when his spouse does not work.

Finally, in passing we can note that as the wife's earnings fall, the budget constraints will tend to become similar whether or not both spouses work. Furthermore, as with the single parent case, the introduction of children into the family tends to reduce the choice set of hours. This is because children raise disposable income at zero hours relative to other working hours by raising Unemployment Benefit and receiving free school meals which are only available at zero hours.

To summarize our findings on working couples, we found that, as in most previous cases, higher wages increase the choice set of hours. Across tenure types we found, unlike previous cases, that mortgagors have larger choice sets although if the wife's wages are high enough to eliminate Housing Benefit, the budget constraints became equivalent. The budget constraints were found to be unaffected by changes in housing costs provided that Housing Benefit is not being received at all or is being received at both zero hours and the beginning of the choice set. We also concluded that working couples would tend to have larger choice sets than those where only one spouse works.

The Effect of the Distribution of Housing Costs on the Budget Constraints

During the preceding analysis, we have constantly assumed that the components of housing costs, rent, mortgage interest payments and rates have moved together as housing costs have altered. For the three levels of housing costs used in this chapter – £32.00, £22.92 and £13.75, rates have accounted for just over 21% of total housing costs.

In this section we analyse the effects of changing the distribution of housing costs between its various components on the receipt of housing rebates. As there exists no 'mortgage rebate', we consider only the case of renters.

As discussed earlier, rent and rate rebates can be modelled as

$$\text{rent rebate} = 0.6 \text{ rent} + 0.25 \text{ (NALL}-Y) \text{ (For NALL}>Y)$$

$$\text{rate rebate} = 0.6 \text{ rates} + 0.08 \text{ (NALL}-Y) \text{ (For NALL}>Y)$$

$$\text{rent rebate} = 0.6 \text{ rent} + 0.17 \text{ (NALL}-Y) \text{ (For NALL}<Y)$$

$$\text{rate rebate} = 0.6 \text{ rates} + 0.06 \text{ (NALL}-Y) \text{ (For NALL}<Y)$$

where Y = relevant income minus disregards
   NALL = needs allowance

By summing the two functions we obtain

total housing rebates = 0.6 (rent + rates) + 0.33 (NALL−Y)
                                 (For NALL>Y)

total housing rebates = 0.6 (rent + rates) + 0.23 (NALL−Y)
                                 (For NALL<Y)

Consequently, it can be seen that for each given level of income and total housing costs, total housing rebates are invariant to the distribution of components of housing costs. This is simply because an increase in one will be offset by the fall in the other. However, this result does not hold if either maximum rent/rate rebates or zero rent/rate rebates are being paid. In these cases changes in the distribution of housing costs between its components can change the total housing rebate received at a given level of income. Consider, for example, two families which receive maximum rate rebates but less than maximum rent rebates. If one family pays £1 more rent than the other (and correspondingly rate payments are £1 less), then it can receive up to £0.60 more in total Housing Benefit than the other identical family. The reason for this is that because both rate rebates are at a maximum, there will be £1 difference between them but only £0.60 difference in the rent rebates.

The interaction of maximum rebates and the actual level of housing costs which, if below the statutory maximum rebates determine the maximum level of benefit, make specific statements about differences in Housing Benefit difficult. However, a stylized view may show little difference in rebates at low levels of income. The variations then increase with income and then fall again as income approaches the needs allowances. As income increases, the level of differences in benefits rises and then declines to zero as Housing Benefit is exhausted, no matter what is the distribution of housing costs. It should be remembered that this stylized profile may be truncated at the beginning depending upon the circumstances of the family. Across levels of housing costs or family types no general comments can be made because the results crucially depend upon exact circumstances.

We can illustrate this point by using Fig. 2.10. The two budget

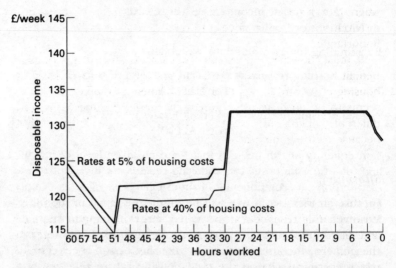

Fig. 2.10 Budget constraints of a married man with 4 children on low wages and high housing costs when the proportion of rates varies

constraints are of a married man with 4 children who has the lowest wage rate. The difference is that in one case rates make up 5% of housing costs and in the other 40%. In order that the full effects be visible the budget constraint has been extended to run to 60 hours of work per week. Along the SB plateau the two households receive the same income but once SB is terminated the budget constraints deviate by £3.68 at 30 hours of work and the difference is still £1.24 after 60 hours of work. Different distributions of housing costs can therefore cause changes in the level of income support which a family receives. However, the differential in disposable income due to changes in housing cost distribution is relatively small when compared to the differences in income due to different family composition, the level of housing costs and tenure type. Moreover, its effect on the choice set of hours is also quite muted. By using the percentage differences in Housing Benefit weighted by the level of housing costs, at that level of income at which the four family types take up Housing Benefit, the maximum difference in disposable income for our sample was found to be £2.00 for the married couple with 4 children. This is less than one hour's pay even at the lowest wage rate. Consequently, the effect of different housing cost distributions on the choice set of hours is unlikely to be of major importance.

It must, however, be stressed that the failure of the Housing Benefit system to guarantee horizontal equity with respect to housing costs can be regarded as a weakness of the system. There seems to be no plausible rationale for similar families to receive different, albeit only slightly different, income levels simply because of the composition of their housing costs.

Summary

In this chapter we have compared the budget constraints of various family types and analysed the effect of changing the level and distribution of housing costs, tenure type and wage rates. In the numerous cases analysed, not one had a choice set of hours which encompassed all the hours available. Indeed, we had some cases where the individual would have had to have worked far in excess of 40 hours per week in order to attain a disposable income in excess of that available on the SB plateau. In the majority of the cases examined the choice set of hours comprises being unemployed or being in 'full-time work'. Only for the single parent family did the budget constraint allow the individual a reasonable choice of working 'part-time' (below, say, 7 hours per week). Moreover, we found that the choice set of hours increased with wage rates, fell as housing costs increased and was larger for a renter than a mortgagor. However, there were a number of exceptions to these findings. For example, in the case of working couples an increase in housing costs will not necessarily reduce the choice set of hours. We also showed how changes in the distribution of housing costs between rent and rates would affect the budget constraints although its practical effects were, for the examples we selected, minimal.

Appendix
The Number of Working Hours at which a Continuous Choice Set Begins and the Replacement Ratio

Category	Single	Married couple, man only works	Married couple, 2 children	Married couple, 4 children	Single parent family, 2 children	Married couple, both work
1	14	20	28	40*	31	16
	0.5836	0.7152	0.8225	1.0001	0.6518	0.7168
2	23	32	40*	40*	40*	26
	0.7634	0.8816	0.9414	1.01098	0.7438	0.8646
3	7	11	14	24	9	9
	0.3277	0.4211	0.5201	0.6711	0.4140	0.5078
4	12	18	23	40*	31	14
	0.4736	0.6272	0.7664	0.9675	0.5853	0.6880
5	19	24	31	40*	31	18
	0.6701	0.7712	0.8648	1.0296	0.7013	0.7516
6	30	39	40*	40*	40*	29
	0.8352	0.9364	0.9826	1.0490	0.7948	0.9066
7	7	10	13	22	9	8
	0.2659	0.3613	0.4646	0.6193	0.3597	0.4874
8	20	26	31	40*	30	14
	0.5481	0.6888	0.8103	1.0028	0.6387	0.7017
9	31	40	40*	40*	26	22
	0.7720	0.9330	1.0031	1.0766	0.7849	0.8407
10	11	14	17	23	13	8
	0.3612	0.4067	0.5036	0.6512	0.4012	0.5019
11	16	22	28	40	30	14
	0.4571	0.6066	0.7441	0.9540	0.5688	0.6938
12	23	29	35	40*	30	14
	0.6464	0.7614	0.8699	1.0511	0.7015	0.7072
13	37	40*	40*	40*	32	22
	0.8721	1.0172	1.0692	1.1262	0.8563	0.8451
14	9	12	13	22	12	8
	0.2607	0.3544	0.4048	0.6090	0.3535	0.4942

Note: 40* indicates that at 40 hours of work per week the level of disposable income is below that available if the family claims SB. The choice set excludes the earnings disregard section, but includes hours excluded by increases in travel costs. Also excluded is the hour at which FIS is received if the following hours are subject to the poverty trap.

Legend

Tenure type	Categories 1–7 rent their accommodation.
	Categories 8–14 have mortgages.
Wage rates	Categories 1, 4, 5, 8, 11 and 12 have average wages.
	Categories 2, 6, 9 and 13 have low wages.
	Categories 3, 7, 10 and 14 have high wages.
Housing costs	Categories 1, 2, 3, 8, 9 and 10 have average housing costs.
	Categories 4, 7, 11 and 14 have low housing costs.
	Categories 5, 6, 12 and 13 have high housing costs.

Notes: Chapter 2

1   See Adler and Du Feu, 1977, for a discussion of their results.
2   See M. O'Higgins's 'Computerizing the social security system: an operational strategy in lieu of a policy strategy', *Public Administration* 1984, vol. 62, no. 2, pp. 201–10.
3   The old system of altering the tax allowances is used rather than the deduction at source introduced in April 1983.
4   *Social Trends* 14, Table 2.4, p. 31.
5   *Social Trends* 14, Table 2.7, p. 32.
6   The probability of these age distributions occurring is rather remote. See Atkinson and Sutherland, 1983.
7   *Social Trends* 14, Table 2.9, p. 33.
8   *Social Trends* 14, Table 2.8, p. 33.
9   *Social Trends* 14, Chart 8.8, p. 121.
10   *New Earnings Survey*, Part A, Table 1, p. A15.
11   Although the model does have the facilities to deal with overtime working.
12   These costs are conservative in comparison with Davies, Minford and Sprague, 1983, who assume £8.25 p.w. in November 1982.

3

A Historical Analysis
of Labour Supply Incentives

Don M. Egginton

Introduction

In this chapter the budget constraints and associated labour
supply incentives of a married man with 2 children are chronicled
between April 1960 and April 1982. As should be clear from
Chapter 2, such households cannot be regarded as representative
of households as a whole. Rather, the aim of the chapter is quite
modest: to explore the way in which changes in social security
and tax arrangements have affected labour supply incentives over
time. To achieve this aim it is illustrative to study just one family
type and we have chosen the married man with 2 children
because this allows a fuller description of the social security
system than say, a married man with no children.

Although we concentrate our attention on the last 25 years, we
begin by sketching the social security arrangements prior to 1960
so that the arrangements made after 1960 can be placed in
context. We have omitted mentioning the changes in other forms
of social security, such as health, not because they are unimportant but because they do not play a direct role in the construction
of budget constraints in which we are ultimately interested.

The Old Poor Law

According to Atkinson (1975, p. 219) the origins of the Supplementary Benefit scheme 'can be traced back to the Elizabethan Act
for the Relief of the Poor'. In a series of Acts between 1597 and
1601, Queen Elizabeth's last two parliaments codified legislation
from the previous forty years. Under these statutes each parish
was to support its own poor by providing 'outdoor' relief for the
aged and the sick, and work for the able-bodied in workhouses. As
a means of reducing social tension, the impoverished were only
entitled to relief within the parish of their birth or where they had
settlement. This restriction on the mobility of labour was liable to
exacerbate the problems of the poor in finding employment and
thereby relieving their own distress. These measures were
financed from rates levied on property. The Poor Laws provided
to Tudor England 'a measure of social security unknown either to
their English forebears or to most of their European contemporaries' (Bindoff, 1950, p. 294).

The Elizabethan Poor Laws were reaffirmed by the Poor Law
Amendment Act of 1664 and this provided the basis of social
security until 1834 although there were wide variations in the
enforcement of these Acts both across time and regions. For
example, Knatchbull's Act of 1722 provided for the building of
new workhouses, but was reversed by Gilbert's Act of 1782 which
was designed to turn workhouses into poorhouses for the old and
infirm while the able-bodied were to be given outdoor relief. The
number of parishes responding to these Acts appears to have been
small. It should be noted that some authors have questioned the
relative importance of Poor Law provision. Jordan (1959) believes
that between Tudor times and the late seventeenth century,
private charity was more important than Poor Law relief.[1]

In the late eighteenth century and the early part of the
nineteenth century relief of the able-bodied had taken numerous
forms. Probably the best known is the Speenhamland system of
1795, which became widespread in the parishes of the South and
Midlands in response to the rise in wheat prices caused by the
French war and the postwar depression. The Speenhamland
system supplemented a man's wage by an amount determined by
his earnings, the size of the man's family and the price of bread. In

the former two aspects the Speenhamland system is akin to FIS. There were numerous local variations to this system. For example, after 1815 payments were made only if the number of children in the family exceeded three. In some areas the bread scales were not used whilst in others payment was in flour rather than money (Marshall, 1968, pp. 13–14). By the early 1830s the Speenhamland system was in decline.

Other systems for subsidizing wages, irrespective of family size, had also evolved. These included the Labour Rate and the Roundsman systems. In the former, ratepayers could choose to employ the able-bodied unemployed at a set wage or pay the difference in rates. Surplus labourers were divided between ratepayers in proportion to the rates they paid. This work was provided for the unemployed at wages which were likely to exceed the market wage rate. This system was estimated to be used in 20% of parishes in 1832. The Roundsman system was less commonly used than the Labour Rate (Marshall, 1968, pp. 13–14). Ratepayers offered employment to the unemployed while part of their wages was paid by the parish.[2]

The New Poor Law

The outdoor relief of the able-bodied was criticized by a number of parliamentary select committees between 1817 and 1828 on two main grounds: that they were responsible for a marked increase in expenditure and that they were injurious to work incentives. In real per capita terms, expenditure was some 39.8% higher in 1833 than in 1802, although it seems unlikely that the increase was wholly due to increased expenditure on outdoor relief.[3] A similar view was forcefully expressed by the Royal Commission on the Poor Laws 1832–4. The Commission attempted to revitalize the idea of 'less eligibility': that is, the able-bodied were not to receive better treatment than the poorest independent labourer. In order to promote this, it was recommended that outdoor relief be abolished and the able-bodied be set to work within workhouses. The resulting Act, the Poor Law Amendment Act 1834, concentrated on administrative details with the appointment of Poor Law commissioners and the grouping of parishes into unions. The commissioners themselves were to regulate the Poor Laws and outdoor relief using the Commission's report to guide them. Under the New Poor Law, as it became known, workhouses were built, the Speenhamland system was ended and the conditions of relief tightened. Yet outdoor relief continued in the form of grants to families of good standing who had fallen on hard times, or by labour tests, that is outdoor relief being dependent upon the undertaking of work. Moreover, the work loads and the relief received varied considerably between localities.[4]

The Experiments with Insurance

The remaining years until the beginning of the twentieth century saw little major legislation regarding poverty relief. The leniency of outdoor relief fluctuated over the period. A notable example was in response to heavy unemployment of Lancashire cotton workers in thr early 1860s, where the Poor Law board ordered the local guardians to grant outdoor relief. During this period, an alternative source of relief appeared in the form of trade union benefits. These not only covered unemployment but also sickness, accident and funeral expenses. Beenstock and Brasse (1986, Table 2.6) estimate that between 1875 and 1910 the maximum number of trade unionists who could have received unemployment benefit rose from just under 18,000 to 50,550. This compares to 800,914 in 1875 and 792,499 in 1900 recipients of both indoor and outdoor relief in England and Wales. Thus the number of recipients of trade union benefits was small, although not insignificant, compared to recipients of Poor Law relief, and the latter accounted for 2.5% of the population in 1900 (Rose, 1972, p. 53). In comparison the income of London charities in 1861 exceeded expenditure on the Poor Law in London (Dilnot *et al.*, 1984, p. 7).

The Infant Welfare State

The period following the 1834 Act saw increased criticism of the Poor Law's inability to deal with recipients on the basis of the causes of their poverty. At the turn of the century, this criticism began to be removed by a spate of legislation. In 1897 the Workmen's (Compensation for Accidents) Act was passed, and by 1906 this covered 13.25 million workers. The Old Age Pension Act of 1908 introduced a means-tested pension for those over 70 and by 1913 this covered 60% of the population over 70. School meals for needy children were provided from 1906 and child tax allowances were reintroduced in the 1909 budget. In 1911 the National Insurance Act introduced, not without opposition from vested interests such as trade unions, unemployment and health insurance. The former covered about 2.25 million mainly skilled workers in 1911 covering seven industries including construction, shipbuilding and engineering.[5] The industries chosen were noted for their seasonal unemployment records, thus the state reduced its commitment by avoiding those industries which suffered chronic unemployment. The state also reduced its liabilities by restricting benefits, of £0.35 per week, to be payable for up to 15 weeks in any one year and then only if five weeks' contributions had been paid in for every one paid out. As a condition of receiving benefit the unemployed had to register as available for work at labour exchanges which had been established by the Unemployed Workmen Act of 1905. Health insurance, administered by approved societies, mainly friendly societies and trade unions, paid both money directly to the sick and certain medical expenses. At the discretion of the society, further payments could be made. This part of the 1911 Act covered about 13 million workers (Pollard, 1969, p. 37). Both these schemes began payments in January 1913.

Shortly after the turn of the century, the social security system had taken up a dual form which in its broad aspects is not dissimilar to the present system, with the Poor Laws providing some security, as SB does today, for those that did not qualify for other benefits. As yet, the relative scarcity of other benefits meant that in 1914, 2% of the population of England and Wales still received relief under the Poor Laws (Rose, 1972, p. 53).

The Interwar Years

The interwar years saw increased legislation on social policy in response to the massive rise in unemployment. In 1916 the unemployment insurance scheme had been extended to cover some 4 million workers (Pollard, 1969, p. 248). At the end of the war the government introduced the Out-of-Work Donation Scheme to deal with the problems of transition to a peacetime economy. The scheme covered nearly all workers and the benefits, which were not contributory, exceeded those available under the 1911 scheme so that the latter was for all intents and purposes suspended. For civilians this scheme was terminated in November 1919 and for ex-servicemen in 1921. It was replaced by the Unemployment Insurance Act of 1920 which maintained the extended coverage of the Out-of-Work Donation Scheme but had similar benefit and contribution levels to the 1911 scheme, which included 'signing on' conditions and limited entitlement of 15 weeks per year. In 1921 this latter condition was extended to 26 weeks and the Unemployed Workers' Dependants Act (1921) provided additional benefits for dependants.

The scheme was soon in trouble, as the rise in the unemployment rate from 3.9% in 1920 to 22.1% at its height in 1932 meant that the increasing numbers of unemployed became ineligible for insurance benefits. The government's response was to introduce amendments to the 1920 Act which eased the contribution conditions for full benefit and allowed supplementary payments to be made. These payments were termed uncovenanted benefit (1921), extended benefit (1924), transitional benefits (1927) and transitional payments (1931). For example, following the Unemployment Act 1927, indefinite rights were granted if 8 contributions had been made in the previous 2 years or 30 at any time. By 1928, there were almost as many unemployed on the 'transitional benefit' as on the full insurance scheme (Pollard, 1969, p. 250). These measures meant that the actuarial basis of the insurance scheme was forsaken with the Treasury having to make up the deficit. This resulted in expenditure reaching 25% of all government expenditure on social services compared to 3–4% in 1920. Yet between 120,000 and 140,000 insured workers slipped through these measures to be dealt with by the Poor Law (Pollard, 1969, p. 250). In part this reflects the 'large number of workers refused benefits' on the grounds that they were not genuinely seeking employment.[6]

Further increase in the numbers of unemployed in 1931 caused the government to reduce the benefits payable by 10%, restrict eligibility to 26 weeks per year, increase the weekly contribution rate to £0.125, and make benefits payable only if 30 contributions had been made in the last 2 years. For those whose benefit was exhausted there were transitional benefits administered by local Public Assistance Committees (PAC) which were responsible for the Poor Law provision after the Local Government Act of 1929. Granting of transitional benefits was dependent upon a stringent means test where the income of other members of the household would be taken into consideration, as was the ownership of property.[7] The impact of this means test resulted in 440,000 persons being excluded either fully or partially from receipt of Unemployment Benefit between November 1931 and the beginning of January 1932 (Deacon and Bradshaw, 1983, p. 17).

There were noticeable regional differences in both the numbers excluded and the generosity of benefits (see, for example, Deacon and Bradshaw, 1983, pp. 20–1). The government responded by introducing the Unemployment Assistance Board (UAB) to standardize benefits by being responsible for the uninsured unemployed. These benefits were to be set so that recourse to the Poor Laws would be unnecessary.

Thus the unemployed were set to become the first group to be excluded from the control of the Poor Laws. The board came into operation in January 1935 and almost within a month its scales were suspended, under the Standstill Act, as nearly 50% of the recipients of the UAB benefits were worse off than under the PACs. It was not until April 1937 that the Board completely administered its own rates and the intervening two years, known as 'the standstill', had seen a mixture of both PAC and UAB rate benefits, whichever was the most favourable to the recipient. 'The standstill' also had the effect that the administrators moved away from a rigid interpretation of the regulations towards a more discretionary approach and by the end of 1935, 20% of claimants were receiving discretionary payments (Deacon and Bradshaw, 1983, p. 25). Thus at the end of the 1930s there was, in effect, a three-tier scheme: the Poor Law, which still dealt with 30,000 unemployed in March 1937, the transitional benefits and the insurance scheme.

Using the data reported in Matthews (1982), we can trace the evolution of benefits paid to a married man with 2 children. The interwar years saw a marked increase in both benefit rates from

£0.57 in 1920 to £1.64 in 1938 for the married man, and from £0.57 to £1.15 over the same period for the representative benefit.[8] The increase is brought out more starkly in Fig. 3.1, where the ratio of Unemployment Benefit against gross earnings is plotted. From a level of 13% in 1920, the ratio rose steeply in the early 1920s and continued to rise throughout the period until it reached a peak of 48.7% in 1936. It should be remembered that the ratio is not a strict replacement ratio because we have not allowed for insurance contributions or travel costs. The series from 1948 to 1982 is a replacement ratio and is consistent with the budget constraints calculated for the period 1960–82 in the later sections of this chapter. These replacement ratios make allowance for National Insurance contributions, housing costs, Supplementary Benefit, Unemployment Benefit, Earnings Related Supplement, Family Allowances and income tax.[9] A comparison of the two periods indicates that despite the substantial rise in the ratio during the interwar period it was well below the levels experienced during the postwar period.

The interwar years, although dominated by the need to devise short-term schemes to meet the challenge of mass unemployment and the continued failure of insurance-based benefits, also saw

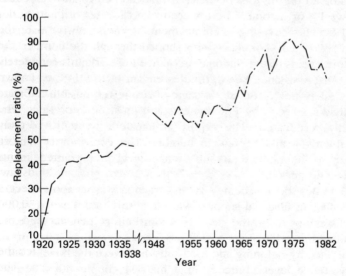

Fig. 3.1 Replacement ratios 1920-82

83

continued development of other aspects of social security. By 1939, 112 local authorities in England and Wales, 8.6%, had introduced rent rebates of some form for council tenants (Legg and Brion, n.d., p. 20). Overall about 2% of tenants received a rebate (Deacon and Bradshaw, 1983, p. 13). Pensions had also been extended with the age of retirement reduced to 60 for women, the income limits increased and the level of pension raised. Furthermore, a contributory pension scheme was introduced with a retirement age of 65 for men. Thus by the beginning of the Second World War, Britain had experience with many of the elements which were to form part of the postwar social security system.

The Beveridge Scheme

The postwar social security system is based on the Beveridge plan devised during the Second World War. We will not attempt to describe the system in any detail. The salient features, in so far as they affect budget constraints, will be described in a later section. Instead a few general points will be made. The Beveridge scheme was based on the idea of social insurance open to all irrespective of wealth or income. There were to be flat rates of contribution and benefits covering unemployment, sickness, injury, maternity and retirement. For those who slipped through the contributory sector, means-tested National Assistance to be administered by the National Assistance Board, the descendant of the UAB, was to act as a safety net. National Assistance became responsible for those individuals receiving PAC benefits and thus the Poor Laws were finally terminated. The report anticipated, wrongly, that the recipients would be few in number. The contributory benefits were to be pitched at subsistence level and granted for an indefinite period.

The Beveridge scheme's great attraction was its apparent offer of sufficient financial support without resort to a means test. Yet this was not to be the case. The contributory benefits were not granted for an indefinite period nor, because wartime inflation was repressed by rationing and food subsidies, were the benefits set at subsistence levels. Indeed, for a married couple the difference between Unemployment Benefit and National Assistance was only

£0.10 in July 1948, and once allowance for housing costs are made the couple would have been better off by claiming both benefits. Consequently a large number of persons, 873,000 at the end of 1950, were dependent upon means-tested benefits even if they were eligible for contributory benefits.

The second problem with the scheme was that, by making contributions flat-rated and the scheme open to all, contributions were tied to the amount affordable by the lowest paid. The least of the scheme's worries was that with benefits being determined by needs the actuarial basis of the contributory sector was violated. More importantly, the relationship between flat-rated contributions determined by groups on low pay and benefits determined by needs, would place the scheme in a financial quandary. The eventual 'solution' was to make contributions earnings related and receive support from general taxation.

Finally, the Beveridge scheme did little to help the working poor. Its major contribution was the introduction of child allowance for families with two or more children, under the Family Allowance Act of 1945. Thus many families would receive no help at all if they were in work.

The introduction of Beveridge's scheme in July 1948 saw the termination of the last vestiges of the Poor Law, which had underlain English social security for the previous 350 years. Over this span of time the Poor Law acted as a safety net, albeit a feared one, and about this various insurance schemes were woven. Thus the Beveridge scheme stands within the (very) broadly interpreted tradition of English social security measures, and it is the Beveridge scheme, with a number of modifications, which itself underlies the system which we analyse, from the standpoint of budget constraints, in the remainder of this chapter.

Budget Constraints

In this and the remaining sections of the chapter we describe the system which arose from the modifications of Beveridge's plan. Unlike the previous section we also describe the resulting budget constraints for a married man with 2 children over the period 1960 to 1982. Before we can attempt this a few points need to be raised. First, until the late 1960s the implementation of rent rebates was the responsibility of each local authority, and consequently the budget constraints which we estimate would not be applicable to every region of Britain. Secondly, over this period there were changes in the interpretation of social security law which are not amenable to modelling. One example of this, noted by Layard (1982, p. 42), is the reduced probability of being disqualified from receiving Unemployment Benefit. Allowing for the effects of these types of changes on the budget constraint would prove rather difficult and is not attempted, but they need to be borne in mind. Finally there are two methods of analysing changes in the budget constraints over time. One approach is to abstract from changes in exogenous variables by fixing them in proportion to wage rates at a given date. Thus rent, rates and travel costs would be determined by changes in wage rates which in turn may be linked to the price level to give a constant real wage level. Thus the budget constraint would indicate the changes in social security arrangements alone. Yet work incentives are not determined solely by social security arrangements, and we have decided to allow the exogenous variables to vary against each other. Using this approach it is necessary to specify the wage rate, housing costs and travel costs in each year. These assumptions are given in Table 3.1. The wage rate is based on the average earnings of manual men whose pay was not affected by absence. As in Chapter 2, we assume that the wife does not work and there is no other source of income.

The data for rental costs were based on the average rent for all local authorities at April of each year, except for 1973, when the figure is for May. Between 1965 and 1968 rents were calculated by taking the rent income received by each local authority in six English and Welsh regions minus income from other amenities. This total income was then divided by the total number of dwellings and then weighted by the proportion of the population in that region. Between 1960 and 1965 the data is simply extrapolated from the other available data. We have not therefore attempted to make rent payments consistent with the size of the families we analyse in the following sections. From 1974 to 1980 the rate statistics are based on the average domestic rate payment for all authorities in England and Wales. Between 1964 and 1973 rates were calculated as the product of the average domestic rateable value times the average rate in the pound in April of each

Table 3.1 The Assumptions Used to Calculate the Budget Constraints (£)

Year	Hourly wage rate	Rent per week	Rates per week	Travel costs per week	Value of free school meals per week
1960	0.29	0.99	0.50	0.36	0.19
1961	0.32	1.04	0.53	0.38	0.19
1962	0.33	1.08	0.57	0.40	0.19
1963	0.34	1.13	0.59	0.41	0.19
1964	0.37	1.21	0.62	0.44	0.19
1965	0.40	1.35	0.70	0.47	0.19
1966	0.44	1.51	0.78	0.50	0.19
1967	0.45	1.69	0.81	0.53	0.19
1968	0.48	1.90	0.86	0.56	0.28
1969	0.52	2.04	0.93	0.60	0.28
1970	0.53	2.23	1.01	0.71	0.33
1971	0.62	2.48	1.16	0.78	0.45
1972	0.69	2.75	1.30	0.83	0.45
1973	0.79	3.44	1.48	0.88	0.45
1974	0.91	3.78	1.58	1.02	0.45
1975	1.19	4.16	1.79	1.53	0.56
1976	1.41	4.77	1.94	1.75	0.56
1977	1.54	5.52	2.24	2.00	0.56
1978	1.73	5.85	2.45	2.10	0.94
1979	1.97	6.40	2.92	2.45	0.94
1980	2.46	9.06	4.40	3.55	1.31
1981	2.69	11.37	4.58	4.40	1.69
1982	2.95	13.50	5.30	5.50	1.69

year. For the years prior to 1964 the rate payments were extrapolated back from the data already obtained. The data for housing costs are therefore an approximation which applies only to local authority tenants. Travel costs are based on the weekly travel costs in November 1982 from the DHSS Tax-Benefit model tables and an index of travel costs derived from the Annual Abstract of Statistics. The travel costs were incremented after every 9 hours of work. In each year the budget constraint is evaluated up to 44 hours of work. The value of free school meals is taken as being the cost of school meals times the number of school days per year. The cost of school meals is derived from Department of Education statistics.

As can be seen from Table 3.1, there have been some marked changes in the relative levels of housing costs, travel costs and wage rates. For example, in 1960, rent payments are assumed to be 3.4 times the hourly wage rate, 4.2 times in 1970, 3.4 times in 1978, and 4.6 times in 1982. Thus changes in the budget constraints between years are also due to assumptions we have made. Although we cannot claim that these assumptions, or indeed any other set of assumptions we could make, are representative, we hope that they at least provide an informed illustration of the changes in both relative and nominal values. We now turn to the social security and tax systems which underlay the budget constraints between 1960 and 1965.

The Components of the Budget Constraints 1960–5

In this section we analyse the budget constraints facing a married man with 2 children during the period 1960–5. In comparison to later periods there were fewer benefits which would effect the budget constraint. However, a number of the taxes and benefits had different forms from those in operation during the 1980s. We begin with a description of income taxation.

The most notable change between this period and the 1980s is in income taxation. During this period income was classified under five schedules: A to E. Only schedule E, which deals with income from office employment or pension, will concern us. Statutory income was defined as joint gross income minus all payments made under legal obligation, such as bank interest and mortgage interest. This was further differentiated into earned and other income with earned income attracting earned income relief. There were also a number of allowances which could be set against tax, the main ones being personal and child allowances. These are the main factors which determine the threshold at which income becomes taxable. A further feature of this period was the allowance paid against National Insurance contributions. This relief was withdrawn in April 1965 and replaced by an increase in the personal allowances. Between 1960 and 1962 the personal and child tax allowances remained constant at £240 and £100 respectively for each child aged under 11. In 1963 these were raised to £200 and £115 per annum and in 1965 the married man's allowance was raised by a further £20. Relief for National Insurance contributions was £18 until 1963 when it was increased to £22.

Earned income relief, EIR, also acts as a tax allowance except that its value varies with the amount of earned income. Over the whole of this period EIR was 2/9 of the earned income up to £4,005 and 1/9 of the next £5,940. EIR is calculated on the joint earned income of the family or on statutory income, whichever is smaller.

During the period 1960–5, the standard rate of tax was 38.75%, from 1960/1 to 1964/5 and in 1965/6 this was increased to 41.25%. Before income tax at the standard rate became payable there were, until 1962, three reduced tax bands which covered the first £360 of taxable income. In these bands the rate of tax ranged from 8.75% to 31.25%. In 1963 the third reduced tax band was abolished and although the widths of the remaining tax bands were raised only the first £300 of taxable income was covered. The tax rates were also raised to 20% and 30% in the first and second tax bands respectively. The effect of EIR was to reduce the effective marginal rate by the amount of the relief fraction. For example in 1965 the standard rate of tax was 41.25% but the effective marginal rate, for those earning less than the limit, was 32%.

National Insurance contributions were a fixed amount, which ranged from £0.49 p.w. in 1961 to £0.68 p.w. in 1965. These rates were for an employed male who was not contracted out of the graduated pension scheme. From April 1961 an additional percentage on gross earnings of 4¼% was payable on earnings between £9 and £15 per week. In June 1963 the upper limit was increased to £18.

A problem exists for calculating budget constraints, as it is not clear at what level of earnings an individual became liable to pay the fixed-level contribution. The Act of 1946 states that National Insurance contributions shall not be paid on 'unsubstantial hours of work'. We arbitrarily define this as being 10 hours p.w. This assumption has the effect that no kink will be visible in the budget constraints because its effect will be hidden below the SB plateau.

We have had to make further assumptions about the rent rebates the individual receives. This is because we lack specific details about the rent rebate schemes run by local authorities. The scarcity of details should not be interpreted that such schemes, for council tenants at least, were rare. *New Society* (27 February 1964, p. 25) reported that in March 1963, 42% of local authorities 'were operating some form of rent rebate or differential rent scheme'. Legg and Brion (n.d., p. 22) report that 'by 1972 75% of local authorities were operating rebate schemes but some of these ensured that only a very small minority of tenants were eligible'. According to Legg and Brion (n.d., p. 21) the two most common schemes up to the 1970s were:

(1) The guarantee to every family, according to its size, of a minimum subsistence income after the payment of rent.
(2) The limitation of the gross rent payable to a certain proportion of family income, usually one-fifth or one-sixth.

There were, however, important exceptions to the above generalization. For example, the GLC in its scheme introduced in 1965 had one-seventh as the proportion of family income, Nevitt (1966, p. 142). For the purposes of constructing budget constraints we assume that a differential rent scheme is in operation, having the following features:

(1) Net rents will be set at one-sixth of net income (i.e. after tax and National Insurance contributions have been paid).
(2) If the family is receiving National Assistance (Supplementary Benefit) they are not entitled to a reduction in rents. (See Cullingworth, 1979, p. 52, for support for this assumption.)

It can be argued that this approach is highly artificial and at worst amounts to inventing budget constraints to suit. However for illustrative purposes assuming the form of the rent rebates functions from a set of possible functions is no worse than assuming level of rents or family type.

Both National Assistance and Unemployment benefit operated under similar rules as described in Chapter 2, National Assistance being the forerunner of Supplementary Benefit. As in that chapter we assume that the families have no capital which may be treated as income for purposes of calculating National Assistance. Two features need to be noted. First, the definition of 'remunerative full time work' which would exclude the family from receiving

National Assistance was not fully articulated until 1981. For the purposes of this study we take full-time work to be 30 hours per week and over. Secondly during this period the 'wage stop' operated on Unemployment Benefit. This ensured that Unemployment Benefit did not exceed 85% of the individual's net weekly earnings if he was in full-time work.

Having outlined the tax and social security arrangements we now describe the budget constraints which resulted during this period.

The Budget Constraints
1960–5

The budget constraints of a married man with 2 children for each year between April 1960 and April 1965 are depicted in Fig. 3.2. As can be seen from Fig. 3.2 the basic shape of the Budget constraint is similar to those which were discussed in Chapter 2. At lower levels of hours of work National Assistance imposes an implicit marginal rate of tax of 100% which excludes the hours covered by National Assistance from consideration in the choice

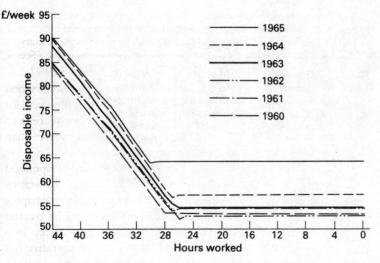

Fig. 3.2 Budget constraints 1960-5 (1982 prices)

set.[10] With the exception of 1960 and 1963 the termination of National Assistance involves a minor loss of disposable income of, at most, £0.10 (in 1962). In each of these years the loss of income is made up after one hour's extra work. The termination hours of National Assistance are given in Table 3.2.

Above the National Assistance plateau disposable income increases consistently with each extra hour of work. Over this section the implicit marginal rate of tax is very low. This is due to a number of factors. First, income tax is not paid until high levels of hours are worked, these are given in Table 3.2. Secondly, in none of the years does the individual receive a rent rebate and there are no deductions from this source. Thirdly, between 1961 and 1963 the termination of National Assistance is at a level of hours such that earnings are below the lower earnings limit. Thus, apart from the fixed amount, no extra National Insurance is paid for a short period (up to 3 hours in 1961 and 1962). For 1960 no extra NI is ever paid. The relatively high level of the income tax threshold and the lower earnings limit imply that there is a zero marginal tax rate operating over a short section of the Budget constraint.[11] By 1964 this has been eliminated because the lower earnings limit on NI contributions begins before National Assistance is terminated. It should be recalled that during this period NI contributions

Table 3.2 Hours of Work at which Selected Benefits Start and Terminate 1960–5

Year	Hour at which National Assistance is terminated	Hour at which Income Tax begins to be paid	Hour at which National Insurance contributions (excl. fixed amount) begins to be paid	Hour at which second tax band is entered
1960	27	39	–	44
1961	26	37	29	41
1962	25	35	28	39
1963	26	42	27	49
1964	26	39	25	46
1965	29	36	23	42

were only paid on earnings between the earnings limits so that implicit marginal tax rates in excess of 100% cannot occur on this account.

The implicit marginal tax rate rises not only because of the different starting points of National Insurance and income tax but also because the individual passes over the threshold from the first tax band into the second. The highest implicit marginal tax rate occurs in 1965 at 27.58% but because the second tax band is not entered until relatively high levels of working hours (see Table 3.2) the average implicit tax rates are much lower, being at most 19.39% in 1965 and as low as 6.58% in 1960. The highest marginal and the average tax rates are given in Table 3.3. The average implicit tax rate is calculated from the beginning of the choice set to 44 hours of work and includes the effect of increases in travel costs.

From Table 3.3 it can be seen that both the average and marginal implicit tax rates have oscillated over this period due to the uprating of the tax threshold in 1963. This offsets the decline in the hour at which the lower earnings limit becomes effective.[12] However the average implicit tax rates are much lower than those discussed in Chapter 2.

At zero hours the individual receives Unemployment Benefit and in each year this is augmented by National Assistance. As there is no earnings disregard during this period, the levels of disposable income at both zero hours and along the National Assistance plateau are determined by National Assistance (see Table 3.4). From this table it can be seen that in nominal terms the level of disposable income increased over this period. This

Table 3.3   Implicit Tax Rates, 1960–5

Year	Highest implicit marginal tax rate above the National Assistance plateau (%)	Average implicit tax rate operating on the choice set of hours (%)
1960	11.06	6.58
1961	20.78	13.29
1962	20.78	14.59
1963	17.59	10.56
1964	19.81	13.70
1965	27.58	19.39

reflects the increase in nominal housing costs over this period and the upward drift of the National Assistance itself. Between 1960 and 1964 National Assistance increased by £1.71 (in nominal terms) and this small increase was offset by other changes so that the termination hour of the National Assistance plateau was the same in 1964 as it had been in 1960. However, 1965 saw an increase of £1.68 (in nominal terms) over 1964 and this increased the hour of leaving National Assistance by 3, to 29 hours.

In real terms, disposable income at zero hours and along the National Assistance plateau oscillated with lowest income in 1962 and the highest in 1965 which was slightly under £11 higher (1982 prices) than the 1960 figure.[13] The replacement ratio, also given in Table 3.4, compares disposable income at zero hours with that attainable at 44 hours of work. It can be seen that the replacement ratio reached its lowest level of 61.8% in 1963 before reaching 71.0% in 1965.

In summing up, the period 1960 to 1965 saw, for the most part, only minor changes in the budget constraints of a married man with 2 children. This was due to the unchanged structure and the tendency for changes in benefits to be offset by changes in the tax thresholds and wage rates. The only revaluation which had a noticeable effect by increasing the plateau and the real disposable income of the unemployed was the uprating of National Assistance in March 1965.

Table 3.4 Disposable Income, the Choice Set and Replacement Ratio 1960–5

Year	Disposable income at zero hours (in £)	Disposable income at zero hours (in £, 1982 prices)	Length of implicit National Assistance plateau	Replacement ratio at zero hours (%)
1960	7.83	53.27	27	63.4
1961	8.26	54.34	27	64.0
1962	8.34	52.78	26	62.2
1963	8.79	54.57	26	61.8
1964	9.54	57.16	27	63.7
1965	11.22	64.09	30	71.0

For the years previous to this there was no clear trend in changes of real disposable income or the length of the National Assistance plateau. However, over this period the lower earnings limit on National Insurance contributions slipped below the number of hours at which the family would still claim National Assistance and therefore there is a trend towards higher marginal implicit tax rates. Overall this period has shown no dramatic change in the budget constraints for a married man with 2 children under our assumptions of housing type, housing costs and wage rate.

The Components of the Budget Constraints 1966–70

This period saw two major innovations to the system outlined in the previous section. These were the introduction of the Earnings Related Supplement to Unemployment Benefit in the National Insurance Act 1966 and rate rebates in the General Rate Act of 1967.

The Earnings Related Supplement (ERS) was calculated as one-third of reckonable weekly earnings in the previous tax year between £9.00 and £30.00 per week, which corresponds to the NI lower and upper earnings limits. This gave a maximum payment of ERS of £7.00 per week. Reckonable weekly earnings were calculated as one-fiftieth of annual earnings which were liable to be assessed under schedule E income tax. The amount of ERS payable was limited so that basic UB plus ERS did not exceed 85% of reckonable weekly earnings. The flat-rate benefit was not affected by this condition. For the purposes of calculating the budget constraints we have calculated reckonable weekly earnings as being the average weekly hours worked in the previous April by manual workers times manual hourly earnings in the previous year times 1.04. As we evaluate the budget constraints in April of each year ERS, which was introduced in October 1966, will not affect the budget constraints until 1967.

At first sight it may appear that the introduction of ERS to Unemployment Benefit would unambiguously alter the budget constraint. This is not the case because the increase in Unemployment Benefit will be offset by a reduction of Supplementary Benefit. In extreme cases, where ERS is small or housing costs are large, ERS will not affect the budget constraint. Moreover, there will be a differential effect between renters and mortgagors because the former may have the reduction of their National Assistance offset by claiming rent rebates. An extension of this is that the ability of ERS to influence the budget constraint was enhanced by the introduction of a rate rebate scheme which again may offset the reduction in National Assistance.

ERS could only be claimed after the 13th day of unemployment and payments ceased after 156 days. In so far as ERS affects the budget constraints it will be only for a limited period. It is therefore necessary to distinguish between the short term, when ERS is being received and the long term when ERS is exhausted. The budget constraints in this chapter are based on the premiss that ERS is received.

The second innovation of this period was the introduction of rate rebates in 1967. Domestic occupiers were entitled to a rebate of two-thirds of the amount by which their reckonable rates for a 6-month period exceeded £3.75 provided that the reckonable income in the previous 6 months was below a given amount. If income exceeded the limit then the rate rebate was reduced by 25% of the excess income. The rebate period began on either 1 April or 1 October with the relevant earnings being determined in the previous 6 months ending on 31 December or 30 June respectively. For the purposes of the budget constraints we calculate reckonable weekly income as the wage rate in the previous year times the average hours worked per week in that year. This makes the calculation of rate rebates consistent with our assumptions regarding ERS. Initially the income limit for a 2-child family was set at £13.00 p.w. and from 1 October 1968 this was increased to £15.00 p.w. As the rate rebate depended upon income in the previous 6 months the rebate is invariant to changes in current income. Thus the rate rebate does not impose an extra implicit marginal tax rate on the family. The lack of an income taper on income below the income limit means that the scheme was rather inequitable in that identical rebates could be awarded to families with different income levels.

We assume that the family's rate payments increased from £0.78 in 1966 to £1.01 in 1970, an increase of 29.5%. We have also assumed that the rent rebate system described in the previous section remains in force and that rents increase by 47.7% from £1.51 in 1966 to £2.23 in 1970.

During this period the basic Unemployment Benefit rate increased from £8.35 to £10.30 p.w. for a 2-child family, an increase of 23.4%. It can be noted that the payment in respect of the children was reduced in April and October 1968 to partially offset increases in family allowances. The increases for the second child from £0.40 to £0.75 in April and £0.90 in October 1968 were the first since October 1956. The increase in family allowances was also offset by a fall in the income tax threshold of £72.00 in 1968, although by 1970 the threshold was £41.00 above its 1966 level. The earned income relief limits and fractions and the standard rate of tax remained the same as in 1965. The reduced rates of tax and their tax bands remained unchanged until 1969. In 1969 the second band was abolished and the tax rate on the first £260.00 of taxable income was set at 30.0%. In 1970 the final reduced rate was abolished.

The national requirement of National Assistance, which from November 1966 became Supplementary Benefit, increased consistently by 24.2% over this period from £8.98 in 1966 to £11.15 in 1970. This change in name also brought the introduction of an earnings disregard of £1 which would be ignored in the calculation of Supplementary Benefit. Thus disposable income along the Supplementary Benefit plateau could be higher than that received at zero hours of work.

National Insurance contributions were levied at a rate of 4.25% in 1966, 4.75% in 1967–9 and 0.5% in 1970 on earnings between £9 and £18. From 1967 onwards earnings between £18 and £30 p.w. attracted contributions of 0.5% (for 1967–9) and 3.25% in 1970. The fixed amount contribution remained in force and this increased from 68p in 1966 to 88p in 1970.

Having outlined the social security and tax systems of the period we now describe the budget constraints that were produced.

The Budget Constraints
1966–70

The budget constraints of a married man with 2 children are depicted in Fig. 3.3. With the exception of 1966 the termination point of SB is 29 hours, the maximum possible. In each of the years, 1966–70, the termination of SB involves a loss of disposable income of between £1.05 in 1968 and £0.07 in 1966. The loss of disposable income is made up after a maximum of 4 hours in 1968 and 1969, after 3 hours for 1967 and 1970 and 2 hours in 1966. The loss occurs, in part, because once the family has left the SB plateau they receive no support with their housing costs as their relative income level is too high.

The absence of Housing Benefit means that above the SB plateau, the implicit marginal tax rates are determined by income tax, National Insurance contributions and travel costs. However, because of the structure of NI contributions and income tax, they interact to produce a number of kinks in the budget constraints (BC) as the implicit marginal tax rate changes. In each of the years, payment of extra NI contributions begins before the end of the SB plateau. Therefore NI contributions only produce a kink in the BC as the middle earnings limit is passed. These hours are given in Table 3.5 and the fall over time reflects the increase in wage rates over time. Moving from the lower hour segment to the higher one involved a fall in the contribution rate of 4.25% in 1967–69, and a rise in 1970 of 2.75%. Imposed upon this kink are

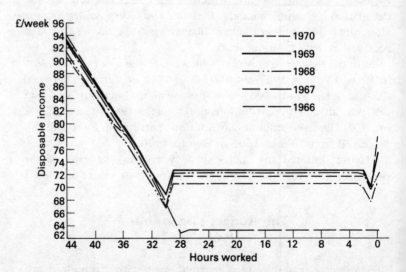

Fig. 3.3 Budget constraints 1966-70 (1982 prices)

Table 3.5 Hour at which Selected Benefits Start and Terminate, 1966–70

Year	Hour at which SB terminates	Hour at which implicit SB plateau terminates	Hour at which income tax is payable	Hour at which NI contributions (excl. fixed amount) begin to be paid	Hour at which income passes middle earning limit	Hour at which second tax band is entered	Hour at which third tax band is entered
1966	27	29	33	21	—	38	50
1967	29	32	32	21	41	38	49
1968	29	33	26	19	38	31	41*
1969	29	33	26	18	35	38*	—
1970	29	32	29	19	34	—	—

* begins to pay basic rate of income tax

those caused by income tax as the family's earnings exceed the relevant tax thresholds for higher rates of tax. The hours at which these thresholds are passed are given in Table 3.5. A number of features can be noted. In 1966 and 1967 income tax was not paid until 6 and 3 hours respectively after the termination of the SB plateau. Up to this level of hours the implicit marginal rate of tax was determined by NI contributions at the rates of 4.25% and 4.75% in 1966 and 1967 respectively. These represent the lowest implicit marginal tax rates above the SB plateau of the whole period.

From 1968 onwards income tax is paid before SB is terminated, thus the lowest marginal tax rate on an extra hour's work increases markedly, reaching 32.6% in 1970. In 1968 the reduction in the tax threshold means that the family enters the basic rate of tax at 41 hours of work, having passed through the two reduced bands. Consequently, the number of segments on this part of the budget constraint does not decline between 1967 and 1968 even though in the latter year tax is paid before SB is withdrawn. As can be seen in Fig. 3.3, in 1969 and 1970 the number of segments declined reflecting the abolition of the second reduced rate in 1969 and the first reduced rate in 1970. By 1970 there were only two segments on the budget constraint above the

Table 3.6   Implicit Tax Rates, 1966–70

Year	Lowest implicit marginal tax rates from the end of the SB plateau (%)[a]	Highest implicit marginal tax rate from the end of the SB plateau (%)[a]	Average implicit tax rate from end of the SB plateau (%)[b]	Average implicit tax rate over the choice set of hours when ERS is exhausted (%)[b,c]
1966	4.25	27.6	19.1	20.2
1967	4.75	28.1	22.9	25.4
1968	22.8	32.6	29.3	30.0
1969	27.9	32.6	31.1	32.0
1970	32.6	35.3	36.5	37.3

a   Excluding travel costs.
b   Including travel costs.
c   As determined by the SB plateau.

SB plateau reflecting the different NI rates above and below the middle earnings limit. These changes have led to a large increase in the average implicit tax rate from the end of the SB plateau to 44 hours of work, from 19.1% in 1966 to 36.5% in 1970 (see Table 3.6).

Although the introduction of rate rebates had no effect on the budget constraints of this family, the second major change, the introduction of ERS did have an impact. Payment of ERS increased from £3.95 in 1967 to £5.16 in 1970 (see Table 3.7). These payments, together with the receipt of rent rebates in 1969 and 1970, lifted disposable income above that available on the SB plateau. For these two years it was the level of disposable income at zero hours which determined the choice set of hours and reduced the choice set by 1 and 4 hours in 1969 and 1970 respectively over that determined by the SB plateau. During 1967 and 1968 the presence of ERS ensured that SB was not claimed at zero hours of work but the introduction of the earnings disregard on SB in 1967 raised the level of income on the SB plateau above disposable income at zero hours. Thus between 1966 and 1968 it was the SB plateau that determined the choice set of hours.

Overall these changes increased the level of real disposable income by £14.57 (23.0%) at zero hours and by £8.49 (13.4%) on the SB plateau over this period. This rise in income was relatively greater than that available at 44 hours per week, which fell, in real terms, by 3.7% in 1970 over 1966. Consequently this period saw a fall in the choice set of hours by some 7 hours and a rise in the average implicit tax rate over the period of some 18.5%. By comparing Tables 3.6 and 3.7 for the years 1969 and 1970, we can see that the introduction of ERS had the effect not only of reducing the choice set but of increasing the average implicit tax rates. This is because the reduction in the choice set eliminates low implicit tax hours and thus the average tax rate rises. As we shall see in the next section the introduction of Housing Benefits can reverse this ordering.

We can also note that the introduciton of ERS increased the replacement ratio in 1967 and 1968 by 8.1% and 7.1% (as a percentage of the ratio without ERS). However, this did not affect either the choice set, except for the earnings disregard section, or the average tax rate over the choice set. This suggests that the use of replacement ratios to model the labour supply decision does

Table 3.7 Income of the Unemployed, the Choice Set and Replacement Ratio, 1966–70

Year	ERS	Rent rebate at zero hours of work	Disposable income at zero hours (1982 prices)	Real disposable income on the SB plateau (1982 prices)	Choice set of hours begins	Average implicit tax rate over the choice set of hours[a]	Replacement ratio
1966	—	0.0	11.46	63.29	29	20.2	67.3
1967	3.95	0.23	13.12	70.65	32	25.4	76.0
1968	3.99	0.0	14.02	72.26	33	30.0	78.7
1969	4.62	0.33	15.48	72.68	34	32.4	81.0
1970	5.16	0.36	17.05	71.78	36	38.7	86.0

a To 44 hours of work and including travel costs

not pay sufficient attention to the interaction of social security and may therefore generate misleading results.

To summarize the changes in the budget constraints, there have been major increases in the level of disposable income at zero hours and in the average implicit tax rate over the choice set. This is true both over the period 1966–70 and when comparing this period with the period 1960–5. The changes in disposable income and choice set over the period 1968 to 1970 is due to ERS. When ERS is removed there are no major changes in either disposable income or the choice set between 1968 and 1970, although the former is still larger and the latter smaller than in the period 1960–5.

The Components of the Budget Constraints
1971–5

Further changes were made to the social security and tax systems during the five years 1971 to 1975. These included the introduction of Family Income Supplement (FIS), a national rent rebate scheme and a new rate rebate scheme. The period also saw the introduction of the unified income tax system. All these changes had the capacity to alter the shape of the budget constraint.

FIS was introduced in the Family Income Supplement Act 1970 and became operational in August 1971. It was designed to help families with children, where the head of the household was in full-time work of 30 or more hours per week. As such it was a marked change in the social security system which, except for family allowances, previously catered only for those who were not working.

FIS was intended to be a temporary measure to reduce poverty in families with children. The Green Paper 'Proposals for a Tax-Credit System' (1972) would have eliminated the need for FIS except for those below the tax threshold. These proposals were dropped with the election of a new government in 1974. This anticipated temporary nature had an effect on the structure which was kept relatively simple. There are, for example, no allowances made for the ages of the children. On its own FIS could not therefore be expected to provide the same coverage for low pay working families that National Assistance provided.

FIS was originally awarded for 6 months and this was increased to one year after the Pensioners and Family Income Supplement Payments Act 1972. As in Chapter 2, this feature is ignored and therefore the budget constraints only apply to those who were not previously entitled or whose entitlement was exhausted. The removal of this assumption would only affect those portions of the budget constraint where SB is not received because FIS counts in full against SB payments. Granting of FIS for a year has the effect of reducing the implicit marginal tax rates but it may increase or decrease the choice set of hours depending upon the exact amount previously claimed and the interactions with Housing Benefit. FIS also guarantees eligibility for other benefits such as free prescriptions, but the only one we have modelled is free school meals because of its relative simplicity.

FIS payments are calculated at one-half the difference between a prescribed income, determined by number of children and marital status, and gross income after account has been taken of disregards. For our purposes, the disregards are Child Benefit and rent and rate rebates.

Over this period the prescribed income level increased from £22.00 to £28.00 per week. FIS was also subject to a maximum payment condition and this remained at £10.00 during 1971–4. In 1975 the maximum was raised to £11.00. Family Allowances were also increased in April of that year to £1.50 per week for the second child, having been £0.90 since October 1968.

The Housing Finance Act 1972 introduced the rent rebate schemes which replaced the rent schemes previously operated by the local authorities. There was still some discretion allowed by the Act, local authorities could make payments of up to 10% in excess of the payments specified in the model scheme. In calculating the budget constraints, this feature will be ignored. Rent rebates are based on a needs allowance, which varies with family type, and the income tapers. If income equals the needs allowance the weekly rent rebate is 60% of the weekly rent. If income is greater than the needs allowance the rent rebate is 60% of the rent minus 17% of the difference between income and the needs allowance. If income is less than the needs allowance the rent rebate is 60% of the rent plus 25% of the difference between the needs allowance and the person's income. Income was defined as gross income plus family allowances, FIS and any other social security payments. Rent rebates could not be claimed if the family was receiving Supplementary Benefit because SB contains a payment for housing costs. Thus as in previous periods the rent rebate scheme also gave rise to a 'better-off' problem. We assume that the family always chooses that combination of benefits which maximizes its disposable income. Over this period the needs allowance rose from £23.75 per week in 1972 to £34.85 in 1975, a rise of 46.7%. Rents over the whole period are assumed to increase by 67.7% from £2.48 to £4.16 per week.

Another major change was brought about by the Local Government Act of 1974 which introduced, from April 1974, a replacement rate rebate scheme from the one operating under the General Rate Act of 1967. The rate rebate scheme uses the same format as the rent rebate scheme, including the same needs allowance, except that the income tapers are 6% if income exceeds the needs allowance and 8% otherwise. The old rate scheme operated up until 1974 and in August 1970 and February 1972 the income limits were raised to £16.25 and £19.75 per week respectively from £15.00. The allowance set against rates remained at £0.14 per week. We have assumed that rates increased from £1.16 in 1971 to £1.79 per week in 1975.

The 1974 rate rebate scheme, by introducing a taper on income below the needs allowance, removed the inequity involved in the 1967 scheme. Moreover because the new rate scheme is assumed to be evaluated on current income the scheme is sensitive to current rather than past needs. However, in becoming sensitive to present needs the rate scheme has introduced another source of implicit tax into the budget constraints which together with FIS, rent rebates, NI contributions and income tax can produce, in theory, very high implicit marginal tax rates.

The final change of this period was the abandonment of the distinction between earned and unearned income with the introduction of the unified taxation system in 1973. This involved the removal of the earned income fractions and the corresponding income limits. To compensate for this, the standard rate of tax was reduced to 30% in 1973, which was equivalent to 38.75% under the old system which was the rate prevailing in the previous two years. The basic tax rate was, however, raised in both 1974 and 1975 to 33% and 35% respectively. These rates are equivalent to

42.4% and 45% under the old system, much higher than the basic rates previously experienced. This was offset by large increases in the tax thresholds from £691 in 1971 to £1331 in 1975, an increase of 92.6%. The increase in thresholds also outpaced the increase in wage rates which grew by 91.9% over the period.

Between 1971 and 1973 National Insurance contributions were paid at a rate of 0.5% on earnings in excess of £9.00 per week up to £18.00 per week. Above the middle earnings limit up to upper limits of £30.00, £42.00 and £48.00 rates of 3.25%, 4.35% and 4.75% were charged in 1971, 1972 and 1973 respectively. A fixed amount of £0.88 was also payable. From 1974 the middle limit was abolished and rates of 5% and 5.5% were payable up to £54.00 and £69.00 in 1974 and 1975 respectively. A fixed amount of £0.84 was payable in 1974 and in 1975 this was replaced by the condition that once the lower limit was exceeded, NI contributions became payable on all gross earnings. As the hour at which the lower limit is exceeded depends on the prevailing wage rate the hour condition on NI payments has also been eliminated. The change did not remove the problem of high implicit marginal tax rates at the point where NI becomes payable

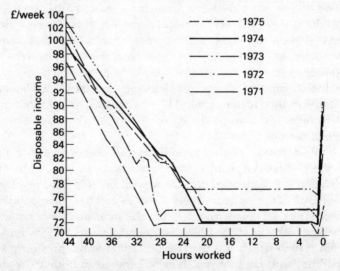

Fig. 3.4 Budget constraints 1971-5 (1982 prices)

although compared to 1974 the problem was eased because only £0.45 became due, rather than £0.84.

The ERS component of Unemployment Benefit was revised during this period. From January 1974 recipients claimed a third of reckonable earnings between £10 and £30 plus 15% of reckonable earnings between £30.00 and £42.00. In 1975 the maximum earnings limit was raised to £48.00. This raised the maximum ERS receivable to £8.47 and £9.37 per week in 1974 and 1975 respectively. Prior to this the maximum had been £7.00. The basic UB level for a 2-child family was increased each year from £10.30 in 1971 to £20.60 in 1975. The normal requirements of SB were also increased each year from £12.10 in 1971 to £22.25 in 1975.

Using these benefit rates we now turn to the budget constraint facing a married man with 2 children over the period 1971 to 1975.

The Budget Constraints
1971–5

As can be seen from Fig. 3.4 and Table 3.8 the termination of the SB plateau saw a marked fall in the length of the SB plateau from 1973 onwards. This can be attributed to the introduction of first rent rebates and then rate rebates which by 1975 were together covering over 99% of the family's housing costs at the end of the SB plateau. This high level of support allowed the family to make itself better off by choosing to relinquish SB at a lower level of hours. As can be seen from Table 3.8 support from Housing Benefits continues to high levels of working hours. Consequently the marginal and average tax rates of the budget constraint above the SB plateau reflect the income tapers on Housing Benefits as well as income tax and National Insurance.

The interaction of these features leads to the operation of high marginal rates of tax as well as providing a number of kinks to the budget constraint. This latter feature is compounded by the presence of travel cost increases and in 1972 the presence of FIS. In each of the years NI contributions start being paid and, with the exception of 1971, the middle earnings limit (where applicable) was exceeded before the SB plateau was terminated. As the upper

Table 3.8 Hour at which Selected Benefits Start and Terminate
1971–5

Year	Termination hour of SB plateau	Start of choice set of hours when ERS exhausted	% of housing costs paid by Housing Benefits at the end of the SB plateau	Hour at which rent rebates terminate	Hour at which rate rebates terminate	Hour at which income tax threshold is exceeded
1971	28	30	0	—	—	28
1972	27	29	0	—	—	30
1973	24	25	57.5	44	—	26
1974	21	22	95.7	43	46	27
1975	20	21	99.2	41	44	22

earnings limit is never exceeded by earnings over this period, the years 1972–5 have a constant NI contribution rate, and thus no kinks in the budget constraint derive from this source. Moreover in 1971 the level of hours at which the middle earnings limit is exceeded, 29, coincides with the termination of the SB plateau and in practical terms the NI contribution rate change is of little importance.

As the individual only pays tax at the standard rate, kinks can only be derived from passing the threshold. As can be seen from Table 3.8, with the exception of 1971, the threshold is passed when working hours exceed the SB plateau. In 1971 the absence of Housing Benefits or FIS implies that, with the exception of those caused by travel costs, there are no kinks in the budget constraint above the SB plateau. In 1972 the beginning of income tax and FIS payments coincide and at 30 hours of work the marginal tax rate increases from 4.35% to 84.35%, the latter being the highest marginal rate of the period. FIS payments are only made for a further hour and its termination causes a further kink at 32 hours of work. Consequently, the 1972 budget constraint has three segments above the SB plateau.

The final three years of this period all have four segments above the SB plateau and all are due to the same causes. These are the crossing of the tax threshold, the Housing Benefit needs allowance and finally the exhaustion of Housing Benefits.

The differences between the source of kinks in 1971 and 1972 compared with 1973 to 1975 is also reflected in a marked difference in the average tax rates of the long-term choice set. From Table 3.9 it can be seen that for the former two years the rates were on average some 24% lower than in the latter three years, a fact which reflects the introduction of Housing Benefits. Apart from the changes in structure of the social security system the average tax rate will reflect the relative levels of the needs allowance, travel costs, Supplementary Benefit, tax thresholds and wage rates as well as the implicit tax levels. Thus in 1972, although the NI contribution was 1.1% higher and FIS with a 50% deduction rate was in operation, the average tax rate was the same as 1971 because of the increase in the number of hours between the SB plateau and the tax threshold. Compared with the years 1966 to 1970 the average tax rates in 1971 and 1972 are broadly similar to those experienced in the second half of the period. As would be expected, the later years have much higher rates and the average rate for 1975 is over three times that prevailing in 1966. These rates apply to the long-term budget constraint and in the short term, when ERS is being paid, the rates will be different. It is to the level of disposable income at zero hours that we now turn our attention.

In each of the years the receipt of ERS lifts disposable income at zero hours above that available on the SB plateau. As can be seen from Table 3.9 there was a noticeable rise in real disposable income over this period and by 1975 real disposable income including ERS was 21.9% above its 1971 level. In comparison, income support when ERS was exhausted grew by 5.6% over the same period. Although ERS and UB payments increased in each year, only 72.4% of the increase can be attributed to this source. A further 22.7% was increases in Housing Benefits which by 1975 covered 82.0% of housing costs. The remainder of the increases came from changes in family allowances and in the value of free school meals. The effects of introducing Housing Benefit on the choice set of hours should not be underestimated. Table 3.9 shows that over the period the short-term choice set fell by some 7 hours so that by 1975 it began at 38 hours per week, its highest starting point not only of this period but of any year since 1960. However, if the unemployed were not eligible for Housing Benefits the choice set of hours would have increased over the period by 5 hours. Without Housing Benefit a comparison of

Table 3.9 Income of the Unemployed and the Choice Set, 1971–5

Year	Real disposable income at zero hours	Real disposable income at zero hours excluding ERS	Hour at which choice set begins	% of housing costs covered at zero hours when ERS claimed	Hour at which disposable income that at zero hours excluding Housing Benefit	Average implicit tax rate over choice set of hours (%)	Average implicit tax rate over choice set of hours when ERS is excluded (%)
1971	74.10	67.74	31	16.8	29*	35.4	35.1
1972	82.30	70.12	33	12.8	30	36.6	35.1
1973	89.70	73.55	34	50.4	27	53.9	55.0
1974	89.09	69.01	35	74.3	24	61.7	58.9
1975	90.34	71.54	38	87.9	24	51.9	63.5

* excluding SB plateau

Tables 3.8 and 3.9 reveals that the choice sets would have been on average only 1.4 hours greater in the short term than the long term and in 1971 the choice set in both the long and the short term would have been determined by the SB plateau.

Paradoxically, the introduction of rent and rate rebates, which were intended to help the working poor, would appear to have reduced the choice set available to those who could claim ERS. The reason for this is straightforward. At the hour at which net earnings equal UB plus ERS the individual receives relatively less Housing Benefits because Housing Benefits are calculated on gross earnings.[14] Thus the presence of Housing Benefits reduces his level of income relative to that at zero hours and thereby decreases the choice set. If the individual was not subject to income tax, National Insurance contributions or other implicit taxation at the hour the choice set began, then the introduction of Housing Benefits would not affect the choice set. Using the budget constraints we estimate that Housing Benefits reduce the choice set of hours by 4 and 6 hours in 1974 and 1975 respectively. This problem would be eliminated if Housing Benefit was calculated on net earnings; in this manner the effect on the choice set would cancel out. Alternatively, withdrawing ERS, so that the unemployed did not claim Housing Benefit, would ensure that the introduction of Housing Benefit would increase the choice set. Indeed for the long-term unemployed the provision of Housing Benefit did improve the choice set. In 1974 and 1975 the increases for the long-term unemployed were 6 and 8 hours respectively. The introduction of Housing Benefits altered the budget constraint in two distinct ways depending upon the individual's ability to claim enough UB plus ERS so that it exceeded the SB plateau.

The final aspect of disposable income exceeding the SB plateau which we want to discuss is its effect on the average implicit tax rate over the choice set. As ERS reduces the choice set the average implicit tax rate rises or falls depending upon whether the eliminated hours were taxed at higher or lower rates than the average. In 1971, 1972 and 1974 this resulted in the average tax rate rising by an average of 1.5% when ERS was available because the reduced choice set excluded hours over which no income tax was being paid. Thus the average rate rose when ERS was available. In 1974 this effect was large enough to cancel the effect of eliminating the high implicit tax rates from Housing Benefits. It is the removal of these high tax rates which in 1973 and 1975 causes the short-term average rate to lie below the long-term average tax rates. The feature is most pronounced in 1975 when the difference in average tax rates is 11.6%. It is this latter pattern which the budget constraints calculated for 1976–81 follow.

To sum up, the budget constraints over the period 1971–5 saw noticeable changes. The introduction of Housing Benefits had by the end of the period caused significant differences to emerge between the short-term budget constraint, where ERS is available, and the long-term budget constraint, where ERS is exhausted. In the former case real disposable income at zero hours rose by 21.9% over the period and by 1975 this was the highest level analysed in any period. This also applies to the choice set which began at 38 hours in 1975. Yet, for the reason explained above, when ERS is exhausted the choice set begins at 21 hours in 1975, which is the earliest start analysed in this or in any of the other previous periods. Finally, we may note the effect Housing Benefits had on raising the average implicit tax rates in both the short- and long-term budget constraints.

The Components of the Budget Constraints 1976–82

The major change to the social security system during this period was the abolition of the Earnings Related Supplement to Unemployment Benefit from January 1982 for new claimants and 30 June 1982 for all claimants. During 1981 a move had been made to limit budget constraint payments by reducing the percentage payable on earnings between the limits to 10% from 15%. This had the effect of reducing the maximum ERS payment to £14.00; in the previous year, 1980, it had been £17.67. Prior to this the maximum payment had, during this period increased in each year so that in 1980 it was some 72% higher than in 1976. By 1982 the basic UB rate was 61.7% higher than in 1976, well below the increase in the retail price index of 114.3%. It can also be noted that the amount paid in respect of each child fell from a high of £3.00 in November 1977 to £0.80 in November 1981.

The years 1977 and 1978 saw the reintroduction, after an

absence of 8 years, of a reduced rate tax band of 25%. During this period the tax threshold for a married man with 2 children increased by 54.7% but this entailed a minor fall in the threshold in 1978 as the married man's allowance was not uprated sufficiently to compensate for the withdrawal of child allowances. The removal of child allowances had begun in 1977 with a reduction of £130 per child in the threshold regardless of age. This was in part offset by the removal of the Family Allowance deduction which was worth £52 in 1976. In 1978 a further £70 was removed from the child tax allowance and in 1979 it was phased out completely. For the purposes of calculating budget constraints from 1979 onwards, only the married man's allowance plays any part although numerous other allowances, such as those on mortgage interest payments, exist.

There were also two changes in the rules applying to both the income disregards on housing benefit and SB. In 1980 came the introduction of a disregard on income for the purposes of calculating housing benefit. Initially the value of this was £5.00 and by 1982 it had risen to £15.95. The introduction of the disregard had the effect of increasing the effective value of the needs allowance by 136.7% compared to the 97.4% increase in the needs allowance alone (comparing 1982 with 1976). The disregard on SB was increased twice during this period by £1.00 in 1977 and by £2.00 in 1981. The scale rate of SB increased from 1976 to 1982 by 112.1%.

As a replacement for child tax allowances the government introduced Child Benefit from April 1977. This benefit was not taxable and was payable for the first child which Family Allowance was not. Although the payment for the first child was £1.00, £0.50 lower than for subsequent children, by April 1978 the rates were equivalent across children. The value of Child Benefit increased throughout this period (in nominal terms) and by 1982 was worth £5.25 per child, an increase of 600% and 320% for a 2-child family over 1976 and 1977 respectively.

Apart from these changes to the structure of the social security system, changes in the value of other benefits, housing costs and wage rates also play their part in determining the budget constraint. Between 1976 and 1982 the level of housing costs increased by 180.2%, wage rates by 109.0%, and the prescribed income level for FIS by 134.3%. The large rise in the FIS income level did not allow it to make any impact on the budget constraints of this family and thus the poverty trap in its strictest sense is avoided.

The Budget Constraints
1976–82

The budget constraints for the 2-child family are depicted in Fig. 3.5. As with the budget constraints from 1967 onwards, the choice set of hours is determined by disposable income received at zero hours of work and not by the SB plateau. The exception to this is the 1982 budget constraint when the abolition of the ERS component of UB implies that the choice set is determined by the level of SB and the income disregard on SB. For each of the years SB payments are terminated well before the compulsory termination point. These hours are given in Table 3.10.

The contraction in the SB plateau in 1979 reflects the increase of nearly 74% in the value of Child Benefit over 1978. Had Child Benefit remained at its 1978 value the end of the SB plateau in 1979 would have been around 21 hours. The termination point of

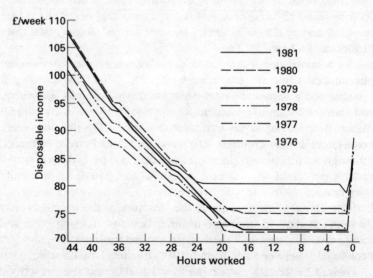

Fig. 3.5 Budget constraints 1976–81 (1982 prices)

Table 3.10 Hour at which Housing Benefit and SB Terminate 1976–82

Year	Hour at which SB terminates	% of housing cost covered by rent and rate rebates at end of SB plateau	Hour at which rent rebates terminte	Hour at which rate rebates terminate
1976	19	99.1	38	39
1977	21	89.7	39	40
1978	22	76.4	37	39
1979	17	91.9	33	37
1980	17	93.6	36	41
1981	23	73.3	41	43
1982	22	83.3	44	45

the SB plateau remained at 17 hours in 1980 even though the reduced rate of tax of 25% was withdrawn and the level of housing costs and the personal scale rate increased (raising disposable income on the SB plateau by £11.06 – nearly 23%). This was offset by the increase in the gross wage rate of nearly 25% to leave the end of the SB plateau unchanged. In 1981 the level of disposable income on the SB plateau increased by a further £11.67 (19.7%) and as the tax threshold did not change the 9.4% increase in the gross wage rate was unable to stop the SB plateau extending to 23 hours.

Once SB is terminated the family receives, in each year, rent and rate rebates worth between 73% and 99% of housing costs. Although the two lowest ratios of housing benefits to housing costs occur in the years with the longest SB plateaux, 1981 and 1978, Table 3.10 shows no clear relationship between these two variables. The voluntary termination of SB implies that in each of the years the family is not made worse off by accepting Housing Benefits. Rent rebates are claimed between 11 hours in 1980 and 22 hours in 1982, and rate rebates are claimed for 16 hours in 1980 and 23 hours in 1982. Thus Housing Benefits have a prolonged influence in the shape of the budget constraint.

Table 3.11 gives the level of hours at which income for the purposes of Housing Benefits have surpassed the needs allowance.

Table 3.11 Hour at which Income Tax and National Insurance are payable, 1976–82

Year	Hour at which income tax is payable	Hour at which NI contributions are payable	Hour at which the Housing Benefit needs allowance is passed	Average tax rate from the end of the SB plateau to 44 hours (%)
1976	22	10	28	60.2
1977	23	10	27	62.1
1978	20	11	26	57.5
1979	18	10	23	54.7
1980	17	10	24	59.8
1981	16	11	27	62.8
1982	16	11	28	67.2

At hours greater than these the income taper on Housing Benefits is 23% while below them it is 33%. However, this picture is complicated by the following features which create kinks in the budget constraints. First, for 1976 and 1977 the income tax threshold is not passed until after SB has been terminated. Secondly, in 1978 and 1979 there was a reduced tax rate of 25% operating for the first £14.42 p.w. of taxable income. The lower tax rate provides a further kink in the budget constraint. This becomes operative above the hour at which the needs allowance is passed because the lower tax band operates for 8 and 7 hours in 1978 and 1979 respectively while the needs allowance is surpassed 6 and 5 hours respectively after tax becomes payable. Thirdly, in 1976 the family receives the maximum rent rebate at 20 hours, hence between 20 and 21 hours implicit tax rate on Housing Benefits is only 12.1% rather than 33%. Finally, above the needs allowances the different termination hours of rent and rate rebates noted in Table 3.10 provide another source of kinks in the budget constraint. Although not all of these features are active on each budget constraint, the segment above the SB plateau can involve up to six kinks. The budget constraint is further complicated by the increases in travel costs. However, a number of these features will overlap, for example, lower tax band and Housing Benefits below the needs allowance, so that they do not cause extra kinks. Moreover a number of the segments will be of only short duration, for example, the reduced rate of taper on housing benefits in 1978 only lasts one hour, so that the multiplicity of implicit tax rates should not be over-emphasized. In passing we can note that for each of the years 1976–82 no FIS is received and that payment of National Insurance contributions begins before the end of the SB plateau.

All the above features, including travel costs, combine to produce average implicit tax rates of between 54.7% in 1979 and 67.2% in 1982 from the end of the SB plateau to 44 hours of work. The low average tax rate in 1979 reflects not only the reduced tax rate band and the reduction of 3% in the basic tax rate but also the relatively low hours at which Housing Benefits are terminated. Since 1979 the average implicit tax rate has increased by an average of about 4% each year. This mainly reflects the increase in housing costs and the needs allowance over this period which extended the hours over which Housing Benefits operate from 32 hours in 1979 to 43 hours, for rent rebate, in 1982. This extension was only partially offset by the increase in the hour at which the SB plateau terminates. Between 1979 and 1982 the National Insurance rate also increased by 2.25% and this also enhanced the increase in the average implicit tax rate.

We now turn to the level of disposable income at zero hours of work. As we noted earlier it is the level of disposable income at zero hours which determines the short-term choice set. With the exception of 1982, income at zero hours is made up of UB, ERS and Housing Benefits, the latter covering between 71.4% and 87.7% of housing costs. Although in nominal terms short-term income at zero hours continued to rise over the period in real terms its value declined so that by 1982 its value was slightly below that of 1971. In contrast, real disposable income for those claiming SB rose over the period with 1982 being the second highest value since 1960.

The reduction in the difference between short-term and long-term income support resulted in the difference in the choice set of hours declining over the period from 15 in 1976 to 3 in 1981. The decline in hours between the choice sets also causes a decline in the implicit average tax rates between the long- and short-term budget constraints. Although in a number of years

117

income tax is not paid until after the termination of SB the removal of these tax-free hours from the budget constraint is insufficient to outweigh the removal of high implicit tax rates from the income tapers on Housing Benefit. Consequently between 1976 and 1981 the short-term average tax rates were always below the long-term rate. In 1976 this had resulted in a differential of 7.1% but with the reduction in the difference between the choice sets this had fallen to just 1.1% in 1981. We can also note that in 1982 the average implicit tax rate over the choice set was the highest experienced since 1960.

Finally in both 1980 and 1981 the level of UB plus ERS is insufficient, without recourse to Housing Benefits, to raise the level of disposable income above the SB plateau. Consequently in these two years the presence of Housing Benefits does not necessarily imply that its elimination would improve the choice set. Indeed in 1980 the short-term choice set would have improved by 1 hour and in 1981 it would have worsened by 5 hours had Housing Benefits been eliminated. This is because in 1980 the ratio of Unemployment Benefit plus ERS to SB is much higher than in 1981, 79.8% compared to 67.8%. Thus in 1981 the SB plateau provides a relatively higher barrier against which gains in the choice set might have been achieved if Housing Benefits were eliminated.

The final period of our analysis has provided some interesting features: the decline of short-term and the rise of long-term real disposable income of the unemployed, the increase in the short-term choice set and the eventual elimination of the distinction between long- and short-term budget constraints. How important these changes, and indeed the changes over the whole period, are in determining hours worked and participation is an empirical matter but this chapter indicates that researchers are unlikely to be hampered by lack of variation in the underlying budget constraints.

Overview

In this section we provide an overview of the budget constraints over the period 1960–82. Table 3.13 summarizes the budget constraints in terms of three parameters: the level of real

Table 3.12 Disposable Income of the Unemployed and the Choice Set of Hours, 1976–82

Year	Real disposable income at zero hours including ERS, 1982 prices	Real disposable income at zero hours excluding ERS, 1982 prices	% of housing costs covered by Housing Benefits at zero hrs	Hour at which short-term choice set begins	Hour at which long-term choice set begins	Average implicit tax rate over choice set of hours
1976	87.73	69.64	76.6	35	20	53.1
1977	86.35	69.37	71.4	36	22	53.5
1978	88.50	72.60	73.9	34	23	50.9
1979	84.11	69.13	75.8	29	18	47.2
1980	84.49	72.64	74.1	28	18	52.7
1981	83.09	75.87	87.7	27	24	61.7
1982	74.04	74.04	0.0	23	23	67.2

disposable income at zero hours, the hour at which the choice set begins and the average implicit tax rate over the choice set. Two main points can be made.

First, there can be quite large differences between the short-term and the long-term budget constraints due to the presence of ERS. Disposable income at zero hours in the short term when ERS affected the budget constraint was on average 18.0% higher than in the long term, the largest difference being in 1974 of 29.1%. The starting hour of the choice set of hours was on average some 40.0% later in the short term over the period 1969 to 1982. The maximum difference is 81.0% in 1975. For both of these parameters the effect of introducing ERS was unidirectional – it increased both short-term parameters in comparison with the long-term. In the case of the average tax rates over the choice set the effects of ERS, as we have explained, depended upon other factors. Thus over the period 1969–81 the average percentage difference in the average tax rates was reduced by 5.4% but this encompassed a range of values from −13.9% in 1977 to +4.3% in 1972.

Secondly, there have been major changes in these parameters over time for both the short- and the long-term budget constraints. In both the short- and the long-term budget constraints there has been a tendency for real disposable income at zero hours and the average rate of tax to rise so that the former measures were 39% above their 1960 value and the latter 1,463% above the 1960 values. In terms of the hour at which the choice set began there was a decline of 17.9% by 1982 over the 1960 values. None of the series smoothly adjusted over time. Indeed for the level of disposable income at zero hours in the short term the maximum value was reached in 1975 and from that year onwards the series has tended to fall. The hour at which the choice set began also saw a tendency to increase in both the short term and the long term before the downward trend is established.

In the introduction to this chapter it was stated that its aim was to demonstrate that the budget constraints have changed over time. Figure 3.6, which illustrates the budget constraints at 5-yearly intervals, provides the visual confirmation of this statement. How the individual reacts to these changes in the budget constraint depends upon his preferences but the marked changes in incentives would make it surprising if none of the changes in work patterns during the last two decades could be attributed to this source.

Table 3.13 Overview of the Budget Constraints, 1960–82

	Married Man with 2 Children					
Year	Real disposable income at zero hours	Real disposable income at zero hours excluding ERS	Hour at which choice set begins	Hour at which choice set begins when ERS excluded	Average implicit tax rate over choice set	Average implicit tax rate over choice set when ERS excluded
1960	53.27	53.27	28	28	4.3	4.3
1961	54.34	54.34	28	28	11.1	11.1
1962	52.78	52.78	27	27	13.9	13.9
1963	54.57	54.57	27	27	9.9	9.9
1964	57.16	57.16	28	28	11.3	11.3
1965	64.09	64.09	31	31	17.8	17.8
1966	63.29	63.29	29	29	20.2	20.2
1967	70.56	65.27	32	32	25.4	25.4
1968	71.89	67.13	33	33	30.0	30.0
1969	75.52	67.80	34	33	32.4	32.0
1970	77.86	67.21	36	32	38.7	37.3
1971	74.10	67.74	31	30	35.4	35.1
1972	82.30	70.12	33	29	36.6	35.1
1973	89.70	73.55	34	25	53.9	55.0
1974	89.09	69.01	35	22	61.7	58.9
1975	90.34	71.54	38	21	51.9	63.5
1976	87.73	69.64	35	20	53.1	60.2
1977	86.35	69.37	36	22	53.5	62.1
1978	88.50	72.60	34	23	50.9	57.5
1979	84.11	69.13	29	18	47.2	54.7
1980	84.49	72.64	28	18	52.7	59.8
1981	83.09	75.87	27	24	61.7	62.8
1982	74.04	74.04	23	23	67.2	67.2

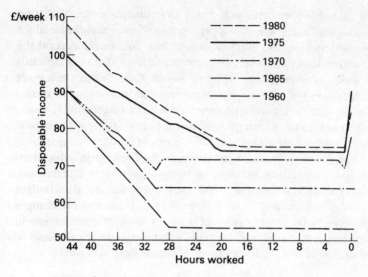

Fig. 3.6 Budget constraints 1960-80 (1982 prices)

Conclusion

We began this chapter with a brief sketch of the 'social security system' as it developed from the early seventeenth century to the Beveridge scheme of the postwar years. We found that in a (very) broad sense the antecedents of today's system can be noted from the past schemes for the relief of poverty. We also noted that the effects of these schemes on labour supply incentives had formed a major part of the discussions of the 1834 Royal Commission on the Poor Laws.

In the second half of the chapter we presented the budget constraints faced by a married man with 2 children over the period 1960–82. In real terms the level of disposable income varied from £52.78 in 1962 to £90.34 in 1975 (including ERS) for the un-employed, the start of the choice set of hours fell by 15 from 38 hours per week in 1975 to 23 in 1982, and the average implicit rate of tax increased by 62.9% over the period 1960 to 1982. The range of variations in these parameters of the budget constraint perhaps implies that it would be fair to suggest that the budget constraints

121

of individuals facing a wide range of circumstances will also have changed. Thus if labour supply decisions are significantly affected by changes in the budget constraints we may expect to see changes in both unemployment and the distribution of hours worked. Furthermore, it is probable that changes in budget constraints will also change the composition of those in terms of family type or tenure type, who work, for example, more than 50 hours per week. Although we have not tested these conjectures, it is an area which appears to be worthy of study.

Finally, we also noted the limited effect ERS initially had on the budget constraints but that over time its effects became more noticeable. Thus similar men except for the duration of their unemployment spell would face different budget constraints. We also used the withdrawal of ERS to illustrate the point that replacement ratios may not be a very precise measure of the budget constraint and hence of labour supply incentives.

Notes: Chapter 3

1 Reported in Checkland and Checkland, 1974, p. 15.
2 For descriptions of the variety of systems operating see the Poor Law Report of 1834, although it should be borne in mind that the systems described may not be an unbiased sample.
3 Calculated from Marshall, 1968, Table 1.
4 See Beenstock and Brasse, 1986, Chapter 2 for examples.
5 The number of workers covered is estimated at 2.5 million by Reform of Social Security, 1985, background paper 3, p. 61. The estimate in the text is from Pollard, 1969, p. 37.
6 Deacon and Bradshaw, 1983, p. 8. This clause dates from 1924.
7 The household means test was abandoned in 1941.
8 The source of the benefit data to 1938 is Matthews, 1982, p. 43. The gross earnings figures are based on Chapman and Knight, 1953, Table 11.
9 Housing and travel costs were interpolated backwards using the April RPI housing and transport components to 1956 using the 1960 levels as the base figure. From 1955 to 1948 the all items RPI was used. The wage data was calculated by the same method using the earnings of manual workers from *British Labour Statistics Historical Abstract.*
10 Assuming that leisure time is a normal good.
11 Ignoring the effects of travel costs.
12 After 1963 declines in the hours at which the lower earnings limit

becomes operative does not affect the average implicit tax rate.
13 A similar pattern also occurs if the housing component is excluded.
14 This analysis assumes that prior to receiving Housing Benefit no SB was received at zero hours.

4

An Informal Empirical Analysis of Labour Supply Decisions in the UK

Don M. Egginton

In Chapter 2 we described the choice set of hours which comprise the set of hours individuals may consider in deciding the number of hours they wish to work per week. The choice set is determined by the interaction of the budget constraint and the individuals' work–leisure preferences which are assumed to obey two postulates; first that individuals prefer more disposable income to less and secondly they prefer more leisure to less. These two postulates imply that the choice set will contain only those hours from which the level of disposable income received is greater than at any other lower level of hours worked. Chapter 2 demonstrated that the budget constraints which determine the choice set of hours should depend upon the individuals' circumstances. If individuals are able to change the level of hours and they behave according to the above postulates, then the differences in the choice set of hours between individuals should be reflected in differences in the level of hours worked per week.

In this chapter we analyse household data to see whether the number of hours worked per week by groups of individuals is consistent with the underlying budget constraint. In this chapter a 'descriptive' approach to the hypothesis is adopted and in Chapter 5 econometric functions are estimated in order to test one specific hypothesis: that the probability of an individual being unemployed is affected by his budget constraint.

The Data

The data used to test our hypothesis were taken from the 1978 and 1981 Family Expenditure Surveys (FES) each of which examined roughly 7,000 households. From these households we select the respondent who is designated as the head of the household; in the majority of cases the individual was male. Our sample, therefore, ignores a number of workers such as wives and dependent children. We further reduced the sample by excluding all heads of households who were retired. The self-employed, the sick and those not seeking work remained in the sample, although the econometric work in the following chapter excludes these individuals.

The number of individuals was further reduced by excluding all households on which no information on wage rates, defined as normal gross wages divided by usual hours worked, nor on the industry in which the individual worked was given. In some cases we were able to impute a wage rate to the individual. This was accomplished by using the average wage rate in April of the appropriate year from the New Earnings Survey (NES) for each industry subdivided into manual and non-manual occupations. The wage rate was defined as average hourly earnings excluding the effects of overtime for full-time males whose pay was not affected by absence. For a number of industries no wage data is given and any individuals who would have received an imputed wage rate were excluded. It should be emphasized that these industries will be represented in the sample provided that some of the survey respondents who were in these industries answered the questions from which wage rates are calculated. This brought the total sample of individuals to 4,881 in 1978 and 5,111 in 1981.

The majority of respondents excluded because of lack of wage data usually worked zero hours per week: 542 out of 544 in 1978. A similar feature occurs in the individuals with imputed wage rates where 433 out of 521 have zero usual hours of work in 1978. Furthermore, only two observations in 1978 gave wage data for those unemployed and as a consequence of this virtually all our wage data for the unemployed is imputed. This is an obvious weakness of our data which is compounded by our scepticism of the imputed wage data. We believe that by using average hourly wages within each industry we have overestimated the wage rate the unemployed would receive if they returned to work because the unemployed tend to face lower-than-average wage rates reflecting their lower-than-average level of skills. Nor are we confident that regressing characteristics such as industry, occupation, sex, marital status, and age, of those working on known wage rates would provide us with an unbiased prediction of the wage rate an unemployed person would receive if they were employed. This is because our data on the educational attainment of the sample is sketchy. Nor do we have data on the health or race of the individuals. It is not clear that the same parameters will be applicable to those who are unemployed if unemployment is taken by an employer as being relevant to the decision of offering a wage rate. Finally if the unemployed have different unobservable characteristics, then any regression performed on observable data will produce biased parameters.

The major reason for using imputed wage rates from the NES concerns an underlying aim of this chapter to evaluate the contribution χ^2 (chi-square) tests can make to analysing the distribution of hours. If an estimated wage function is used to impute wage rates it is relatively easy, in logistic terms, to progress from this to estimating hours functions which can provide a richer set of results than the χ^2 tests. There seems little point in estimating a wage equation and then returning to use χ^2 tests. For this reason we have imputed the wage rates from the NES. However, we are wary of drawing conclusions from data which contain imputed wages and due to this some tests have been carried out on the data which excludes imputed wages; this is tantamount to excluding the unemployed.

Although we have data for both 1978 and 1981, differences between the distributions for given categories should not only be attributed to changes in budget constraints; other factors, such as the fall in aggregate demand, are also likely to be important. However, comparison of categories within a given year control for at least some of these outside factors and thus can be used to deduce the presence or otherwise of budget constraint effects on labour supply behaviour. Consequently, no attempt is made to compare similar categories from 1978 and 1981.

The FES gives a choice of two definitions of hours worked per week: actual hours worked for last weekly or monthly pay, and usual weekly hours. Both these definitions exclude meal breaks but usual weekly hours also excludes overtime. In the analysis below we have defined hours per week as usual weekly hours. The choice of either variable presents some problems. If we use actual hours, the variable will reflect changes in working practices to which the individual is unable to react because of their temporary nature. The use of usual hours, which excludes overtime, minimizes this problem but adds another in that overtime hours may play an important part in the choice of job and hence hours worked per week.

The heads of households were initially divided into 84 categories which were determined by factors which we expected would distinguish the individuals' underlying budget constraints. These factors were sex, wage rates, tenure type and family type. The categories were divided into two wage rate groups – 'low' pay, those earning less than the average manual man's wages, and 'high' pay. There were three tenure types – renter, mortgagor, and owner or rent-free. Seven family types were identified – single; single parent; married, no children; married, 1 child; married, 2 children; married, 3 children; married, more than 3 children. For ease of identification each category was allocated a number as given in Table 4.1.

Within each category the heads of households were separated into 22 cells which were defined in terms of the number of hours usually worked each week. The cells were defined as being zero hours per week, 1 to 5 hours per week, then in steps of 5 hours up to 30 hours per week. From 30 to 50 hours per week the cell size is 2 hours and above 50 the cell size is 5 hours up to 70 hours of work per week which is a 'catch-all' for anyone in excess of 70 hours worked per week, of whom there were 33 in 1978 and 25 in 1981.

For each of these categories we can calculate the distribution of usual hours worked and it is hoped that any differences in the underlying budget constraints which are proxied by controlling for wage rates, family and tenure types, will manifest themselves in different hours distributions between the categories. We test differences in the hours distributions using χ^2 tests.

Although it was intended to divide female heads of households the low numbers, 561 in 1978 and 585 in 1981, precluded this and just two categories, 43 and 44, were used. Male single parents

Table 4.1   The Categories of Household

Category Description

1   Low pay, rented, single
2   Low pay, rented, single parent
3   Low pay, rented, married, no children
4   Low pay, rented, married, 1 child
5   Low pay, rented, married, 2 children
6   Low pay, rented, married, 3 children
7   Low pay, rented, married, more than 3 children
8   Low pay, mortgagor, single
9   Low pay, mortgagor, single parent
10   Low pay, mortgagor, married, no children
11   Low pay, mortgagor, married, 1 child
12   Low pay, mortgagor, married, 2 children
13   Low pay, mortgagor, married, 3 children
14   Low pay, mortgagor, married, more than 3 children
15   Low pay, rent-free/owner, single
16   Low pay, rent-free/owner, single parent
17   Low pay, rent-free/owner, married, no children.
18   Low pay, rent-free/owner, married, 1 child
19   Low pay, rent-free/owner, married, 2 children
20   Low pay, rent-free/owner, married, 3 children
21   Low pay, rent-free/owner, married, more than 3 children
22   High pay, rented, single
23   High pay, rented, single parent
24   High pay, rented, married, no children
25   High pay, rented, married, 1 child
26   High pay, rented, married, 2 children
27   High pay, rented, married, 3 children
28   High pay, rented, married, more than 3 children
29   High pay, mortgagor, single
30   High pay, mortgagor, single parent
31   High pay, mortgagor, married, no children
32   High pay, mortgagor, married, 1 child
33   High pay, mortgagor, married, 2 children
34   High pay, mortgagor, married, 3 children
35   High pay, mortgagor, married, more than 3 children
36   High pay, rent-free/owner, single
37   High pay, rent-free/owner, single parent
38   High pay, rent-free/owner, married, no children
39   High pay, rent-free/owner, married, 1 child
40   High pay, rent-free/owner, married, 2 children
41   High pay, rent-free/owner, married, 3 children
42   High pay, rent-free/owner, married, more than 3 children
43   Female, single
44   Female, single parent family

are also in short supply, 72 and 86 in 1978 and 1981 respectively, and these categories were eliminated. Finally a number of other categories had fewer than 30 observations and these categories were also deleted.

The deleted categories are:

1978	1981
2	2
8	8
9	9
13	14
14	15
16	16
20	20
21	21
23	23
30	30
37	37
42	42

It must be pointed out that this approach is very crude. We have not controlled for the level of housing costs, unearned income or the level of past earnings, which determines the level of earnings related Unemployment Benefit, nor have we controlled in any strict manner the level of wage rates. It is therefore arguable that the differences in individuals' budget constraints within each category may be as large as the differences between categories and consequently analysis of the categories may not provide meaningful results because the categories themselves are too broad. However, further classification of the categories, and hence budget constraint, would result in further losses of degrees of freedom, as some of the categories would again contain too few observations. Furthermore, detailed analysis of this form is best achieved by using the econometric techniques of Chapter 5. This chapter provides an opportunity to evaluate a different method of ascertaining the effect of budget constraints on the distribution of hours.

Two final points need to be noted. First, the analysis of the distribution of hours across categories assumes that work–leisure preferences are randomly distributed across the categories. If this is not the case, then the differences in the distribution of labour supply cannot be interpreted as being wholly due to the underlying budget constraint. Secondly, we also assume that the influence an employer has on the distribution of labour supplied is random. We have made no attempt to exclude those with a secondary job on the basis that this represents constraints being implied on the choice of hours in the primary job. These two factors are ignored in this section, as it is not possible to analyse their effects using this framework.

The distribution of hours of work for 1978, by category, is given in Table 4.2 and the equivalent data for 1981 is given in Table 4.3. In order to ease analysis the data has been converted into percentage terms for larger hours cells. The following discussion ignores the categories with insufficient numbers.

Using usual hours of work data including the imputed wage cases we found that 27 cases out of 31 had the cell 39–40 hours as the mode in 1978. In 1981 the hours 39–40 were the modal cell in 28 out of 31 active categories. From Table 4.2 it can be seen that between 11% and 39% of the observations per category lie within this cell. For 1981 (see Table 4.3) the figures were 10% and 62% respectively. In 1978 between 9% and 84% and in 1981 between 16% and 87% of the sample work less than 39 hours per week (including zero hours) and between 5% and 63%, and 0% and 50% in 1978 and 1981 respectively usually work more than 40 hours per week. There is therefore a high degree of variability in the percentages within these categories. Even within these broad definitions of hours there is a diverse distribution of hours. For example, the unemployment rate ranges from 0% to 32% in 1978 and from 4% to 37% in 1981. At least part of this diversity can be reduced by excluding women from the sample. It can be seen, from Table 4.3, that their hours distributions are quite different from those of males. Between 25% and 37% in 1978, and between 25% and 30% in 1981, of females were working less than 25 hours per week. The corresponding range for males is 0% to 22% in 1978 and 0% to 14% in 1981. Females working more than 40 hours are also rarer, with between 5% and 12% in 1978 and between 3% and 8% in 1981 working these hours. We postpone further discussion of the female distributions until later in the chapter.

A notable feature of the hours distributions for males is the lack of observations of persons working between 1 and 25 hours per week. Indeed, for both years many categories had low numbers of observations up to 20 hours per week and this is apparently consistent with the range of hours covered by the SB plateau as discussed in Chapter 2. However, there are some problems with these conclusions – for example, 5 of the 28 viable male distributions in 1978 had observations in all the five cells which make up the range of hours 1–25. These were categories 1, 3, 15, 17 and 38. Whether or not these categories are significantly different in this respect will be answered in a later section. It should also be noted that in 1981 only two categories, 3 and 17, had entries in all of these five cells.

In contrast to the number of part-time hours observations there is no dramatic fall of hours above a threshold point in 1978 and it is not until the cell 61–65 that a large fall-off in observations occurs. Indeed, between the cell 41–42 and the cell 51–55 there is in general no great difference in the percentage of observations for those categories with significant numbers. Indeed, there are some categories, such as 10, where the number of observations is greater in the cell 51–55 than in the cell 41–42 in both years.

However, this statement is not as valid for the hours distributions in 1981. Whereas in 1978, 53.6% of the viable categories had greater or equivalent number of observations in cell 41–42 hours as in cell 51–55 hours, in 1981 this figure was only 13.3%.

It should also be pointed out that there are four categories in 1981 in which all ten cells between 41 and 71+ hours are filled. These are categories 11, 12, 32 and 33. In 1978 eleven categories, 3, 4, 5, 6, 7, 12, 26, 27, 29, 31 and 33, had observations in all these ten cells.

This extended tail to the distribution above 40 hours of work also appears to be consistent with the budget constraints described in Chapter 2. Since at these higher levels of hours the budget constraint will provide less impediment to the choice of hours.

Superficially, the distribution of hours within the male sample seems to be consistent with the underlying budget constraints suggesting that labour supply incentives influence labour supply decisions. In the following sections we analyse the data in a more systematic manner.

Table 4.2 1978 Percentage Distribution of Hours by Category

Category	No. in category	Unemployment rate %	Hours worked								Average hours worked by the employed
			1–25	1–30	31–38	39–40	41–46	41–50	47–55	51+	
1	95	4	11	12	16	33	15	27	19	8	38.71
2	17	12	8	0	0	47	6	12	24	29	47.73
3	229	3	8	10	7	35	18	31	19	14	41.44
4	136	3	1	1	5	30	19	40	29	21	45.70
5	150	7	3	3	6	31	17	33	23	21	45.22
6	69	9	0	0	0	36	17	30	25	25	46.57
7	46	15	0	0	0	39	17	24	13	22	46.91
8	18	11	6	6	6	33	39	44	6	0	40.41
9	5	0	20	20	0	0	40	40	20	40	43.20
10	121	7	1	1	11	31	19	31	21	20	45.11
11	90	2	1	1	8	29	23	41	23	19	45.97
12	108	6	1	1	5	26	18	35	27	28	47.46
13	22	9	0	0	0	18	14	36	36	36	51.55
14	10	9	0	0	0	50	30	50	20	0	42.70
15	36	3	22	25	8	33	14	25	14	1	36.17
16	6	0	0	0	17	33	17	17	0	33	47.67
17	135	6	16	19	9	27	18	27	14	13	39.07
18	59	0	7	8	3	37	15	34	31	17	42.90
19	45	7	2	2	9	22	13	31	36	29	46.57

20	28	4	0	0	7	43	7	18	14	29	46.8
21	5	0	20	20	0	20	0	0	20	60	53.1
22	87	17	1	6	23	24	13	25	14	5	41.02
23	21	19	0	0	5	43	19	29	10	5	42.53
24	228	11	2	3	19	34	20	28	11	5	40.64
25	172	11	1	1	21	33	17	26	15	9	41.84
26	229	14	0	1	17	28	14	25	20	14	43.42
27	109	16	1	2	6	29	18	31	20	16	44.84
28	65	14	2	3	8	37	11	25	20	14	43.47
29	67	7	0	4	36	16	18	24	9	12	42.22
30	15	7	0	13	13	33	20	27	13	7	39.96
31	404	9	1	4	32	27	13	23	13	6	40.60
32	325	9	0	2	28	22	19	30	15	8	41.88
33	579	11	0	2	26	24	17	27	15	10	42.17
34	151	9	1	5	26	22	20	29	15	10	41.37
35	50	16	0	0	16	20	14	32	22	16	45.31
36	29	31	0	3	17	24	14	17	5	7	41.22
37	8	63	0	0	0	12	12	25	12	0	43.50
38	141	15	6	9	24	23	16	25	10	4	39.06
39	71	11	0	4	18	30	17	31	18	6	41.73
40	84	18	0	2	21	27	13	24	12	7	41.78
41	37	32	0	3	19	19	19	19	3	8	41.82
42	10	28	0	0	11	22	11	22	22	17	46.46
43	318	4	25	33	32	18	9	11	3	1	31.45
44	243	17	37	45	22	11	2	4	2	1	25.67

Note: categories may not sum to 100% because of rounding.

Table 4.3 1981 Percentage Distribution of Hours by Category

Category	Number in category	% Unemployment rate	Hours worked								Average hours worked by the employed
			1–25	1–30	31–38	39–40	41–46	41–50	47–55	51+	
1	80	4	12	14	12	54	10	14	5	2	37.25
2	18	17	0	0	11	72	0	0	0	0	38.83
3	164	5	10	12	14	58	7	9	3	2	37.14
4	119	10	3	3	13	62	5	9	6	3	39.48
5	141	14	1	1	9	55	13	16	6	4	40.50
6	70	17	0	3	4	57	9	13	4	6	41.34
7	35	37	0	0	0	54	0	6	6	3	41.93
8	11	0	9	18	18	27	18	18	9	18	38.50
9	4	25	25	25	0	25	0	0	0	25	39.17
10	92	5	1	2	10	54	9	18	14	10	41.71
11	76	9	1	3	14	42	15	18	8	13	42.73
12	104	17	0	0	12	36	11	20	12	14	44.62
13	34	24	0	3	9	44	12	12	3	9	42.04
14	11	18	0	0	9	55	9	9	0	9	40.89
15	23	13	17	26	4	35	13	13	4	9	34.20
16	5	0	0	20	0	40	0	0	20	40	43.60
17	95	5	14	18	20	35	13	17	5	5	36.99
18	43	12	5	5	16	49	6	7	9	12	42.01
19	31	6	0	0	10	48	6	16	16	19	44.84

20	17	5	0	0	12	53	6	6	6	24	45.56
21	2	0	0	0	0	50	0	0	0	50	57.25
22	97	15	1	2	39	33	3	6	6	4	38.79
23	23	17	4	4	30	35	9	9	0	4	39.61
24	228	13	1	2	25	42	8	10	2	1	38.96
25	209	12	1	2	30	45	9	10	1	1	38.63
26	255	19	0	1	21	47	6	9	3	3	39.78
27	150	15	1	1	21	53	6	8	3	3	39.65
28	75	20	0	0	24	43	5	11	7	3	40.07
29	107	6	3	8	46	25	7	12	6	0	37.98
30	26	27	0	0	31	35	8	8	0	1	38.55
31	469	9	1	3	45	33	7	8	2	3	38.47
32	393	6	2	3	41	34	8	13	5	3	39.29
33	659	15	0	2	40	30	8	10	4	3	39.21
34	204	15	0	3	35	32	8	11	3	2	39.30
35	41	12	2	5	27	34	17	20	2	0	39.07
36	30	30	3	7	33	23	7	7	0	0	37.02
37	3	33	0	0	0	33	0	33	33	3	44.50
38	165	24	4	7	26	32	7	9	2	1	38.03
39	90	16	0	4	28	39	9	12	4	4	38.97
40	85	18	0	4	25	35	11	15	5	0	40.13
41	31	16	6	6	35	35	3	6	3	9	37.54
42	11	18	0	9	27	9	27	27	0	9	41.50
43	324	6	25	31	43	13	4	7	3	1	31.16
44	261	23	30	38	26	10	2	3	1	0	28.04

Note: categories may not sum to 100% because of rounding.

The Maintained Hypotheses

Chapter 2 demonstrated that the budget constraints are highly sensitive to the household's characteristics. If we are to engage in an informal analysis of the FES data we are forced to make some simplifying assumptions about the shape of the budget constraint. Even so it is not always possible to draw forth some unambiguous consequences for the distribution of hours. We concentrate on two measures, the unemployment rate and the average hours worked per week by those employed. Throughout the chapter we ignore the Earnings Related Supplement to Unemployment Benefit, ERS, and assume that the preference function is homothetic, and that preferences are distributed equally across wage, tenure and family types.

Figure 4.1 depicts the budget constraints of two individuals one of whom has a higher wage rate which gives the budget constraint *oabd*. The 'low' wage budget constraint is given by *oaeg*. I_0I_0 is an indifference curve which leaves the 'high' wage individual indifferent to working H_1 hours or being unemployed. If the wage rate was reduced this individual would become unemployed, provided he was not disqualified from receiving benefits, because this is the highest level of utility that can be obtained. If preferences are distributed in a similar manner between 'low' and 'high' wage individuals this leads us to expect that, *ceteris paribus*,

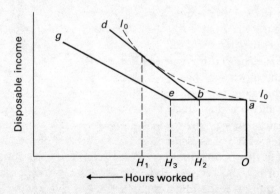

Fig. 4.1 Stylized budget constraints as the wage rate changes

136

'low' wage individuals will have higher unemployment rates. If we had not ignored the presence of ERS the 'high' wage individual may have had a higher level of disposable income at zero hours than the 'low' wage individual. This will tend to raise the unemployment rate for high wage individuals so that the relative magnitude of unemployment rates between the two groups becomes ambiguous between the two groups. Thus only by ignoring ERS, which is assumed to increase with the wage rate, can we derive the result that unemployment rates will be higher for the 'low' wage group.

The comparison of average hours worked by those employed is ambiguous because depending upon the relative magnitude of the substitution and income effects, hours of work may either increase or decrease as wage rates increase. The SB plateau also exerts an extra effect on the average hours of work. The 'low' wage individual will not choose to locate on his budget constraint between the hours of H_2 to H_3 and thus if the income and substitution effects exactly offset each other the 'low' wage individuals would on average have higher hours of work. Thus if the income and choice set effects outweigh the substitution effect the 'low' wage individuals will have, on average, the higher level of working hours. There is no *a priori* method of evaluating these effects and so the model yields no prediction about the level of average hours as the wage rate changes. The presence of ERS will reduce and may reverse the differences in the choice set, that is, low wage individuals may have a larger choice set than their high wage counterparts, therefore the interpretation again depends upon the assumption that ERS is unimportant.

Figure 4.2 depicts the stylised budget constraint as tenure type changes between rented and mortgaged accommodation *ceteris paribus*. The renting individual faces the budget constraint *oabcd* and the mortgagor has the budget constraint *oaeg*. The SB plateau has the same level of disposable income, *oa*, because the family type and housing costs are assumed to be equivalent. The SB plateau is shorter for the renter because of the presence of rent rebates which, it is assumed exceed the value of mortgage interest relief at this point. Housing Benefits increase the implicit marginal rate of tax and consequently the segment *bc* has a steeper slope than the corresponding segment, *eg*, of the mortgagor budget constraint. After *c* on the renter's budget constraint where

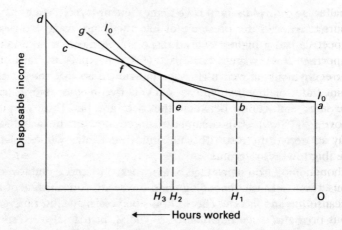

Fig. 4.2 Stylized budget constraints as tenure type changes

housing benefits are exhausted the marginal tax rates become equivalent but the mortgagor has the higher level of disposable income because of the tax relief on mortgage interest payments. Throughout the remainder of this chapter we assume that the sections of the budget constraint above the point f play no role in determining the hours of work individuals choose.

This allows us to draw two unambiguous predictions which can be tested using the FES data. These are first that the renter will have lower unemployment rates than the mortgagor and secondly that average hours for those employed will be higher for the mortgagor. The first hypothesis can be explained as follows; $I_0 I_0$ is an iso-preference curve which leaves the individual indifferent to working H_3 hours or zero hours as the renter's budget constraint becomes more like the mortgagor's it will pivot around point f. This will cause this individual to choose to be unemployed, hence providing that all the points of tangency are not at point f, we would expect the mortgagor to have the higher unemployment rate *ceteris paribus*. The second hypothesis follows from the observation that renters are assumed to face the higher implicit marginal rates of tax and also to have higher disposable income over the section between b and f. Both the income and substitution effects therefore operate to encourage the renters to choose lower hours of work. Furthermore the mortgagor has a

138

smaller choice set by H_1 to H_2 hours and this limits the choice of hours to those above H_2, which is a further reason why we might expect the mortgagors to have higher average hours worked. It is important to keep in mind that these two hypotheses are only correct providing we ignore the budget constraints above the point f. If we allow this to enter our analysis then we cannot draw the same conclusions. To the extent that the budget constraints above f will become more important the higher the wage rate we may anticipate that our hypotheses are less likely to hold true in the high wage rate comparisons we perform. Note also that although we have separate data on owner-occupier or rent-free households we do not use these in the tests of tenure type because this involves changes in housing costs, and no unambiguous prediction can be drawn.

Our final set of tests involves changing family type, holding wage rates and tenure type constant. The stylised budget constraints are depicted in Fig. 4.3. Here *oabc* represents the budget constraint of the smaller family and *odef* the budget constraint of the larger family. The distance *cf* represents a combination of greater child allowances and tax thresholds available for the larger family. It is assumed that the income granted on SB for the extra member of the family, *ad*, exceeds the difference observable on the choice set of hours. We ignore the effects family type may have on Housing Benefits and assume that

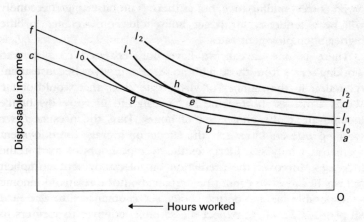

Fig. 4.3 Stylized budget constraints as family size changes

the tax thresholds are always passed before the end of the SB plateau is reached. Along the segments *bc* and *ef* the marginal tax rates are equivalent and consequently there is no substitution effect in operation. The income effect will tend to reduce the average number of hours worked by larger family types but this may be offset by the reduced choice of hours available to them because their choice set is smaller. Consequently if larger families tend to work longer hours this is because the choice set effect outweighs the income effect. The analysis of average hours worked by those in employment as family size changes is a test of the relative magnitude of the income and choice set effects, providing the underlying assumptions are correct.

The model can also be used to predict that the larger the family size the higher will be the unemployment rate. This is because the increase in income on the SB plateau is assumed to be more than is gained along the choice set. If the individual was originally in equilibrium at *g* and his family circumstances change, without altering his preferences, then the individual will choose to be unemployed. If the individual was forced to remain on the upward sloping portion of his budget constraint he would choose point *h*, on the indifference curve I_1I_1, but this indifference curve intersects the budget constraint and therefore the individual can reach higher indifference curves by reducing his hours of work. This process stops when I_2I_2 is reached when the individual is unemployed. This effect will not occur for every initial hour of work, corresponding to, *g*, but as there is no offsetting effect there will be a tendency for larger households, on average, to have higher unemployment rates.

There is one caveat: we have not separated couples with working wives from those with non-working wives because of the reduction in the number of viable categories that would occur. Wives' earnings shorten the SB plateau and increase disposable income along the choice set of hours. Thus the presence of a working wife could reverse the effects on average hours of work so that as family size increases the average hours of work could increase. Moreover the prediction on unemployment no longer follows because we cannot be certain about the relative increases in disposable income on the choice set as compared to along the SB plateau. We might expect the earnings of wives to vary across family types because the presence of children may limit the level of earnings a wife can obtain or alternatively the absence of children may indicate that the wife is older, perhaps past retirement age, and this may, in part, mitigate the above factor. Thus it is unlikely that the effects of wives' earnings will cancel out. The comparison where the reversal of the hypotheses is perhaps most likely is in the comparison of single males with childless married couples as there are no offsetting earnings for the single male.

We may summarize the tests and hypotheses as follows: for the comparison across wage groups the hypothesis predicts that the 'low' wage group has the highest unemployment rate, but that the average level of hours worked is ambiguous, as it depends upon the relative magnitude of the income, choice set and substitution effects. If the former effects are larger than the substitution effect the 'low' wage group will have the higher level of hours.

For the comparison across tenure types the hypotheses are that the renter will have lower unemployment rates than the mortgagor. The renter will also have lower average hours for those employed compared to the mortgagor. Finally across family types the hypotheses predict that the unemployment rate will increase with family size. The hypotheses also predict that the effect of the budget constraint on average hours will be ambiguous because the income and choice set effect work in opposite directions. If the larger families have higher average hours this is because the choice set effect is larger than the income effect.

Bearing in mind the strong assumptions we have had to make to derive these predictions we turn to testing them on the FES data. We begin with tests across wage rates.

The Effects of Wages on Male
Labour Supply

1978

In this section we are primarily interested in how the distribution of hours changes as we alter the wage rate between a 'low' wage and a 'high' wage rate holding, as best we can, tenure and family type constant. To do this, we follow Plant (1984) and use χ^2

tests for homogeneity. If two distributions are homogeneous, i.e. the proportion within each cell is not statistically different from the expected number in the cell, then we cannot reject the hypothesis that the two samples were drawn from the same distribution. The χ^2 test, however, cannot inform us about the form of the underlying distribution and for this we rely on further descriptive statistics. In order to control for tenure and family type all comparisions are made between a 'low' wage rate and 'high' wage rate individual within the same tenure and family classes. This gave us 12 comparisons in 1978 and 13 in 1981 because some categories had to be rejected due to their small size.

The results from the χ^2 tests which are reported in Table 4.4 indicate that in 83.3% of the comparisons we could reject the hypothesis of homogeneity. The two cases in which this hypothesis was not rejected were for the married male renter with 3 children and the married male renter with more than 3 children. There seems little to explain why these categories have income substitution and choice set effects which cancel out as the wage rate changes when the other ten categories do not.

In general the 'low' wage groups tend to have fewer households working less than 39 hours per week, with the figures ranging from 8.7% to 36.1%. The corresponding figures for the 'high' wage group are 23.9% and 54.1%. Comparing each category with 'low' pay against the corresponding category with 'high' pay there were no instances of the proportion working less than 39 hours per week being greater in the 'low' pay categories. A similar case can be made, with the exception of single males in rented accommodation, that 'high' wage groups have fewer cases of individuals working more than 40 hours per week than the corresponding 'low' wage groups.

Table 4.2 reports the average hours per category when the unemployed are excluded. The average hours of work for the 'low' wage group is 43.7 hours and for the 'high' wage group 39.5 hours. Using the t-distribution to test for differences between the means, a statistically significant difference was found and this indicates that we cannot reject the hypothesis that the two samples were drawn from different populations. Comparing each viable 'low' wage category with its corresponding 'high' wage category we find that in only one comparison (from twelve) did

Table 4.4 χ^2 Tests of Homogeneity by Wage Rate, Holding Family and Tenure Types Constant – Including Unemployed

	Rented	Mortgagor	Rent-free/owner
Single	√	—	—
Married couple, no children	√	√	√
Married couple, 1 child	√	√	√
Married couple, 2 children	√	√	√
Married couple, 3 children	x	—	—
Married couple, more than 3 children	x	—	—

√ = reject x = cannot reject at the 5% level of significance.

the average hours (excluding the unemployed) of the 'high' pay categories exceed that of the corresponding 'low' pay category. It would appear that the evidence is, at first sight, consistent with the income and choice set effects outweighing the substitution effects so that 'low' wage individuals work longer hours, *ceteris paribus*.

However, we do not know whether the lower mean level of hours worked is statistically significant in comparisons across individual categories. Nor with our present data set can we construct tests of this. We can re-run the χ^2 tests, comparing 'low' and 'high' wage rate categories when the unemployed are removed from the samples. These are reported in Table 4.5. We could not reject the hypothesis of homogeneity in five of the twelve comparisons. These included the previous two non-rejections (with the unemployed included) together with the comparisons of married men with 2 children in rented accommodation, single men in rented accommodation and married men with 1 child in rent-free accommodation. The comparison of single males who rent (categories 1 and 22) resulted in a statistically significant χ^2 but the 'low' wage category had lower average hours of work. Thus in this case it would appear that the substitution effect outweighs the income and choice set effects. On the individual comparison of categories the 1978 FES

Table 4.5 χ^2 Test of Homogeneity by Wage Rate, Holding Family and Tenure Types Constant – Excluding Unemployed

	Rented	Mortgagor	Rent-free/owner
Single	x	—	—
Married couple, no children	√	√	√
Married couple, 1 child	√	√	x
Married couple, 2 children	x	√	√
Married couple, 3 children	x	—	—
Married couple, more than 3 children	x	—	—

√ = reject x = cannot reject at the 5% level of significance.

reveals that the net magnitude of the income, substitution and choice set effects is not consistent enough for it to overcome differences in the preference functions or the different magnitude of changes in the budget constraints between various tenure and housing types.

This control failure may be compounded by another possibility: namely, that the cases where we cannot reject homogeneity do not have very large differences in their respective wage rates. This may be the case in the rented categories where four of the five non-rejection cases occur. If there is a threshold wage rate at which individuals decide to buy their own homes, then this will place a ceiling on the wage rates of those in rented accommodation. This will tend to reduce the differences in the budget constraints within the rented categories compared to the other housing categories. Consequently, the effect of wage rates on the distribution of hours within the rented sector may not be as significant as in the other sectors.

The above analysis indicates that the unemployed, in at least three of the comparisons, had a significant effect on the distribution of hours. If the maintained hypothesis is correct we would expect that the 'low' wage categories would have the higher unemployment rate. Using Table 4.2 we can see that in all but one of the twelve comparisons this expectation is not borne out, with the 'high' wage categories often having substantially higher unemployment rates. The only categories which do not are married couples with more than 3 children in rented accommodation, categories 7 and 28. The average unemployment rate was 13.7% for the 'high' wage groups and 5.5% for the 'low' wage rate categories. These averages were significantly different at the 1% level and this seems to provide a strong argument against the maintained hypothesis concerning labour supply incentives.

The incidence of higher unemployment rates amongst 'high' wage earners seems to contradict our knowledge of the unemployed who predominately consist of relatively 'low' wage individuals. This leads us to suspect that the wages imputed to the unemployed have a significant upward bias and this results in a number of the unemployed being allocated to 'high' wage categories to which they do not belong. Alternatively these results may be due to our failure to control housing costs which may be higher for the 'high' wage individuals. However, this does not seem a very convincing explanation.

Why, if we do not believe our imputed wage data to be very good, did we not seek a replacement? There are three reasons for this. First, as we have stated before, given our available data set we did not believe that any improvement on the imputed wage rates would be more than marginal. Secondly, from a methodological point of view it is not acceptable to change a variable simply because it gives results which are unexpected. Finally if the hypotheses are correct then it might be expected that this would be visible even if the imputed wage data has some biases. That this does not occur suggests, at the least, that the hypotheses are not robust to alternative specifications of imputed wages.

Setting aside the results from comparing unemployment rates it seems hard to avoid the conclusion, for the 1978 FES, that the effect of wages on the hours distribution has not provided any clear-cut indication about the relative magnitude of income, substitution or choice set effects. We now turn our attentions to the 1981 FES to analyse the effect of wages on hours of work.

1981

Using data from 1981 we could make thirteen comparisons of categories which differed in their wage rates. These are reported in Table 4.6. We found that in twelve of the cases the hypothesis

Table 4.6 χ^2 Test of Homogeneity by Wage Rate, Holding Family and Tenure Type Constant, Including Unemployed, 1981

	Rented	*Mortgagor*	*Rent-free/owner*
Single	√	—	—
Married couple, no children	√	√	√
Married couple, 1 child	√	√	√
Married couple, 2 children	√	√	√
Married couple, 3 children	x	√	—
Married couple, more than 3 children	√	—	—

√ = reject x = cannot reject at the 5% level of significance.

of homogeneous distributions could be rejected using χ^2 tests. The comparison where homogeneity could not be rejected was for categories 6 and 27.

We find that 'high' wage categories have lower average hours worked by those in employment compared to 'low' wage categories in ten of the thirteen categories. The categories which do not conform to the above result are: 1 and 22, 3 and 24, and 17 and 38. The average hours worked by those in employment with 'high' wages is 39.18 hours compared to 40.98 hours by those with 'low' wages (in viable categories). The difference between these means using the *t*-distribution is statistically significant at the 1% level.

With the unemployed excluded we re-ran the χ^2 tests and the results are presented in Table 4.7. This indicated that we could not reject the hypothesis of homogeneity in three cases: 6 and 27 (which we were unable to reject when the unemployed were included) together with categories 18 and 39, and 17 and 38. This latter comparison is one which had higher average hours worked by 'high' wage earners.

Overall, three comparisons cannot be distinguished on the basis of their distribution of hours for those employed. In a further two comparisons we can distinguish between the distributions and these comparisons seem to indicate that the substitution

Table 4.7 χ^2 Test of Homogeneity by Wage Rate, Holding Family and Tenure Type Constant, Excluding Unemployment, 1981

	Rented	*Mortgagor*	*Rent-free/owner*
Single	√	—	—
Married couple, no children	√	√	x
Married couple, 1 child	√	√	x
Married couple, 2 children	√	√	—
Married couple, 3 children	x	—	—
Married couple, more than 3 children	—	—	—

√ = reject x = cannot reject at the 5% level of significance.

effect outweighs the income and choice set effects. The remaining eight comparisons have average hours worked which are lower for the 'high' wage categories who have distributions of hours which are statistically significantly different from their 'low' wage counterparts. It would appear that the 1981 FES data is slightly more supportive of a consistent net effect between categories than the 1978 FES and this might be due to the reduced importance of ERS in 1981.

We now turn to our second hypothesis, that 'high' wage categories will have lower unemployment rates than 'low' wage categories. Unlike the 1978 data, where only one 'low' wage category, 7, was found to have a higher unemployment rate than its 'high' wage counterpart, the 1981 data produced five such examples. These are the comparisons of categories: 6 and 27, 7 and 28, 11 and 32, 12 and 33, and 13 and 34. Furthermore, although the average unemployment rate for all viable 'low' wage categories, 12.8%, is lower than the average for 'high' wage categories, 15.2%, this difference was not found to be statistically significant. The 1981 data again seems to be more supportive of the maintained hypothesis than the 1978 data, but it would be unwise to suggest that these results gave more than the barest support to the hypothesis that the unemployment rate decreases with the average rate.

The Effects of Tenure Type on
Male Labour Supply

1978

In this section, we test the homogeneity of the distribution using χ^2 tests after controlling for the wage rate and family type using the 1978 FES. This gives nine tests – three in the 'low' wage and six in the 'high' wage rate categories (these we report in Table 4.8). In only four cases could we reject the hypothesis that the proportions within each cell came from the same underlying distribution. These comparisons were: 3 and 10, 24 and 31, 25 and 32, and 27 and 34.

All of the three 'low' wage comparisons had average hours for those in employment which were consistent with the hypothesis. For the 'high' wage comparisons only half were consistent with the hypothesis. These were the comparisons of single individuals, married couples with 1 child, and married couples with more than 3 children.

Table 4.8 χ^2 Test of Homogeneity Between Renters and Mortgagors, Holding Family Type and Wage Rate Constant, Including Unemployed, 1978

'Low' wage rates	M(0)	M(1)	M(2)		
M(0)	√				
M(1)		x			
M(2)			x		

'High' wage rates	S	M(0)	M(1)	M(2)	M(3)	M>(3)
S	x					
M(0)		√				
M(1)			√			
M(2)				x		
M(3)					√	
M>(3)						x

√ = reject x = cannot reject at the 5% level of significance.
For nomenclature see Table 4.9.

To test whether these differences were significant we re-ran the χ^2 tests excluding the unemployed. These are reported in Table 4.9. We still found four statistically significant distributions, but these were not all the same as when the unemployed were included. There were no comparisons of 'low' wage categories in which statistically different distributions could be found but the 'high' wage rate of the married couple with 2 children revealed a statistically different distribution between renters and mortgagors. When the unemployed are excluded from the distributions only one comparison from nine is both statistically significant and supports the maintained hypothesis (married, 1 child, high wages). Yet three comparisons do not conform with the

Table 4.9 χ^2 Test of Homogeneity Between Renters and Mortgagors, Holding Family Type and Wage Rate Constant, Excluding Unemployed, 1978

'Low' wage rates	M(0)	M(1)	M(2)		
M(0)	x				
M(1)		x			
M(2)			x		

'High' wage rates	S	M(0)	M(1)	M(2)	M(3)	M>(3)
S	x					
M(0)		√				
M(1)			√			
M(2)				√		
M(3)					√	
M>(3)						x

√ = reject x = cannot reject at the 5% level of significance.

Nomenclature

S   = single
M(0) = married couple, no children
M(1) = married couple, 1 child
M(2) = married couple, 2 children
M(3) = married couple, 3 children
M>(3) = married couple, more than 3 children

hypothesis and are also statistically significant. On the whole, therefore there appears to be virtually no evidence from average hours of work from the 1978 FES to support the hypothesis that budget constraints influence labour supply decisions.

If we compare unemployment rates between categories to analyse the effects of tenure type we find that in only two comparisons out of nine are unemployment rates consistent with the maintained hypothesis. These were the comparison of 'low' wage, childless married couples and the 'high' wage rate married with more than 3 children. In the 'low' wage case the mortgagors' unemployment rate exceeds the renters' by 4% and in the 'high' wage case the difference is 2%. In those comparisons which do not support the maintained hypothesis the renters' unemployment rate exceeds the mortgagors' by an average of 3.7%. Using the *t*-distribution we find that we cannot reject the hypothesis that the mean unemployment rate of the renting categories (10.7%) is the same as that of the mortgagors (8.4%).

The 1978 FES data does not provide evidence with which to support the maintained hypothesis on unemployment rates. Moreover, there are no instances of unemployment rates and average hours of work being jointly consistent with the maintained hypothesis which are statistically significant when each hypothesis is tested on its own. On the basis of these results we are forced to conclude that there appears to be no significant or systematic effect on the distribution of hours induced by the effects of tenure type on budget lines.

This finding is perhaps not too surprising. We have already noted that the maintained hypothesis depends upon ignoring the effect of mortgage interest relief and we have also failed to make any allowance for differences in housing costs, except in so far as we controlled wage rates, or make any allowance for differences in preferences.

1981

Tables 4.10 and 4.11 report the χ^2 tests carried out on the 1981 FES data for evidence of tenure type affecting the distribution of hours. This data set gave ten viable comparisons and nine when the unemployed were excluded. In seven comparisons the hypothesis of homogeneity was rejected by data including the

Table 4.10 χ^2 Tests of Homogeneity Between Renters and Mortgagors, Holding Family Type and Wage Rate Constant, Including Unemployed, 1981

'Low' wage rates	M(0)	M(1)	M(2)	M(3)
M(0)	√			
M(1)		√		
M(2)			√	
M(3)				x

'High' wage rates	S	M(0)	M(1)	M(2)	M(3)	M>(3)
S	x					
M(0)		√				
M(1)			√			
M(2)				√		
M(3)					√	
M>(3)						x

√ = reject   x = cannot reject at the 5% level of significance.

Nomenclature as in Table 4.9

unemployed. In not one of the comparisons did the inclusion or exclusion of the unemployed alter the conclusions on homogeneity.

Of the nine comparisons, with the unemployed excluded, four had average hours for those employed which were consistent with the hypothesis. These comprised all of the viable comparisons in the 'low' wage categories, together with the high wage married couple, 1-child comparison. All four of these comparisons which were consistent with the hypothesis proved to be statistically different distributions. Alternatively, three comparisons: married couples with zero, 2 or 3 children, all with high wages, were statistically non-homogeneous and also exhibited average hours for those employed which were inconsistent with the hypothesis. Thus there is almost as much evidence against the hypothesis as there is supporting it. It can be noted that the results may indicate an asymmetry between the two wage rates and, as suggested in the previous section, this might be due to the increased relative

Table 4.11 χ^2 Tests of Homogeneity Between Renters and Mortgagors, Holding Family Type and Wage Rate Constant, Excluding Unemployed, 1981

'Low' wage rates	M(0)	M(1)	M(2)		
M(0)	✓				
M(1)		✓			
M(2)			✓		

'High' wage rates	S	M(0)	M(1)	M(2)	M(3)	M>(3)
S	x					
M(0)		✓				
M(1)			✓			
M(2)				✓		
M(3)					✓	
M>(3)						x

✓ = reject x = cannot reject at the 5% level of significance.

Nomenclature as in Table 4.9.

importance of mortgage interest relief at higher wage rates.

The composition of unemployment rates reveal that two out of ten were consistent with the hypothesis but, using χ^2 tests of the whole distributions only one was statistically non-homogeneous. This was the 'low' wage rate married with 2 children comparison. However there were four comparisons which had unemployment rates which were statistically inconsistent with the maintained hypothesis on the basis of the χ^2 tests. All of these were from high wage rate comparisons and this may also be evidence that mortgage interest relief is important for high wage rate individuals, although other interpretations are possible. We also subjected the mean unemployment rates to a test of statistical difference by dividing the sample into renter and mortgagor groups. The means were 11.5% and 13.8% for the renting and mortgage groups with 'low' wages and 15.7% and 10.5% for the respective groups with 'high' wages. The means proved to be significantly different for 'high' wage rates but statistically insignificantly different for the 'low' wage comparisons. These results therefore provide no support for the maintained hypothesis but again provide evidence of the asymmetry between the 'high' and 'low' wage groups.

It is noticeable that there were only two comparisons in which hours and unemployment data were both consistent with the hypothesis. The other eight comparisons were either statistically insignficant or did not support the hypothesis. On this basis we have to conclude that the evidence has not favoured the maintained hypothesis that renters will have lower average hours of work of those employed and lower unemployment rates than mortgagors.

The Effects of Family Composition on Labour Supply

1978

In this section we analyse the distribution of hours in each category by family type, holding wage rates and tenure type constant. This gave 60 comparisons, 24 being in the 'low' wage categories and 36 in 'high' wage categories. Due to the lack of observations there are no comparisons of single parent families in either wage category and there are only three comparisons in the 'low' wage mortgage categories.

We begin with the comparison of average hours of those employed, of which there are 57 with three comparisons (38 and 41, 39 and 41 and 40 and 41) being lost due to lack of degrees of freedom. These comparisons are reported in Table 4.12. Of these comparisons, 48 indicated that the larger families had higher average working hours for those employed than smaller families. The majority of the results which gave the opposite result were, by far, in the 'high' wage categories, eight from a possible nine. Again there appears to be some asymmetry between 'low' and 'high' wage categories, although it should be pointed out that four of these opposite results in the 'high' wage comparisons all concerned category 29, the single person with a mortgage. So if this result is atypical the asymmetry may not be as great as it appears at first sight. Moreover not one of the nine comparisons which had lower average working hours for the larger families is statistically different using χ^2 tests.

153

Table 4.12 χ^2 Tests of Homogeneity by Family Type, Holding Wages and Tenure Type Constant, Excluding Unemployed, 1978

Rented:

	'Low' wage rate					'High' wage rate				
	M(0)	M(1)	M(2)	M(3)	M>(3)	M(0)	M(1)	M(2)	M(3)	M>(3)
Single	×	✓	✓	✓	✓	×	✓	✓	✓	✓
M(0)	—	×	×	✓	✓	—	×	×	✓	×
M(1)		—	×	×	×		—	×	✓	×
M(2)			—	×	×			—	×	✓
M(3)				—	×				—	✓

Mortgage:

	'Low' wage rate					'High' wage rate				
	M(0)	M(1)	M(2)	M(3)	M>(3)	M(0)	M(1)	M(2)	M(3)	M>(3)
Single	×	✓	✓	✓	×	×	×	×	×	×
M(0)	—	×	×	✓	×	—	×	×	×	✓
M(1)		—	×	×	×		—	×	×	×
M(2)			—	×	×			—	×	×
M(3)				—	×				—	✓

Rent-free/Owner-occupier:

	'Low' wage rate			'High' wage rate		
	M(0)	M(1)	M(2)	M(1)	M(2)	
Single	×	×	✓	—	✓	
M(0)	—	×	✓	×	×	
M(1)		—	×	—	×	

✓ = reject × = cannot reject at the 5% level of significance.
See Table 4.9 for nomenclature.

Of the 48 comparisons which indicate higher average hours for larger families, only 18 were found to be significantly different using χ^2 tests with 12 of these comparisons being between 'high' wage categories. It is noticeable that eight of these comparisons concern single persons renting on both 'high' and 'low' wages. The only categories against which categories 1 and 22 were not statistically significantly different were 3 and 24, the married couple with no children. Indeed, of the four comparisons using childless married couples against single persons none of the distributions were found to be statistically different, which may be indicating that our caveat about working wives in childless married couples has some foundation.

Summing up the comparison of average working hours by family type it would appear that the results are better than we might have expected from previous experience; 18 of the 57 comparisons were found to have statistically higher average hours of work by larger family types. This is consistent with the magnitude of the choice set effect exceeding that of the income effect. Of the nine comparisons which were consistent with the reverse conclusion not one had a statistically different distribution of hours. Even so these results are not particularly impressive as over 68% of the comparisons fail to provide an estimate for the qualitative effects of the choice set effect as opposed to the income effect.

We now turn to the distribution of hours including the unemployed, which gave us 60 comparisons. Of these 41 reveal unemployment rates which are consistent with the hypothesis that they should increase with family size – 16 of these comparisons were in the 'low' wage category. However, Table 4.13 shows that only 12 of the 41 comparisons with unemployment rates consistent with the hypothesis have statistically different hours distributions (six in each wage category). This compares with five comparisons of unemployment rates which contradicted the hypothesis and were found to be derived from statistically different hours distributions.

Of the 57 comparisons on which χ^2 tests have been completed on the data both excluding and including the unemployed, the majority, 36 comparisons, remained non-significant regardless of the inclusion or exclusion of the unemployed. In 14 of the cases the distributions remained statistically different whether the

Table 4.13 χ^2 Tests of Homogeneity by Family Type, Holding Wage Rates and Tenure Type Constant, Including Unemployed, 1978

Rented:	'Low' wage rate					'High' wage rate				
	M(0)	M(1)	M(2)	M(3)	M>(3)	M(0)	M(1)	M(2)	M(3)	M>(3)
Single	x	√	√	√	√	x	x	√	√	x
M(0)	—	x	x	√	x	—	x	√	√	x
M(1)		—	x	x	x		—	x	√	x
M(2)			—	x	x			—	x	x
M(3)				—	x				—	x

Mortgage:	'Low' wage rate					'High' wage rate				
	M(0)	M(1)	M(2)	M(3)	M>(3)	M(0)	M(1)	M(2)	M(3)	M>(3)
Single	x	x	√	√	√	x	x	x	x	x
M(0)	—	x	x	√	x	—	x	x	x	√
M(1)		—	x	x	x		—	x	x	x
M(2)			—	x	x			—	x	√
M(3)				—	x				—	√

Rent-free/Owner-occupier:	'Low' wage rate			'High' wage rate		
	M(0)	M(1)	M(2)	M(1)	M(2)	M(3)
Single	x	√	√	√	√	—
M(0)	—	√	x	x	x	x
M(1)		—	x		x	x
M(2)			—			—

√ = reject x = cannot reject at the 5% level of significance.
See Table 4.9 for nomenclature.

unemployed were included or excluded. In seven cases the introduction of the unemployed into the distribution caused a change in the statistical status of the comparisons. In four cases, 22 and 25, 22 and 28, 24 and 28, and 31 and 34, the introduction of the unemployed turned the distribution of hours from being statistically different to being statistically indistinguishable to the χ^2 tests. The reverse occurred in the comparisons of categories 15 and 18, 17 and 18, and 17 and 19. It is noticeable that three of these seven comparisons come from the 'low' wage rate, rent-free categories and are also inconsistent with the hypothesis. Of the three comparisons which became statistically different on the introduction of the unemployed, two are not consistent with the hypothesis that unemployment rates increase with family size. Thus the χ^2 tests do not provide a source of information to confirm or reject the unemployment rate hypothesis. We therefore turn to analysing the unemployment rates using t-distribution.

The comparisons were divided into six groups which were determined by the wage rate and tenure type. Within the groups the unemployment rates from each comparison are separated into a 'low' unemployment and a 'high' unemployment set on the basis of family size. Using the t-distribution we then test for significant differences in the means of each set within the group. With the exception of the low pay mortgagor group the mean unemployment rates were consistent with the hypothesis that larger families have higher unemployment rates. For four of the six groups, including low pay mortgagor, we could not reject the hypothesis that the means were equivalent. The groups containing 'low' wage rate renting families and high pay rent-free/owner families both had mean unemployment rates which were consistent with the hypothesis and statistically significant. In the former case the unemployment rate of large families exceeded that of the comparison with smaller families by an average of 5.1% and in the latter case by 9.7%, on average. But even in these groups four, from 21, of the comparisons are inconsistent with the hypothesis. On the basis of these results it seems fair to conclude that the effect of the budget constraint on unemployment rates is not well established. The main support given to the hypothesis is the lack of contradictory evidence but it would be unwise to find such evidence convincing.

1981

The 1981 FES data gave 64 comparisons between viable categories when the unemployed were included and 47 when they were excluded. These are reported on Tables 4.14 and 4.15 respectively.

We begin the analysis by considering the average hours undertaken by those in work: 40 comparisons from a possible 47, are consistent with the choice set effect dominating the income effect and of these ten are statistically different using the χ^2 test. The majority of these, six, are derived from the 'low' wage renter comparisons which contain only ten of the viable cases. If this performance was repeated over all the remaining categories we would have expected a further three statistically different hours distributions to be found in the 'high' wage renting comparisons. It would appear that there may be some form of interaction between tenure type and family type which causes significantly different distributions to predominate in the renting sector.

An alternative explanation is that renters have the majority of viable categories containing single people. As single persons represent one end of the spectrum of family size we might expect this to produce rather more statistically significant differences than a comparison based on, say, a married couple with 1 child. Hence, we might anticipate that the rented sector would produce more statistically significant distributions, not because tenure and family types interact, but because of the distribution of viable categories in our data. This argument is weakened when one notes that for the five comparisons of single persons against married couples with 3 or more children, from both 1978 and 1981, only two produced significantly different distributions of hours worked. It is clear then that an interaction between tenure and family type cannot be ruled out. Of the seven comparisons which are consistent with the income effect dominating the choice set effect, none of the distributions of hours worked proved to be statistically significantly different. Summing up this evidence, it would appear that there is some support for the choice set effect outweighing the income effect but, as the majority of the comparisons between distributions were not statistically significantly different, the results are far from convincing.

We now turn our attention to the hypothesis that as 'family

Table 4.14 χ² Tests of Homogeneity by Family Type, Holding Wage Rates and Tenure Type Constant, Excluding Unemployment, 1981

Rented:

	'Low' wage rate				'High' wage rate				
	M(0)	M(1)	M(2)	M(3)	M(0)	M(1)	M(2)	M(3)	M>(3)
Single	x	√	√	√	√	x	√	√	x
M(0)	—	√	√	√	—	x	x	x	x
M(1)	—	—	x	x	—	—	x	x	x
M(2)	—	—	—	x	—	—	—	x	x
M(3)	—	—	—	—	—	—	—	—	x

Mortgage:

	'Low' wage rate				'High' wage rate				
	M(0)	M(1)	M(2)	M(3)	M(0)	M(1)	M(2)	M(3)	M>(3)
Single	√	x	x		√	x	x	x	x
M(0)	—	x	x		—	x	x	x	x
M(1)	—	—	x		—	—	x	x	x
M(2)	—	—	—		—	—	—	x	x
M(3)	—	—	—		—	—	—	—	x

Rent-free/Owner occupier:

	'Low' wage rate	'High' wage rate	
	M(1)	M(1)	M(2)
M(0)	x	x	x
M(1)	—	—	x

See Table 4.9 for nomenclature.
√ = reject x = cannot reject at the 5% level of significance.

Table 4.15 χ^2 Tests of Homogeneity by Family Type, Holding Wage Rates and Tenure Type Constant, Including Unemployed, 1981

Rented:	'Low' wage rate					'High' wage rate				
	M(0)	M(1)	M(2)	M(3)	M>(3)	M(0)	M(1)	M(2)	M(3)	M>(3)
Single	x	✓	✓	x	x	✓	x	✓	✓	x
M(0)	—	x	✓	✓	✓	—	x	✓	x	x
M(1)	—	—	x	x	x	—	—	✓	x	x
M(2)	—	—	—	—	x	—	—	—	x	x
M(3)	—	—	—	—	x	—	—	—	—	x

Mortgage:	'Low' wage rate			'High' wage rate				
	M(1)	M(2)	M(3)	M(0)	M(1)	M(2)	M(3)	M>(3)
Single	—	—	—	✓	x	✓	✓	x
M(0)	x	x	x	—	x	x	x	x
M(1)	—	x	x	—	—	x	x	x
M(2)	—	—	—	—	—	—	x	x
M(3)	—	—	—	—	—	—	—	x

Rent-free/Owner-occupier:	'Low' wage rate		'High' wage rate			
	M(1)	M(2)	M(0)	M(1)	M(2)	M(3)
Single	—	—	x	x	x	x
M(0)	x	x	—	x	x	x
M(1)	—	x	—	—	—	x
M(2)	—	—	—	—	—	x

✓ = reject x = cannot reject at the 5% level of significance.
Nomenclature as in Table 4.9.

size' increases the unemployment rate should also increase. Of the 64 viable comparisons, 48 were consistent with the hypothesis. Of the 48 comparisons, only seven are statistically different both with and without the unemployed. It should be remembered that the χ^2 test when the unemployed are included is not a test of the degree of difference between unemployment rates but rather a test on the whole hours distribution. We cannot tell whether the unemployed on their own are statistically different, so that the best conclusion we can draw is that only seven comparisons from 47 reveal statistically different distributions as a whole.

The introduction of the unemployed causes five of the comparisons to change their distinctive statistical properties. In three cases, comparisons 25 and 26, 29 and 33, and 29 and 34, the introduction of the unemployed resulted in insignificantly different distributions becoming significant on the χ^2 test. In the comparison of categories 1 and 6 and 3 and 4 the converse occurred. We may note, without reading too much into it, that the former three comparisons are all 'high' wage cases while the latter two are 'low' wage groups.

We can use the change in statistical significance to illustrate a weakness in the use of χ^2 tests for analysing the hours data. For the three comparisions which became statistically significant upon the introduction of the unemployed the difference in the unemployment rates range from 6.8% between categories 25 and 26 to 9.6% between categories 29 and 34. With such large differences in the unemployment rates it is to be expected that the distributions would become statistically different. However, the comparison of categories 1 and 6 gave an even larger difference in the unemployment rates, 13.4%. Why then did the distributions of hours become statistically indistinguishable after the introduction of the unemployed? The answer lies in the χ^2 test's requirement that no cells can be empty. To overcome this problem the program used to calculate the χ^2 statistic amalgamates cells. For example, in the comparison of categories 1 and 6 the program reduces the number of cells from 22 to 4. In the comparison of categories 1 and 6 the introduction of the unemployed together with the amalgamation procedure reduced the differences between the distributions. Without the unemployed the percentages working between 1 and 25 hours per week were 12.5% and 0% for categories 1 and 6 respectively.

With the unemployed included, the percentages became 16.3% and 17.1% respectively. Under such conditions it is not surprising that the distributions became statistically indistinguishable when the unemployed were included even though visual inspection would seem to indicate that the unemployment rates are very different. Thus the use of χ^2 tests when the cells are the product of amalgamation may make the tests unreliable due to the masking of information.

To evaluate the effect of budget constraints on the unemployment rate we turn to testing the difference between the mean unemployment rates. The categories were separated into six groups on the basis of wage rates and tenure type. Within each of these groups two sets of unemployment rates corresponding to the 'high' unemployment (large families) and 'low' unemployment (small families) were constructed from the comparisons. The mean of the unemployment rates were then tested using the t-distribution. With the exception of the 'high' wage rate rent-free/owner-occupier categories, each of the mean unemployment rates was found to be consistent with the hypothesis that unemployment rates increase with family size. Of these five categories four were found to be statistically different at the 5% level of significance with differences in the unemployment rates of between 2.5% and 10.8%. The 'low' wage rate rent-free/owner-occupiers also proved to be statistically different. These results are noticeably better than those derived from the 1978 FES at supporting the hypothesis. Yet 34 of the comparisons revealed no statistical difference between the distributions whether or not the unemployed were included. On this basis it would be unwise to suggest that the unemployment rates gave more than modest support to the hypothesis.

To summarize the analysis of hours distributions by family type, it would be fair to conclude that both the 1978 and 1981 FES data gave at best slight evidence that the choice set effect offsets the income effect and that the unemployment rate increases with family size as predicted by the budget constraints.

Female Labour Supply

In an earlier section of this chapter we noted that the distribution of hours for the female categories did not appear to take the same form as those for male categories. The major difference is that a much higher proportion of females work part-time, and thereby work hours over which we would expect the SB plateau to operate (at least for 1978).

One problem with the female categories we have obtained is that they are not distinguished by wage rate, or tenure type but only by a crude distinction between the numbers of children. It may be the case that if we had treated the male categories in a similar fashion then their observed distributions may not have been different. To test this we amalgamated the male distributions into seven categories based on family type and irrespective of wage rates and tenure type. These categories give enough observations of male single parent families, 72 in 1978 and 79 in 1981, to make them viable.

By comparing the single and single parent family cases for both sexes, we can rule out the effect of amalgamation as the cause of the female differences because in both 1978 and 1981 the distributions prove to be statistically different at the 1% level according to the χ^2 test. Nor was this result altered if the unemployed were excluded. Consequently it is not the lack of refined data which produces these results. The analysis also revealed that the female distributions were statistically different from each other in both years whether or not the unemployed were excluded. Hence different factors appear to determine the distribution of the two female categories. An obvious candidate to explain the difference may be the presence of children which single parent females have to look after. This of course does not explain why females in 1978 chose to work hours which would seem to imply that they faced marginal tax rates of 100%.

In 1981 the alteration to the earnings disregard rule on SB, for those who receive it, would further tend to encourage part-time rather than full-time working. The difference in the distributions of single male and female workers may result from females having on average lower wage rates and preference functions which caused the substitution effects to exceed the income and choice set effects.

Summary

In the above sections we have analysed the distributions of male hours of work from the 1978 and 1981 FES data sets. We have concentrated on the effects which three distinguishing features, wage rates, tenure type and family type, have upon average hours of work for those employed and the unemployment rate between categories. The results on the whole provide little to no support for the hypotheses, where they are explicit in either of the years or by wage rates, family or tenure types. This can be contrasted with our description of the distribution which, for males, had few observations over hours on which the SB plateau may operate. For the female distribution of hours there was not even this superficial consistency with the budget constraints assumed to underlay their labour supply incentives. Where theory produced no prediction of which category should produce the highest average hours for those employed we found no systematic effect from the comparisons. This is consistent with preferences being specific to the characteristics of the category and the magnitude of the changes in the budget constraints varying between comparisons.

There are a number of factors which may also contribute to the nondescript nature of these results. First, it may be the case that individuals simply do not or cannot respond to their budget constraints. This may be due to the inability of employees to move between jobs to achieve the desired mix of hours and earnings whether because there are no vacancies or because the new job would require extra training which may be prohibitively expensive. In such cases the budget constraint and the work–leisure preference function are not tangential because the workers have no choice about the number of hours they work. One explanation of the few observations of part-time working, for males, is that employers have costs associated with the number of employees, which are invariant to the number of hours worked by each employee. Consequently employers will tend to prefer full-time employees to part-timers. Under these circumstances we would expect more full-time hours to be worked but these may not necessarily be optimal from the employee's point of view. Hence we would not expect effects of wages, tenure and family type on budget constraints to be reflected in the distribution of hours.

Secondly, we have assumed that the distribution of work–leisure preferences is symmetrical between the various categories. However, this may not be the case; those with mortgages may prefer work to leisure in comparison with a similar person in rented accommodation because they wish to reduce the amount of mortgage owing. Alternatively, building societies and banks may only lend to those on high earnings and perhaps hours. Consequently we have failed to control properly for these interactions and, under such circumstances, we might have failed to discern any systematic effects of budget constraints on hours of work.

Thirdly, we have also failed to control other elements which would have affected the budget constraints. For example, we have ignored the level of housing costs which, as Chapter 2 demonstrated, can have a significant effect on the budget constraint. Other important aspects which have been ignored include the level of wives' earnings, the presence of ERS and mortgage interest relief, all of which can have significant effects on the budget constraint. Under these circumstances, we cannot be sure what the underlying budget constraints actually are and hence the hypotheses are partially speculative. It may be that families are reacting to the budget constraints to optimize their work–leisure preferences, but that the differences between the budget constraints are so minimal that differences in hours are insignificant.

Fourthly, as discussed in an earlier section we may have inappropriately allocated the unemployed to higher wage categories because our imputed wage rates overestimate earnings. If this is correct our hypotheses about unemployment rates might perform poorly and little can be inferred about the effect of budget constraints upon the propensity to be unemployed.

Finally, the use of χ^2 tests as a method of analysing the effect of budget constraints has also been under consideration in this chapter. The problems noted above may make χ^2 tests too blunt an instrument to be of any significant use when used with the FES. Moreover, even if more data were collected which would allow the categories to be refined it is not obvious that the use of χ^2 tests could provide additional information to that which could be derived from econometric studies.

5

Econometric Analysis of Labour Supply and Work Incentives

Michael Beenstock and Alan Dalziel

I
Introduction

Chapter 4 contained an informal analysis of the relationship between budget constraints and hours worked. The aim of this chapter is to examine the issue more rigorously to see if we can draw any firm conclusions about work incentives and their effects upon labour supply.

The subject of labour supply has been the focus of much research and controversy over the years. This is probably due to the difficult economic and statistical problems encountered in the area, and also perhaps due to the sensitive nature of the subject matter. Early attempts to assess the impact of the state on work behaviour employed a questionnaire approach (e.g. Royal Commission on the Taxation of Profits and Income, 1954; Break, 1957; and Fields and Stanbury, 1971). Men and women were directly asked how the tax system influenced the hours they worked, and from their replies the researchers tried to establish whether taxes were responsible for any significant incentive or disincentive effects.

The results of these surveys were inconclusive. This was partly due to their construction and partly due to the inherent weakness of the technique. Considerable care has to be taken in the wording of the questions to ensure that the respondents understand what is being asked. Even if they understand, they may deliberately mislead the interviewer giving replies which they feel are more socially acceptable, or, if they suspect a link between the survey and future revisions of the tax system they may well provide a more strategically motivated reply. The method of sampling is also important. The survey needs to be truly representative of the working population rather than being confined to specific occupational or income groups.

After interviewing is completed, problems still exist as it is very difficult to quantify the net influence of the tax regime, especially the implied income and substitution effects. Most surveys just reported the number of households which had overall incentive and disincentive effects. Thus the findings tended to be rather imprecise and heavily dependent upon the interviewee's subjective interpretation of the question.

In recent years, econometric techniques have come to the fore. Although such work still relies on interview-based data, the information requirements are less. It is not necessary to question people's psychological attitudes to work. All that is required is information on payment rates, working hours and personal circumstances.

One of the first cross-sectional econometric studies in the UK was carried out by Brown, Levin and Ulph (1976). Using a specially commissioned survey of weekly paid workers in Great Britain they found incentive effects were generally weak. From a sample of married men they estimated a substitution elasticity of 0.18, an income elasticity of -0.0111 and a price elasticity of -0.179, the latter implying that a 1% increase in the disposable wage rate lowered hours supplied by 0.179%.

This work, however, did not adequately tackle the problem of a non-linear budget constraint and its associated multiple marginal wage rates. Like Hall (1973) they linearized the budget constraint about observed hours of work and then regressed hours of work against the corresponding net wage, and the intercept of the line on the vertical through zero hours. In a stochastic specification of the model this causes correlation between the exogenous variables and the disturbance term (endogeneity bias) and leads to biased and inconsistent parameter estimates. This can be seen in Fig. 5.1. Take the case of a convex piecewise budget constraint. Point O represents zero hours of work. Suppose an individual

167

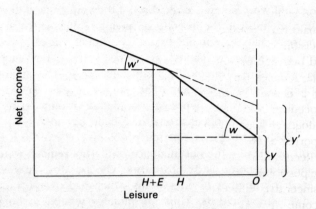

Fig. 5.1 Piecewise linear budget constraints

locates at *H* and works *OH* hours. Linearizing the budget line around *H* would give him a wage rate of *w* and an intercept of the segment on the vertical of *y* (this intercept is sometimes called 'virtual income'). If there was another individual who differed from the last only by the influences captured in the error term of the model, he could quite possibly find himself on another segment of the budget constraint. In this case he would work *O*(*H* + *E*) hours, have a virtual income of *y'* and face a wage rate of *w'*. This means that when a worker chooses his hours of work, he at the same time chooses his net marginal wage rate, and an estimation procedure should take this into account.

Solutions to this problem were suggested by Burtless and Hausman (1978), Wales and Woodland (1979) and Ashworth and Ulph (1981). They were very similar and involved parameterizing each segment of the budget line and then locating the utility-maximizing point by positing a specific type of utility function. Ashworth and Ulph using the same data set as Brown, Levin and Ulph (1976) estimated for married men, an elasticity of substitution between 0.36 and 0.58 depending upon the utility function assumed. This is higher than in the original work and confirms suggestions that previous methods led to estimates that were downwardly biased.

Some of the UK work has also addressed the question of labour force participation, for example, Greenhalgh (1980), Zabalza

(1983) and Blundell *et al.* (1984). This work concentrated on female participation and probably reflects a belief that the work decisions of married women are most sensitive to changes in taxes and benefits. Greenhalgh, using 1971 General Household Survey data, found a participation elasticity for married women of 0.36 for a change in the wife's gross hourly wage. Her estimation procedure did not fully take account of the problem of endogeneity, and Zabalza, who utilized a CES utility function, reported a stronger effect.

Recent discussions of unemployment have drawn attention to the possibility that state benefits as well as taxes can have a strong disincentive effect on labour supply. The difference between income in work and income out of work may be so small that some workers do not find it worthwhile to work many hours or to work at all and are 'trapped' into a low standard of living. The case of non-participation in the labour force is especially interesting. Some commentators such as Minford *et al.* (1983) have cited the level of state benefits as a major cause of the present high rates of unemployment. The analysis presented below, while in no way discounting the effect of benefits and taxes on the *variation* in hours worked, focuses on the decision to work or not to work. The issue is investigated in a microeconomic setting. That is, in common with the other econometric work, it is based upon standard utility-maximizing behaviour by the individual.

A worker, facing a market-determined wage, selects a point in his budget set which yields the highest level of utility. Utility, itself, is assumed to be a continuous function of hours of leisure, and units consumed of a composite consumption good (income). As the shape of the budget constraint crucially affects the number of hours an individual will work, any non-linearities induced by the tax-benefit system must be taken into account. To tackle this problem we used a version of the tax-benefit model described in Chapter 2. With this information, we endeavoured to explain the participation decision in terms of parameters describing the individual's budget constraint, and other relevant variables.

II
Econometric Methodology

Budget Constraint Parameterization

The tax-benefit model was used to calculate net income accruing to an individual for all hours worked in the range from zero to 80 hours. As has been seen, the model takes into account not just the tax and National Insurance systems, but also overtime pay, Child Benefits, rent and rate rebates and several other benefits, and includes any interaction between them. Several criticisms, though, can be levelled at this kind of computation and the two most important will be discussed.

First, because of institutional rigidities, it is argued that a worker cannot freely vary his hours, and hence his choice set is effectively only a subset of the points along the budget constraint. This claim is probably true for many jobs but to some extent a person can choose his hours of work by choosing his job, whether that job be part-time or full-time. (The choice of job, however, is not endogenous to the models presented here.)

Secondly, people are often considered to misperceive their true budget constraints, owing to their less than perfect knowledge of the complexities of the tax-benefit system. Hence their labour market decisions may be based on a rather different set of criteria than those suggested here. The weight of this objection is ultimately an empirical issue. It is acknowledged that the statistical techniques employed cannot discriminate between people's lack of awareness of their true work incentives, and a simple failure to act as rational economic men. With these reservations in mind, we decided nevertheless to proceed with the analysis.

There have been a number of studies of participation in the labour force, mostly referring to women. This study examines the participation decision of heads of households, with particular emphasis on the work incentives they face.

The decision to work or not to work is hypothesized to depend upon γ, a vector of parameters describing an individual's budget constraint, Φ, a vector of other variables, mainly personal characteristics and demand effects, and Σ, a random error term with zero mean.

$$Y = \varrho(\gamma, \Phi, \Sigma) \tag{1}$$

Such a model implicitly assumes that, for a married couple, the husband's work decision is independent of the wife's, except for the income effect from her earnings. The wife's behaviour is assumed to be unaffected by the husband's. It is also noted there is no allowance for variations in income–leisure preferences between people having the same set of observations on the independent variables, and so the effect will be carried over into the disturbance term. It now remains to describe the parameterization of the budget constraint, and the theory underlying the model.

Computer runs of the tax-benefit model have revealed a wide range of shapes for the budget lines, and quite a few instances of net marginal rates of taxation above 100%. However, the most common basic shape for 1978 and 1981, the years chosen for the analysis, is that shown in Fig. 5.2. In general, there is a 'spike' at zero hours, caused by the earnings related supplement on Unemployment Benefit,[1] followed by a dip down towards the 'earnings disregard' slope. The plateau to the left arises directly from the Supplementary Benefit system where payments are reduced by £1 for every additional £1 earned. After 29 hours Supplementary Benefit is no longer available. People typically come off Supplementary Benefit before 29 hours and experience a

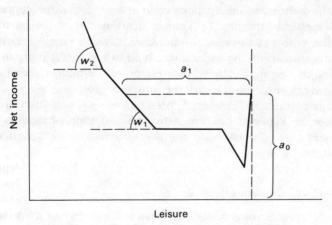

Fig. 5.2 Stylized version of a typical budget line

171

rise in net income. By the time normal hours (i.e. normal hours for the job excluding overtime and meal breaks) are reached, net income is rising and, if the worker is eligible for overtime payments, an outward kink in the budget line may occur.

It was thought that the best approach would be to describe the budget line in as few parameters as possible, making sure that each parameter had some theoretical significance. The parameters are as follows.

Parameter 'a_0' is the level of net household income if the head of the household is unemployed and consists principally of Unemployment Benefit, and if appropriate, wife's earnings. Parameter 'a_1' is defined by constructing a horizontal line from the level of income for zero hours, 'a_0', to the intersection with the budget constraint. For the conventional case of convex indifference curves this section defines the non-optimal region of the budget constraint (it also constitutes one definition of the extent of the 'poverty trap').

It could be argued that the kink point itself and a small adjacent region along the slope is also non-optimal. The size of such a region depends, of course, on the class of utility function assumed. The more general the class, the smaller the area where optimization cannot occur, and hence this objection is not considered a serious one. Parameter 'w_1' is the slope of the budget line from the end of the plateau to normal hours and is thus the average rate of retained income.

The fourth and final parameter 'w_2' is similar to the previous, and applies to the first 20 hours of overtime.[2]

The object of this exercise has been similar to that of Burtless and Hausman (1978) and Ashworth and Ulph (1981), that is, to define the economically feasible region of the budget constraint. However, in contrast with the other approaches, no explicit representation of individual preferences is made. A further difference between this and Ashworth and Ulph is that, in the present case, the UK state transfer system is more completely modelled.

The Participation Decision

It now remains to describe the relationship between the budget line parameters and an individual's participation decision. Con-

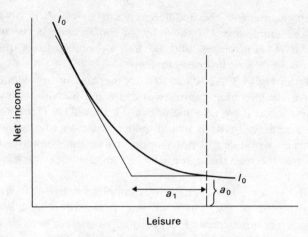

Fig. 5.3 The marginal worker

sider an individual who is indifferent between working and not working, given the market wage and the tax-benefit system. (Fig. 5.3). For the moment, we will exclude the possibility of overtime payments.

If 'a_0' is increased, *ceteris paribus*, there is a vertical shift in the budget constraint (Fig. 5.4). The result of this pure income effect is ambiguous. The individual may find a higher level of utility in

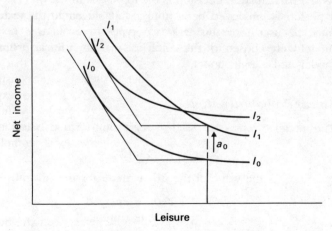

Fig. 5.4 Effects of autonomous benefits on labour supply

173

unemployment if the indifference curve was I_1I_1, or he may choose employment if the relevant indifference curve was, say, I_2I_2. If 'a_1' is increased, and 'a_0' and 'w_1' remain fixed, utility will always be higher in unemployment.

From Fig. 5.3 it is clear that an increase in 'w_1' alone, given convex indifference curves, will cause the individual to join the labour force. If we now include 'w_2' it is unlikely that a change in the parameter by itself would induce a person who is indifferent between working and not working to become employed. But if this was the case the sign for the effect should be the same as for 'w_1'.

There are, however, few examples where a change in government policy will alter one parameter and leave other parameters unaffected. Indeed, the parameters are, in general, interdependent. Therefore, for most of the changes in the tax-benefit system, the effect on all the work incentive parameters would have to be ascertained, before the impact of the measures could be calculated from the econometric model.

III
Empirical Analysis

As the participation decision is dichotomous in nature (i.e. either a person is employed or is not) a suitable empirical technique must be used. For this task two types of qualitative response model were chosen for the empirical analysis, a linear probability model, and a logit model.

Linear Probability Model

The model can be expressed in regression form as below.

$$Y_i = \alpha_0 + \sum_{j=1}^{k} \alpha_j X_{ij} + e_i \qquad (2)$$

where X_{ij} is the value of the jth attribute for the ith individual,

$$Y_i = \begin{cases} 1 \text{ if } i \text{ is employed} \\ 0 \text{ if } i \text{ is unemployed} \end{cases}$$

and e_i is random error term.

174

Equation (2) can easily be interpreted as describing the probability that an individual will choose a certain option given his attributes (see Pindyck and Rubinfeld, 1976). That is, more formally,

$$P_i = \begin{cases} 0 & \text{if } \hat{\alpha}_o + \Sigma\hat{\alpha}_j X_{ij} < 0 \\ \hat{\alpha}_o + \Sigma\hat{\alpha}_j X_{ij} & \text{if } \hat{\alpha}_o + \Sigma\hat{\alpha}_j X_{ij} < 1 \\ 1 & \text{if } \hat{\alpha}_o + \Sigma\hat{\alpha}_j X_{ij} > 1 \end{cases}$$

where P_i is the probability of choosing employment.

A problem with this procedure is that Ordinary Least Squares (OLS) estimation of equation (2) does not guarantee that P_i will be constrained to the (0,1) interval. Predictions outside the interval will have to be arbitrarily bounded, or the observations simply ignored. Both these responses are unsatisfactory, and therefore the transformation of the model by a cumulative probability function is often suggested. This leads, for example, to the logit, and probit models.

A further criticism of the linear probability model can be made. That is, the error term is heteroscedastic. In an attempt to overcome this, Weighted Least Squares (WLS) was employed using a consistent estimator of the error variance suggested by Goldberger (1964).

A final word of warning is in order. As the error distribution is not normal, the 't' statistics, and corresponding confidence intervals are biased. Despite these problems, the linear probability model has the virtue of computational simplicity and allows us to gain a quick impression of the data.

Logit Model

The logit model can be written in the form below:

$$\log\left(\frac{P_i}{1 - P_i}\right) = \alpha_o + \sum_{j=1}^{k} \alpha_j X_{ij} + v_i \tag{3}$$

It is clear that equation (3) cannot be estimated directly by OLS as values of P_i close to 1 or 0 will mean that the dependent variable is undefined. This, coupled with the continuous nature of most of the explanatory variables, implies that numerical methods must be employed, and a maximum likelihood procedure is adopted here.

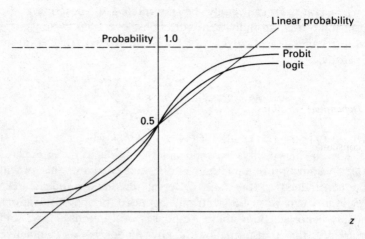

Fig. 5.5 Functional forms for the probability of employment

The two specifications together with a probit formulation are illustrated in Fig. 5.5.

Data

The data used throughout the study is taken from the Family Expenditure Surveys for the years 1978 and 1981. The sample was restricted to the first quarter of each year due to limitations in computing capacity. The version of the tax-benefit model selected is for the corresponding periods.

Results

From the discussion in Section II, we would expect the sign on the 'a_0' parameter to be either positive or negative, the sign on 'a_1' to be negative, and the signs on 'w_1' and 'w_2' to both be positive. It was decided, however, to exclude 'w_2' from the equation on the grounds that overtime rates are unlikely to affect participation decisions.

The results for 1978 are presented in Table 5.1. The regressions include terms for demand-side effects as well as for supply-side influences.

Table 5.1 Models of Unemployment in 1978 Q1

Dependent variables	Linear probability model (1) P_i	Logit model (2) $ln\left(\dfrac{P_i}{1-p_i}\right)$	Adjusted linear probability model (3) P_i^*
constant	0.6805 (7.6)	2.47 (1.2)	
a_0	0.0002 (0.7)	0.0175 (1.2)	0.0006 (2.9)
a_1	0.0020 (2.2)	0.0472 (1.7)	−0.0010 (1.9)
w_1	0.0216 (1.8)	0.6242 (1.4)	−0.0036 (0.5)
peage	0.0107 (2.4)	0.1818 (1.9)	0.0024 (0.7)
peagesq	−0.0001 (2.4)	−0.0022 (1.9)	−0.00002 (0.6)
idch	−0.0174 (2.7)	−0.4547 (2.7)	−0.0038 (0.8)
indup	−0.5436 (2.7)	−9.756 (2.3)	−0.4548 (2.4)
morg	0.0450 (3.1)	1.273 (2.8)	0.0359 (3.4)
$\dfrac{1}{\hat{\sigma}_i}$			0.9194 (13.0)
Method	OLS	Maximum likelihood	WLS
No. of observations	1014	1014	1014
Goodness of fit	$R^2=0.04$	McFadden's $R^2=0.13$ Chi-square (8)=45.9	$R^2=0.98$

Notes 1 Variables for WLS have been transformed.
   2 't' values for logit model are asymptotic.
Definitions
peage = age of head of household.
peagesq = peage squared.
idch = number of children.
indup = industry unemployment rate (proportion).
morg = dummy for possession of mortgage. Equals 1 if have mortgage, 0 if not.

It is sometimes argued that the productivity of young and old members of the labour force is lower than that of workers in the middle age range, and therefore there is less demand for their services. This may lead to a U-shaped relation between age and unemployment rates. Labour supply considerations are likely to enhance the effect. According to the life-cycle hypotheses, individuals reach their peak earnings potential during middle age, and hence the opportunity cost of leisure time is then at a maximum. Thus during this stage of their career they will be less willing to substitute leisure for consumption, and their labour supply is likely to be higher. The inclusion of the age of the individual and its square was intended as a test of this phenomenon. The results seemed to corroborate this well-known finding (e.g. Nickell, 1979).

As regards other variables which may be important, no evidence could be found for any independent effect of the level of education or the occupational status of the individual on his probability of being employed.

As the OLS regression estimates are not efficient, Weighted Least Squares was employed using the estimate of the error variance given below,

$$\hat{\sigma}_i^2 = \hat{P}_i(1 - \hat{P}_i)$$

Weighting by the reciprocal of the standard deviation of the error term gives the WLS estimates of equation (3) in Table 5.1. As predictions outside the $(0,1)$ interval were bounded in the calculation of $\hat{\sigma}_i^2$, estimates are unlikely to be efficient.

The high correlation between the reciprocal of the standard error, and the dependent variable is not surprising. As in 1978, for example, more than 95% of the sample is employed, the dependent variable will equal the independent variable for more than 95% of the observations.

For the logit models two measures of goodness of fit are reported. The first is McFadden's R^2 (Amemiya, 1981, p. 1505) which equals

$$1 - \frac{L(\beta)}{L(\beta_0)}$$

where $L(\beta)$ is the log likelihood function of the model and $L(\beta^0)$ is the log likelihood function of the null model where all slope coefficients are set equal to zero. The statistic varies between 0 and 1. The second, which is related to the first, is a likelihood ratio test between the selected model and the null model, where $LR = 2L(\beta) - 2L(\beta_0)$. The statistic is distributed as a χ^2 with r degrees of freedom where r is the number of independent parameters in the chosen model (excluding the intercept term). As the critical value for the χ^2 distribution for 8 degrees of freedom at the 5% level is 15.5, it can be seen that both logit models appear to be statistically significant.

From the estimates in Tables 5.1 and 5.2 it can be seen that the overall fit of the model is poor. The contribution of the work incentive variables is generally weak. Parameter 'a_0' is positive and implies leisure is an inferior good. The sign on parameter 'a_1' varies and is never significant in the logit model, whereas parameter 'w_1' is positive in 1978 and 1981 (save for 1978 (3)), though in 1981 it is in no instance significant. The only persistently strong effects seem to come from the industry unemployment term and the age variables which suggests that demand has a stronger influence than supply considerations.

There are a number of possible explanations for the poor performance of the models. The first is mis-specification. A large number of hypotheses were tested, however. The logit model was considered a better formulation than the linear probability model, and its estimates appeared to be marginally better. A possible third model was the probit. As people have a simple choice between working and not working we would expect the predictions to be in the tails of the probability distributions, the only region where the logistic and the cumulative normal distributions are markedly different. Such was the poor data coherence of both models that the results were similar and so only the logit estimates are reported.

A 'balanced sample' approach was also tried for both years. Here, all the unemployed, and an equal number of randomly selected, employed people were analysed in order to increase the representation of the unemployed in the sample. Doubts exist about the validity of this procedure. The results were similar to those already reported except that predicted probabilities were closer to their actual values.

Another explanation for the poor fit of the models is, as mentioned earlier, that people may not fully understand the tax

Table 5.2 Models of Unemployment 1981 Q1

Dependent variable	Linear probability model (1) P_i	Logit model (2) $\ln \frac{P_i}{1-P_i}$	Adjusted linear probability model (3) P_i^*
constant	0.637 (5.0)	−0.882 (0.6)	
a_0	0.0007 (2.5)	0.0198 (3.2)	0.0005 (3.1)
a_1	0.00007 (0.1)	−0.0024 (0.1)	−0.0014 (1.4)
w_1	0.0092 (1.0)	0.1703 (0.9)	0.0041 (0.9)
peage	0.0163 (2.5)	0.1706 (1.9)	0.0068 (1.2)
peagesq	−0.0002 (2.7)	−0.0023 (2.5)	−0.0001 (1.6)
idch	−0.0387 (4.1)	−0.5642 (4.6)	−0.0103 (1.3)
indup	−0.6996 (4.8)	−8.043 (4.9)	−0.492 (3.2)
morg	0.0283 (1.4)	0.3728 (1.9)	−0.0059 (0.4)
$\frac{1}{\hat{\sigma}_1}$			0.876 (7.6)
Method	OLS	Maximum likelihood	WLS
No. of observations	1014	1014	1014
Goodness of fit	$R^2=0.06$	McFadden's $R^2=0.12$ Chi-square (8) = 72.4	$R^2=0.96$

and social security arrangements, and make their work decisions on incorrect information. A third reason is that people may act irrationally contrary to economic theory. Finally, the survey data may be of insufficiently high quality. That is, incorrect responses may be given to questions on income received, mortgages and rates paid, and so on, so that the budget lines constructed here may not be the ones upon which people actually base their choices. This point is explored in more detail in the next section.

IV
The Reliability of FES Data

The aim of this short subsection is to provide an indication of potential sources of bias in the Family Expenditure Survey data, which may have a bearing upon the results reported above. To the extent that interviewees' responses to questions asked by FES interviewers are unreliable, our hypothetical budget constraints will not accurately reflect the labour market choices available to individuals within the sample, adding an extra dimension of uncertainty to the interpretation of estimated coefficients.

First, misreporting of any element which enters into the calculation of income at zero hours of work is likely to bias the 'a_0' parameters of the budget constraints. Over-reporting will bias 'a_0' and hence, the whole budget profile, upwards, whilst under-reporting will have the opposite effect. Evidence of the direction and magnitude of these biases is by nature scarce, but Kemsley, Redpath and Holmes (1980) provide some details which are of interest. Of the items which were found to be unreliably reported in the housing schedule (on the basis of an exercise using data from the fourth quarter of 1978), one was of particular relevance to this study. Mortgage interest payments are utilized within the tax-benefit model in the calculation of 'housing additions' to benefit claimants who are classified as owner-occupiers, but this item was found to have an index of reliability of less than 80%. Unfortunately, no indication of the direction of bias is available and so we can only surmise that the 'a_0' parameters will be biased in the manner described above.

Secondly, perhaps the most important of the potential sources of error relates to the earnings data. In Chapter 2, the tax-benefit model was described and from this, the importance of correctly reported earnings is clear. If these are overstated, then the 'w_1' parameter will appear steeper than it should be and the benefit plateau shorter. If understatement occurs, then 'w_1' will be biased downwards and the plateau will appear longer than it should be, with a lower level of utility suggested than would be given in the presence of the true wage rate.

FES earnings data is collected on a 'current-rate' basis and last earnings are assumed to be representative of usual earnings.

However, if last pay is atypical respondents are also asked to supply details of their gross and net usual pay, or, if this varies, to report their average pay. But neither usual pay nor the period over which it is to be calculated is defined; this is left to the subjective interpretation of the respondent. A feasibility study undertaken in June 1979 (Kemsley, Redpath and Holmes, op. cit. Chapter 17.8) considered these issues using an effective sample of 466 from 520, and found that for 34% of weekly paid workers (99 of 292), last pay was not usual. For monthly paid workers the proportion was somewhat less, at 25% (43 of 174).

When last pay differed from usual, the study suggested that some 35% of this grouping calculated usual pay over a period of only one month and only 5% of weekly paid workers consulted documents, compared to 34% of those paid calendar monthly. So, overall, it was suggested that 59% of the former and 57% of the latter group adopted a 'considered statistical approach' in arriving at their estimates of usual earnings. Although generalizations should be viewed with caution, these results would suggest that for a given survey, of the numbers reporting a wage, this is likely to be inaccurate in some 17% of cases. Again, the direction of bias unfortunately cannot be ascertained and so neither can the direct implications for our budget constraint parameters.

A third potential source of error relates to earnings of the householder's spouse (if applicable). The general effect here, given accurate reporting, will be reflected in the 'a_0' parameter and any under- or non-reporting will produce a budget profile which is artificially high, given payment of Supplementary Benefit, or artificially low, given Unemployment, but no Supplementary Benefit.

Despite shortcomings in the FES, it appears that earnings should perhaps not be singled out in particular. Atkinson and Micklewright (1983), for instance, compared FES with 'Blue Book' information as a check on its external consistency and their conclusions were generally favourable.

Estimates of aggregate earnings on the basis of the FES were some 5–10% below the National Accounts figures, but were not considered to be especially unreliable. Investment income, on the other hand, was found to be 45–50% below Blue Book aggregates and clearly very unreliable. Suggested reasons for this divergence were inaccurate reporting (intentional or otherwise) and a possible under-representation of top income groups in the FES. The consequences of this are of some importance since under- or non-reported investment income may produce the following effects. If Unemployment (but no Supplementary) Benefit is payable, the 'a_0' parameter may be understated. Hence, 'a_0' and 'w_1' will probably be inaccurate. If the true level of investment exceeds the Supplementary Benefit disallowance level, then 'a_0' in this case will include benefit payments to which there is no entitlement. Finally, if investment income is relatively high and to the extent that state benefits are not claimed, then 'a_0' will again be understated, 'w_1' understated, and 'a_1' again inaccurate.

The foregoing comments have provided an illustration of the biases to be expected in our hypothetical budget constraint parameters arising from use of the Family Expenditure Survey data. However, the discussion does not suggest any pronounced reasons for the anomalous signs reported in Tables 5.1 and 5.2.

V
Summary

This chapter has briefly surveyed UK research into work incentives and labour supply, and has presented some analysis of its own. The examination of the determinants of labour force participation encountered many of the econometric problems typically found in this field. It is acknowledged that not all of them were adequately resolved, and, as a result, the findings have to be viewed somewhat circumspectly. Nevertheless, it seems from this analysis that the structure of the tax-benefit system has, in general, only a weak effect on the probability of being unemployed. Demand factors, and other factors such as, for instance, social pressure to work, may well exert a stronger influence. But this is still to some extent a matter for conjecture. Although considerable advances have been made in the analysis of labour supply in recent years, comparatively few firm conclusions can be drawn. Serious areas of disagreement still remain.

Notes: Chapter 5

We are indebted to Michael Parker who wrote Section IV.

1   Earnings Related Supplement was abolished in 1982 and this accounts for the main difference between the budget lines illustrated here and those in Chapter 2.
2   In some cases, unemployment income is less than the level of income experienced on the Supplementary Benefit plateau. For these instances an adjustment term was added to 'a_0', to bring it to the level of plateau income. This effectively rules out optimization in the 'earnings disregard' section.

6

Labour Supply Incentives
for the Retired

Peter Warburton

I
The Third Dimension

Previous chapters have sought to provide a framework of analysis for the hours per week decision regarding the supply of labour and to shed some light on the weeks per year decision. The purpose of this chapter is to analyse the third dimension of labour supply decisions, the years per life decision. In the early years of this century a person's working life typically consisted of 50 hours per week, 50 weeks per year and 50 years per life. Average weekly hours worked are now down to less than 45 for manual workers and less than 40 for non-manuals, whilst additional holidays have reduced the number of standard working weeks per year to 46 or 47. Perhaps the most startling change to work patterns, concomitant with increased prosperity on the one hand and rapidly changing technological and industrial structure on the other, has occurred in the third dimension. Increased years of education, including retraining, vocational and post-experience courses, have effectively shortened the average working life by about 5 years since 1910. Changes have also occurred in the age of retirement, traditionally 65 for men and 60 for women.

There has been a steady downward drift in participation rates of men aged over 45 over the postwar period. Between 1971 and 1981, however, as Table 6.1 shows, there was a dramatic shift

Table 6.1 Trends in Retirement in Great Britain, 1971–81

		1971	*1981*	*Difference*
Retired:		%	%	%
Males	45–49	0.13	0.16	0.03
	50–54	0.41	0.48	0.07
	55–59	1.23	1.78	0.55
	60–64	7.06	13.70	6.64
	65–69	68.12	79.15	11.91
	70 & over	87.90	89.81	1.91
Permanently sick or				
'other' inactive:		%	%	%
Males	45–49	1.7	2.42	0.72
	50–54	2.21	3.73	1.52
	55–59	3.37	6.69	3.32
	60–64	6.29	11.69	5.40

Sources: 1971 Census Report on Economic Activity, Table 3.
1981 Census Report on Economic Activity, Table 3.

towards earlier retirement. Almost twice as many men had retired before 65 in 1981 compared to 1971. In addition to the early retirement phenomenon, which cannot be attributed to the availability of state pensions, since these become payable only from age 65 for men, there is a health limitation phenomenon. Over 11% of 60–64-year-olds were classified as permanently sick in the 1981 census compared with under 7% ten years before. In essence many older workers who, when unemployment was low, would have struggled on to state pensionable age despite infirmity, now accept state benefits or early retirement inducements and leave the labour force early.

Three explanations for the decline in male participation (both in the UK and the USA) proffer themselves. First, many traditional industries have dramatically reduced their employment levels, and the older employees have borne the brunt of redundancies. Secondly, the incidence of heart attacks, thromboses and cancers amongst middle-aged people has increased, leading many more to opt out of their jobs before they otherwise would. Finally, the advent of more generous pension provisions for the old both from the state and through the mass membership of occupational pension schemes, has also undoubtedly influenced the average age of retirement.

While it is not our intention to attempt to apportion responsibility for declining participation between these three contending explanations, it is necessary to establish whether in any meaningful sense there is a retirement decision. In other words do some people jump or are they all pushed? This issue is raised in Section II where the results of two empirical studies are discussed: Zabalza, Pissarides and Barton (1980) for the UK, and Quinn (1977) for the USA. Some econometric estimates for labour participation in the UK using time-series data are also provided.

In Section III the retirement decision model is presented, beginning with the concept of budget lines and extending the analysis to the dynamic budget line. The dynamic budget line describes a set of *n* annual retirement date options, where *n* is the mean number of years of future life expectancy. The novel concept of a leisure function is also introduced.

Section IV sets out the main results of the model by means of several simulations of the basic parameters of dynamic budget lines. An individual's current age, future life expectancy, lifetime earnings profile, earnings level, and the characteristics of their occupational pension schemes, if any, are examined in turn. The choice of intertemporal discount factors both for income and leisure, the work-lover/work-hater dimension and the role of housing preferences and associated costs are also discussed.

II
Empirical Analysis of the Retirement Decision

The presumption of this chapter, and indeed of most of the others, is that the individual has a meaningful labour supply decision to make. Nowhere has it been suggested that this is an unconstrained decision in real life. The institutional constraints imposed by employers' desire to synchronize production activities and by the structure of the tax and benefits system are examples of effective limits to labour participation. Furthermore, poor health, disability and family circumstances influence labour supply decisions for a given set of earnings and benefit opportunities. All these factors have particular significance for the older age-groups, those for whom the retirement option is a consideration.

Before proceeding to an empirical analysis of the relative contributions of income, health and labour market conditions to the determination of the participation rate in the UK, it is instructive to summarize the findings of other research in this area. Two studies will be considered in some detail: Quinn (1977) and Zabalza, Pissarides and Barton (1980).

Quinn modelled the microeconomic determinants of early retirement amongst white married men aged 58–63 using the US Social Security Administration's Retirement History Study. The analysis was restrictive in that only two labour force states were allowed: participation and non-participation (retirement). The model was therefore constructed on the basis that a set of independent variables collectively determined the probability of being in the labour force. A logit-type transformation of the type used in Chapter 5 was used to prevent expected probabilities straying outside the (0,1) interval. Amongst the list of independent variables were the husband's and spouse's real hourly wage rates, real non-benefit unearned income of the family, a measure of local labour market conditions and dichotomous dummy variables representing different types of benefit entitlement, the existence of a health limitation, the presence of dependants and a number of specific job characteristics. The results from the data set of 4,354 white married men showed that the health limitation dummy was the single most significant regressor. The existence of a limitation reduced the probability of being a labour market participant by over 20 percentage points. Eligibility for social security reduced the probability by over 11 points, eligibility for a pension from another source, by 7 points and dual eligibility by nearly 26 points. Asset income exerted a weak but significant negative effect on the probability of participation whilst the real wage rate effect was insignificantly different from zero at the 5% level. Of the other variables, the existence of dependants increased the probability, as did conditions of low unemployment. Job characteristics, for example, low autonomy or excessive strain, were negative but poorly determined regressors.

The lessons to be learned from this US study are first that to enter the replacement ratio into a participation model is liable to yield misleading results since the coefficients on the wage and other income variables are likely to be very different. The nature of the social security arrangements both in the USA and the UK make labour force membership a condition for receiving means-tested benefits. Secondly, Quinn discusses the dangers of using actual benefits received from the survey data rather than imputed or potential benefits. Because of non-take-up of benefits and because of the under-recording of unearned income by tax-dodgers, recorded benefits tend to be underestimates. Furthermore, the level of benefits received is endogenous to the work–leisure decision.

Zabalza, Pissarides and Barton (1980), for the UK, develop a more elaborate utility framework within which to analyse the probability of being engaged in full-time work, part-time work, and retirement. Whilst the extension to three labour free states is an obvious improvement, the characteristics of part-time workers are much harder to distinguish empirically than those of full-time workers or retirers. On the reasonable assumption of convexity of the (income, leisure) opportunity set, the authors derive a likelihood function in which the arguments are functions of the net income and leisure hours differentials, the elasticity of substitution between work and leisure, and a set of independent variables as before. Each valid case from the cross-section data was allocated to one of the three states on the basis of actual hours worked. The percentage distributions for both men and women are reproduced in our Table 6.2 from their Table 1.

Table 6.2 Percentage Distribution of Men and Women Just Below and Just Above the Statutory Pensionable Age

	Age Group	Full-time	Part-time	Retirement
Men	60–64	79	3	18
	65–69	9	16	75
Women	55–59	39	40	21
	60–64	12	26	62

Source: Zabalza, Pissarides and Barton (1980), Table 1.
Notes: 1 Full-time work is defined as work for pay for more than 30 hours per week. Part-time work is correspondingly defined as work for pay for less than 30 hours per week, and retirement is defined as zero hours of work.
2 The weighted samples consisted of 1,483 men and 1,207 women.

In addition to the determinants of participation considered by Quinn, Zabalza *et al.* included the ages of husband/wife and spouse, and dummy variables for the attainment of statutory pensionable age, the presence of a 'waiting' wife (one who must wait for her spouse to attain eligibility to retirement benefit), marital status and involuntary loss of job. Zabalza *et al.* also estimate potential benefit and other income rather than use eligibility dummies. This has the advantage that pension elasticities can be calculated. The disadvantage of all schemes which require imputation of incomes, however, is that the margins of error so introduced may obscure the objective rather than the reverse.

The elasticities of substitution obtained by the maximum likelihood estimation of the model were rather low, being 0.25 for men and 1.3 for women. The implication of their results is that women are more responsive to economic incentives than are men. Evaluated at the sample means (age 63 for men, 60 for women) the implied wage elasticities were -0.02 for men and 0.37 for women. The (unearned) income elasticities were -0.023 for men and -0.38 for women. This near-symmetry contrasts with the earlier study but since it is a logical consequence of the income differential specification, no conclusion can be drawn.

Once again, poor health and old age are revealed as very significant contributors to the retirement decision. The dummy for the attainment of statutory pensionable age was very significant, implying either that people's tastes for income and leisure change abruptly at this point or, more probably, that the benefit system induces a change in behaviour on account of the sudden availability of retirement benefit.

Finally, Zabalza *et al.* conclude that if the individual concerned has left his main job involuntarily, he will have, at any age, probably due to a discouragement effect, a much higher probability of being retired.

In summary, both studies agree on the importance of the health limitation, although confessing that reliance on subjective assessments of an individual's health is a weakness. They also agree that increasing the wage of the primary earner makes hardly any difference to the probability of being retired. However, whilst Quinn finds a significant negative effect of pension entitlement and of other income, on the probability of participating, Zabalza *et al.*

do not. In Zabalza and Piachaud (1981), using the same model, a simulation of a 20% increase in state retirement pension resulted in only 2.3% of men and 1.9% of women switching from work to retirement, most of those coming from part-time rather than full-time work.

In the light of the foregoing discussion, some estimation on time-series data for the UK was attempted. The reasons for using time-series data are first to provide a check on the validity of the cross-section results and secondly to address the time-series phenomenon of declining labour participation ratios for the over-45s directly. Figures 6.1 and 6.2 display these ratios for various age-groups for men and women, respectively. The model considered for estimation is necessarily basic because of the paucity of data points. Moreover, the form in which the data appear is also restrictive. Degrees of participation are once again not distin-

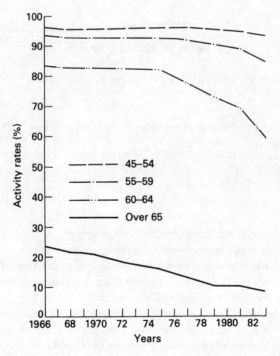

Fig. 6.1 Activity rates for males in Great Britain 1966-83

191

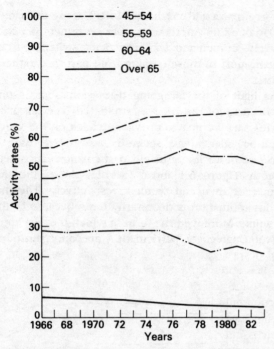

Fig. 6.2 Activity rates for females in Great Britain 1966-83

guished and the width of age-classes is relatively large. The model
is as follows:

$$AR_i = F \left(\frac{AEW_i}{P}, \frac{BEN_i}{P}, UR, RCI_i, DR_i \right) \qquad (1)$$

where:

AR_i is the participation ratio for age-group i,
AEW_i is average net weekly earnings from work,
BEN_i is the amount of weekly income support provided by
the state, according to NI contribution status.
UR is the national unemployment rate,
RCI_i is the rate of certified incapacity for age-group i,
measured in days per cohort member per year,
DR_i is the mortality rate of age group i, and
P is the retail price index.

192

The eight groups under consideration are the age ranges 45–54, 55–59, 60–64 and 65+, for both men and women. Since there are comparatively few degrees of freedom for the individual age-group regressions, the model must be parsimonious. Hence we have omitted variables such as real unearned income (occupational pensions, annuities, investments and so on) and the average duration of unemployment spells. The two health limitation variables, RCI and the death rate, DR, are used as alternatives. Data sources are provided in the Appendix to this chapter.

Table 6.3 presents the results from the estimation of a dynamic form of the specification given in equation (1). On the whole, the results for females are superior to those for males but sign expectations are confirmed in almost all cases. We shall comment on the results by sex, taking the males first.

The income effects were positive, except for the 60–64 age-group, but never significantly different from zero by conventional standards. It is noteworthy, however, that the largest effect was for the youngest age-group. The findings of Quinn and Zabalza *et al.* are thus confirmed in these respects.

The benefits (and pensions) effect is negative for all age-groups, although it is only convincing for the 60–64 group. The 55–59 age-group regression is difficult to interpret in view of the fact that $x_1 + x_2$ exceeds unity. The evidence is consistent with a mild disincentive effect of real income support levels on male participation.

The unemployment rate appears to exert quite a strong disincentive effect by comparison to the real benefits variable. Predictably the effect increases in severity towards pensionable age for men and becomes insignificant beyond that age. Finally, and surprisingly, neither the rate of certified incapacity nor the death rate yielded the expected sign except in the case of the 60–64 age-group. This suggests that health limitations only bite after the age of 60 for men.

Female labour participation is better explained by the model. The income effects are well determined and positive for women under 60, suggesting that the narrowing of the pay differential between men and women during the early 1970s has made an important difference to female participation levels. Real benefits exert a powerful effect for all age-groups. It is clear that the effect is at its peak for the 60–64-year-olds.

Table 6.3 Participation Ratio Equations for Great Britain, 1966–83

General form of the regression:

$$AR_{it} = x_0 + x_1 AR_{it-1} + x_2 AR_{it-2} + x_3 \left(\frac{AEW_{it}}{P_t}\right) + x_4 \left(\frac{AEW_{it-1}}{P_{t-1}}\right) + x_5 \left(\frac{BEN_{it}}{P_t}\right) + x_6 \left(\frac{BEN_{it-1}}{P_{t-1}}\right) + x_7 UR + x_8 RCI_{it} + x_9 DR_{it}$$

	x_0	x_1	x_2	x_3	x_4	x_5	x_6	x_7	x_8	x_9	R^2	SE(%)
Males:												
45–54	24.0 (1.4)	1.148 (5.4)	−0.40 (1.7)		2.026 (1.7)		−11.316 (1.3)	−0.155 (3.1)	0.155 (1.7)		0.972	0.139
55–59	−36.1 (1.0)	0.811 (1.9)	0.668 (0.8)	7.63 (1.1)	0.362 (0.1)	−37.2 (1.2)	−16.22 (0.2)	−0.220 (1.5)	0.083 (0.8)		0.974	0.414
60–65	36.4 (2.8)	1.158 (6.6)	−0.429 (1.9)	−0.90 (0.4)		12.61 (1.2)	−25.93 (3.7)	−0.515 (3.1)	−0.186 (2.8)		0.986	0.461
65+	7.9 (2.5)	1.013 (2.5)	−0.19 (0.5)	2.31 (0.4)		−23.3 (1.3)		−0.027 (0.2)	0.024 (0.3)		0.982	0.600
Females:												
45–54	40.7 (3.4)	0.917 (4.4)	−0.464 (2.1)	23.86 (3.6)			−22.12 (1.7)	−0.144 (1.7)		−3.206 (1.8)	0.993	0.286
55–59	47.8 (2.1)		0.665 (5.5)	17.53 (2.7)		−17.53 (2.7)		−0.196 (1.7)		−2.323 (1.4)	0.900	0.732
60–64	46.7 (4.1)	0.861 (3.5)	−0.907 (4.1)		10.13 (1.6)		−79.68 (2.9)	−0.167 (1.6)	−0.733 (2.6)		0.971	0.523
65+	12.2 (5.4)	0.247 (1.5)		−0.83 (0.77)		−15.42 (2.6)	−22.00 (3.2)	0.15 (7.1)	−0.117 (2.9)		0.989	0.116

'*t*' values are reported in parentheses

The discouraged worker effect is in evidence for the under-65s but is nowhere particularly significant. The rate of certified incapacity is clearly an important limiting factor for the over-60s, and particularly for the 60–64 age-group. Interestingly it is the steadily declining death rate which influences participation in the younger age-groups. Hence progressively lower mortality rates for these age-groups help to encourage higher participation ratios.

In conclusion, there is something to be said for each of the three main arguments with which we began. The income incentive effects are strong for women, a fact which also emerges from the Zabalza study. The benefit and pension disincentive effects are correctly signed but not usually very precisely determined, except for the 60–64 age-group in each case. On this evidence we should expect some response by individuals to changes in their budget line parameters, but not a great deal.

Unemployment, standing for policy-induced and shock-related patterns in economic activity, is clearly an important ingredient of the model. The strongest effects are for 60–64-year-old men. Once again it is this age-group which stands out in terms of the magnitude of the health limitation effect, both for men and women. Brenner (1979) has argued that unemployment, rapid structural change and rapid economic growth increase worker stress and adversely affect mortality. If this analysis is correct, the total unemployment effect will be underestimated by our existing model.

Having examined the recent history of labour participation rates for older men and women in Great Britain, the scene is set for a more detailed analysis of how the income–benefit picture changes through the later stages of a person's working life. The implications that follow for the lifetime participation decision will continue to depend on a great number of personal characteristics in addition to income and benefit levels.

III
The Retirement Decision Model

The aim of this section is to present a model of the individual's retirement decision based on a conventional utility function. The individual is deemed to consider consumption and leisure, both in the present and in the future, as normal goods. In other words, there is no circumstance in which increased leisure for given income or increased income for given leisure would yield a reduction in utility. In order to express utility at time t, a discounting procedure is required to evaluate future income and leisure in terms of present values. The interpretation of the discount factor for income and consumption as the real rate of time preference or the real rate of interest is well established in the literature. The key insight into the unfamiliar concept of leisure discounting is that leisure becomes progressively more valuable towards the end of life. The closer an individual is to his or her expected age at death, the more that individual would be prepared to pay for the privilege of not working. The ageing process, whether or not it is accelerated by ill-health, tends to reduce the supply of physical and mental effort available to the individual. The effort of working a given number of hours per day therefore absorbs an increasing proportion of this available supply with age. This is the main characteristic of the leisure calculation which we propose, but there are other important features and these will be described later.

Thus, whilst future income flows are discounted to the present using a positive discount factor, y per cent per annum, future leisure flows are negatively discounted at l per cent per annum. More formally,

$$Y_t = \frac{Y_{t+1}}{1+y} \qquad y \geq 0 \qquad (2)$$
$$L_t = L_{t+1}(1+l)l \geq 0 \qquad (3)$$

The discount factors y and l, since they relate to different personal characteristics are unlikely to be equal. They may also be age-dependent. For example, a young person may be indifferent towards any income flows more than 5 years into the future, whilst an older person whose human investment has been realized to a greater extent may already be concerned about his or her pension. Finally, an elderly or chronically ill person with a highly uncertain future life expectancy may again have a very high discount factor with respect to income flows for obvious reasons. Similarly, the size of l will vary as individuals' assessment of their state of health varies through life.

Having carried out the discounting procedure for income and

leisure flows, we wish to relate them through a utility function. Since we have no guidelines to help us decide on the form of this function, we propose a simple Cobb–Douglas relationship:

$$U = A_1 . \text{PVY}^\alpha . \text{PVL}^{(1-\alpha)} \qquad (4)$$

where U is utility, PVY and PVL are the discounted present values of income and leisure, respectively, and A_1 is a constant representing exogenous influences on utility. The interpretation of α, the returns to income parameter, is an index of the degree to which the individual enjoys the consumption of goods (and thereby income) relative to leisure. Implicit in the choice of α is a money valuation of an hour of leisure. If α is taken to be 0.5, then the value of leisure in pounds per hour is simply the ratio of PVY to PVL. More generally the hourly value of leisure, HVL is defined by

$$\text{HVL} = \frac{(1-\alpha)}{\alpha} . \frac{\text{PVY}}{\text{PVL}} \qquad (5)$$

The greater the utility derived from goods relative to leisure, the lower the implicit valuation of leisure, and vice versa. In the remainder of this section the detailed method of calculation of the income and leisure flows and the associated leisure function will be discussed.

The starting point of our analysis is the static budget line described in Chapter 2. The three extra ingredients in a pensioner's budget line relative to a standard working person's budget line are the state retirement pension, earnings related pensions and the differential tax allowances granted to persons of state retirement age (65 for men and 60 for women) and above. The flat-rate state retirement pension is available to everyone of state retirement age (SRA) who has a complete National Insurance contributions record. If an individual should choose to retire later than SRA then it may be advantageous, because of the penalty system, to defer receipt of the pension until his retirement. A premium of 7.45% per extra year (up to a maximum of 5 years) is payable in the case of deferred pensions. Five years on from SRA is defined as pensionable age and from this age the state retirement benefits are paid in full regardless of whether the individual is still working or not.

The rules concerning earnings related pensions, of which there are two main types, are different and highly complex, and only the salient features are given here. Approximately 57% of all employees now belong to private occupational pension schemes organized by their employers. Members of such schemes pay a reduced rate of National Insurance contribution but pay an extra regular amount into the appropriate superannuation fund. Each fund has its own rules concerning the age from which benefits are payable, the maximum number of years of reckonable service and, most importantly, the levels of pension benefit appropriate to different lengths of service. The state earnings related pension scheme, to which all employees whose employers have not contracted-out belong, is similar in concept to the private occupational schemes but operates under a quite different set of rules. Earnings related pension contributions and benefits are calculated within two bands of earnings level, an upper band and a lower band. Therefore there is a maximum contribution and benefit which can be paid. Also, whereas most private schemes calculate the pension using the last year's or few years' working income as a benchmark, the state scheme uses the average of the best 20 years' revalued earnings. The revaluation is performed using a price index rather than an earnings index which, as Creedy (1982) points out, can make a significant difference to the level of pension received.

There is a further drawback to the state earnings related scheme if the individual wishes to work beyond SRA. Even though the extra pension is payable from that age, if the person earns more than £57[1] per week or works more than 12 hours per week then entitlement to pension is clawed back on a pound-for-pound basis to the point where it is extinguished. Benefits from private schemes, since only the Inland Revenue comes to hear of them, are not able to be withdrawn.

Finally, the differential tax system increases the marginal gains from working beyond SRA. In the case of a married man with only the man working, the tax allowance for a pensioner is £3,295[1] rather than £2,445[1] for a man aged under 65, provided the pensioner's total taxable income does not exceed £6,700.[1] To the extent that it does, the additional allowance is withdrawn on a two-pounds-for-three basis until extinguished.

The social security system applies to pensioners in much the same way as it does to working-age individuals. The major difference is in the application of the requirement to sign on if unemployed. From the age of 60 a man may deregister, if he has been unemployed for a year or more, and claim Supplementary Benefit at the long-term scale rate. Additional benefits to cover heating costs and a minute age allowance also apply to certain pensioners. Before April 1983, the Housing Benefit system was identical for heads of households under or over SRA, but from that date there is a small difference. For retired households not receiving Supplementary Benefit, and having an income in excess of the prescribed Housing Benefit requirement level, the rent and rate rebates are more generous than for non-pensioners. Essentially, the tapering is more gradual permitting pensioners with higher incomes to qualify for relief from housing costs.

To appreciate the aggregate effect of the differential characteristics of persons over SRA, a series of comparative static budget lines are presented in Figs. 6.3 to 6.8. The six examples selected for presentation here are those of married men engaged in manual work aged 50, 60, 65 and 70, respectively, and of married men employed in a non-manual occupation aged 50 and 60. Few non-manual employees have the opportunity to work beyond the age of 65 (although many self-employed persons do) and so these cases were excluded from the list. The four specific ages chosen have the following significance. The age of 50 is commonly used as the age threshold at which retirement becomes a possibility. For employees in very generous occupational pension schemes, 25 years in the scheme may be sufficient to generate a substantial pension. At 60, long-term Supplementary Benefit, for which no contributions are required, becomes available as it is a means-tested benefit. At 65 a man reaches SRA and at 70 he reaches pensionable age. For the latter age the budget lines are drawn for the deferred pension case. The detailed assumptions underlying the six examples are set out in Table 6.4.

It should be noted, as in so many instances before, that even when the most likely values of each parameter relating to individuals' circumstances are chosen, the end product remains strictly representative of only a very small minority of individuals. However, the important features of the examples are applicable to almost all employed persons in the relevant age-brackets. A further word of caution is necessary. The examples portray six different typical married men, not the same two men at different

Table 6.4 Selected Examples for Budget Lines of Married Men, Sole Earners

Case	A	B	C	D	E	F
Age	50	60	65	70	50	60
Manual/non-manual	M	M	M	M	NM	NM
Number of dependent children	1	0	0	0	1	0
Average weekly earnings*	£136	£124	£108	£95	£200	£174
Basic hours per week	40	40	40	40	40	40
Overtime hours (evaluated at time and a half)	5	5	5	5	0	0
Basic wage rate per hour*	£2.85	£2.67	£2.36	£2.09	£5.00	£4.35
Rent (£ per week)**	14	13	12	11	16	15
Rates (£ per week)**	4	4	4	4	6	6
Work travel costs (£ per day)	0.6	0.6	0.6	0.6	0.6	0.6
Percentage rate of superannuation contributions, where applicable	6	6	6	6	6	6
Number of reckonable years' service in pension scheme	25	35	40	40	25	35
Occupational pension (£ per week), where applicable	42.5	54.25	54	61.75	62.5	76.13
Post-retirement wage rate as a proportion of pre-retirement wage rate, where applicable	0.6	0.6	0.6	0.6	0.6	0.6

* New Earnings Survey 1982, Tables 124 and 127.
** The sum of rent and rates, including water rates, was approximated from Table A, Appendix 8 of the Family Expenditure Survey 1980.

ages. Thus, the assumptions about wage rates and housing costs reflect the national averages for people of given ages and type of work.

Figure 6.3 depicts the case of a manual worker aged 50 who is the sole earner in the household and whose only other dependant is a 15-year-old child. Given the assumptions in Table 6.4, the relevant Supplementary Benefit subsistence level is £74.73 per

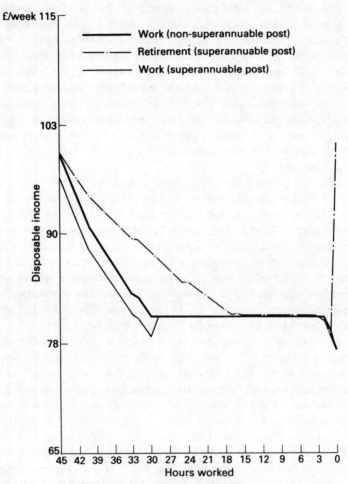

Fig. 6.3 Work and retirement budget lines for a married manual worker aged 50 (Case A in Table 6.4)

week and the net income from a usual week's work, if the job is not superannuable, is just under £100. At the age of 50, retirement without an occupational pension is equivalent to unemployment in the eyes of the state tax-benefit system. The incentive to 'retire' at 50 is small, especially when it is remembered that benefit income will fall when the dependent child leaves home and that the claimant is not entitled to long-term SB until he reaches 60.

The more interesting case is where the job is superannuable. The work option produces a slightly lower profile than before, reflecting the impact of superannuation contributions on net income. The third line, representing the retirement option, drops from a peak of over £96 at zero hours down to the SB level. The zero hours point shows the first-year case only, since Unemployment Benefit ceases after a year, to be replaced by an SB which is means-tested. Superficially, the retirement option offers an equivalent net income to that in work, but at least 3 months' work must be accomplished in each subsequent year for the income level to be maintained.

A similar pattern, shown in Fig. 6.4, obtains for the example of the 60-year-old manual worker. In fact, for the non-superannuable case the percentage of net income from full-time work replaced by benefits is lower than for the preceding example, but only because of the absence of dependent children in the household. The striking difference emerges in the superannuable case as the worker is assumed to have 10 more years' reckonable service and therefore a much higher pension. This boosts the percentage of replaced income in work to 111% for the first-year case, and thereafter, when long-term SB becomes available, to 81%.

Whether or not the employee holds a superannuable job remains a key factor in the retirement decision at age 65 for a manual worker. In frame (a) of Fig. 6.5, where the non-superannuable case is depicted, the replacement ratio rises to 0.71 and, because of the exemption of the first 12 hours of work from having pension withdrawal consequences, the ratio rises to 0.82 under our assumptions. In frame (b), every point on the retirement profile lies above the highest point of the working one. This is partly a result of moving into the advantageous tax regime and partly a consequence of 5 more years' contributions to the occupational pension scheme.

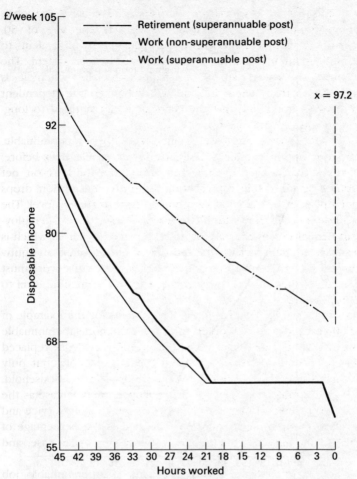

£/week 105

— · — · — Retirement (superannuable post)

————— Work (non-superannuable post)

————— Work (superannuable post)

x = 97.2

92

Disposable income

80

68

55

45 42 39 36 33 30 27 24 21 18 15 12 9 6 3 0

Hours worked

Fig. 6.4 Work and retirement budget lines for a married manual worker aged 60 (Case B in Table 6.4)

Curiously, the comparison between work and retirement incomes closes again for the 70-year-old manual worker. On the assumption that he defers both his state and occupational pension until his 70th birthday to avoid a hefty tax burden, work is distinctly advantageous in the non-superannuable case. This is due to the fact that, on reaching pensionable age, the deferred pension is paid automatically and without penalty. There is much less of a

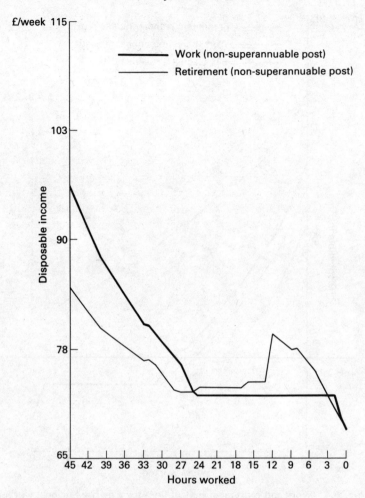

Fig. 6.5 (a) Work and retirement budget lines for a married manual worker aged 65 for the non-superannuable case (Case C in Table 6.4)

difference in the superannuable case, shown in frame (b) of Fig. 6.6, the replacement ratio being 0.88.

The chief differences which emerge from an inspection of Figs. 6.7 and 6.8 relative to 6.3 and 6.4 are a consequence of the fact that the non-manual workers are significantly better paid than their manual contemporaries. The replacement ratios, compared

204

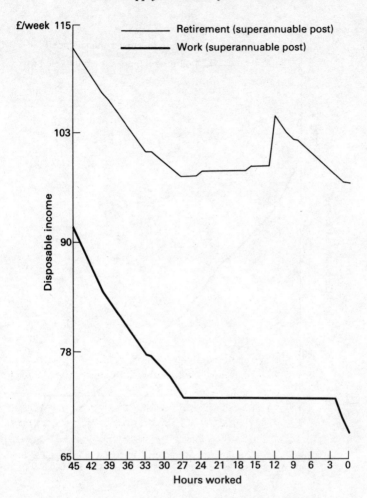

(b) Work and retirement budget lines for a married manual worker aged 65 for the superannuable case (Case C in Table 6.4)

in Table 6.5 demonstrate that, relatively speaking, manual workers stand to lose less by early retirement than non-manuals by virtue of the fixed scale rates for certain benefits. However, the system of rent and rates rebates provides significant additions to the household incomes of non-manual employees in retirement.

These static budget lines can be generalized to represent

205

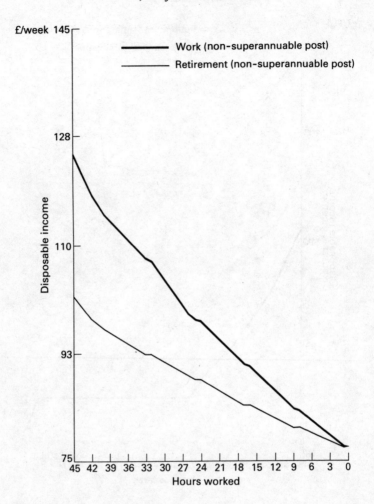

Fig. 6.6 (a) Work and retirement budget lines for a married manual worker aged 70 for the non-superannuable case (Case D in Table 6.4)

illustrative snapshots of weeks in different years of a person's life. To analyse the retirement decision we require a representative budget line for each remaining year of that life. To provide a full description of the labour supply options facing a person in every remaining year would require a multi-dimensional diagram, but to

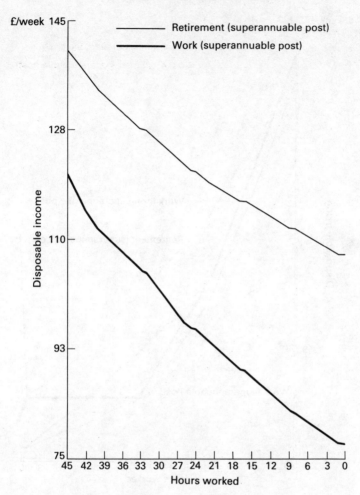

(b) Work and retirement budget lines for a married manual worker aged 70 for the superannuable case (Case D in Table 6.4)

give some idea of the diversity of decision paths open to men aged 50 and over, these are outlined in Fig. 6.9. The unrealistic assumption that decisions are changed only at the discrete ages 60, 65 and 70, is again used for illustrative purposes. The key to the figure lists the set of labour participation states and the figure

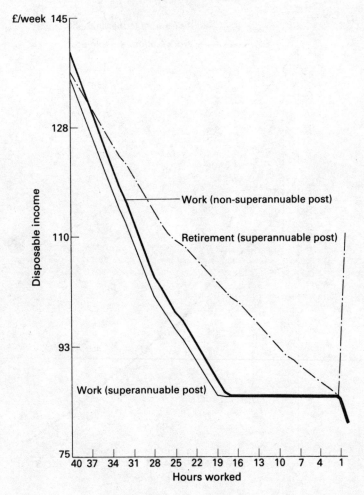

Fig. 6.7 Work and retirement budget lines for a married non-manual worker aged 50 (Case E in Table 6.4)

aims to identify all the remotely likely combinations of states and the associated income flows which are both logically consistent and economically rational. A total of 626 different decision paths are described by the figure. Fortunately out of this large number of paths necessary to account for the complexity of the whole, only a much smaller subset could ever apply to any one

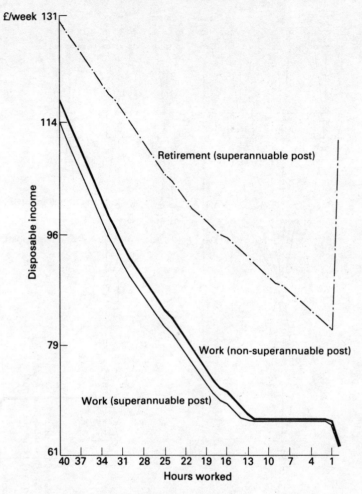

Fig. 6.8 Work and retirement lines for a married non-manual worker aged 60 (Case F in Table 6.4)

individual. If we summarize a series of labour supply decisions by the four decision parameters (A, B, C, D) from the figure then we can identify some of the more likely ones.

By far the most common decision path actually taken is the case represented by (4, 4, 7, 7), the classic case of full-time work until 65 with no pension other than the state pension. Other well-

209

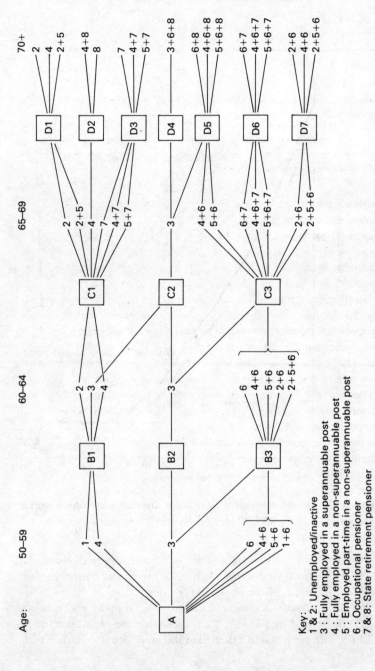

Fig. 6.9 Labour supply options for a 50-year-old man assuming 5-yearly decision intervals

Key:
1 & 2: Unemployed/inactive
3 : Fully employed in a superannuable post
4 : Fully employed in a non-superannuable post
5 : Employed part-time in a non-superannuable post
6 : Occupational pensioner
7 & 8: State retirement pensioner

Table 6.5 Replacement Ratios

Age	Manual				Non-manual	
	50*	60	65	70	50*	60
Non-superannuable post	0.63	0.66	0.71	0.57	0.48	0.53
Superannuable post						
year 1	0.97	1.11	1.02	0.88	0.79	0.95
after year 1	0.66	0.81	1.02	0.88	0.55	0.67

* assuming no dependent children.

trodden paths are (3, 3, 6+7, 6+7), the analogous case for employees in superannuation schemes; (3, 6, 6+7, 6+7), early retirement for such employees; (4, 2, 7, 7) the case of the worker whose work experience ends at 60; and (4, 2, 2, 2) the case of the redundant worker who misses out on state retirement pension altogether because of a poor contributions record and has to rely on Supplementary Benefit. Many of the combinations are required only to permit the possibility of an employee with a small occupational pension returning to part-time or full-time work in a non-superannuable job after retirement to supplement his pension. The paths which include 1+6, 2+6, or 2+5+6 represent cases where the occupational pension is very small.

The Family Expenditure Survey for 1980 gives a detailed decomposition of sources of incomes for sampled households. Retired households, which accounted for 22% of the total, fall into two main groups. Just over half of the retired households had insignificant incomes from occupational pensions and annuities, and were largely dependent on the state retirement pension or other social security benefits. Of this group, two-thirds were single. The second group, which contained equal numbers of single people and couples received average pension and annuity incomes of over £16 per week. A small group, probably no larger than 5% of the total sample of retired households, had occupational pensions averaging £60 per week.

Thus, whilst the existence of occupational pensions generates a large number of additional decision paths, most of these are open to relatively small numbers of retired people at present.

In order to determine the present values of the series of income flows consequent on a given decision path we must

211

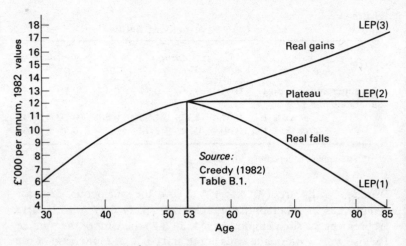

Fig. 6.10 Lifetime earnings profiles

proceed to a formal treatment of the problem. Gross earnings in work in year i are defined as

$$W_i = \phi_1 \phi_2 \text{LEP}_{ij}$$

where LEP_{ij} represents one of three lifetime real earnings profiles. The standard profile is derived from Creedy's analysis and revalued to 1982 real earnings levels and the other options cater for plateau real earnings and permanently rising real earnings. The three profiles are plotted in Fig. 6.10. The constants ϕ_1 and ϕ_2 describe the levels adjustment to the relevant earnings profile and the correction factor for part-time working, respectively. State retirement pension in year i, P_i, is payable from SRA. Earnings related pensions, OCP_i, are assumed to be payable from C, the date of retirement or age 65, whichever is the earlier. Social security benefits, B_i, are payable as a primary source of income whenever the individual is out of work. Social security and Housing Benefits may also be received in addition to other primary sources of income, but this is a complication from which this exposition abstracts. Finally, income tax, T_i, is payable in each year according to the prevailing tax allowances and tax rates. To economize on notation we will simply note that

$$\text{PVY} = \text{PVGY} - \text{PVT} \tag{6}$$

212

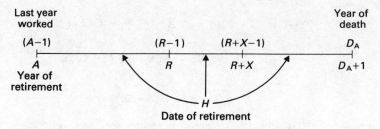

Fig. 6.11 Schematic representation of the remaining years of life

and define the gross income flows, GY.

Figure 6.11 defines the time span over which discounting takes place. The individual's future life expectancy is taken from the actuarial table English Life No. 10 given in the Annual Abstract of Statistics. The individual is assumed to make his first annual decision at the beginning of the current year A, and to die at the end of the final year, effectively at $(D_A + 1)$. The fixed points between A and $(D_A + 1)$ are SRA, denoted R, and pensionable age denoted $R + X$.

Three possibilities arise from Fig. 6.11. Either the actual retirement date occurs before SRA, between SRA and pensionable age, or after pensionable age.

If $H<R$,

$$\text{PVGY} \doteq \sum_{i=0}^{H-A-i1} \gamma^i W_i + \sum_{i=H-A}^{R-A-1} \gamma - (B_i + \text{OCP}_i)$$

$$+ \sum_{i=R-A}^{D_A-A} \gamma^i (P_i + \text{OCP}_i)$$

If $H = R$ then the second expression drops out.

If $R<H< (R+X)$,

$$\text{PVGY} = \sum_{i=0}^{C-A-1} \gamma^i W_i + \sum_{i=C-A}^{H-A-1} \gamma^i (W_i + \text{OCP}_i)$$

$$+ \sum_{i=H-A}^{D_A-A} \gamma^i (P_i(1 + x(H-R)) + \text{OCP}_i)$$

If $H = C$ then the second expression drops out.

If $H > (R+X)$

$$PVGY = \sum_{i=0}^{C-A-1} \gamma^i W_i + \sum_{i=C-A}^{R+X-A-1} \gamma^i(W_i + OCP_i)$$

$$+ \sum_{i=R+X-A}^{H-A-1} \gamma^i(W_i + OCP_i + P_i(1+5x))$$

$$+ \sum_{i=H-A}^{D_A - A} \gamma^i(OCP_i + P_i(1+5x))$$

where $x = 0.07454$, the deferred premium for state retirement pension, and $\gamma = 1/(1+y)$.

The discounted net income variable, PVY, is calculated by a computer program entitled Lifetime Labour Supply Options (LLSO). The program can be used to evaluate the discounted income flows corresponding to the decision paths of Fig. 6.9, where decisions can be changed annually. Table 6.6 compares eight lifetime labour supply options for a 50-year-old married man. His characteristics correspond to Case A of Table 6.4, except that the assumption is now made that there are no dependent children in the household. The real rate of time discount, y, is to be 3% per annum.

The eight options are presented in descending order of their resulting discounted net income flows. The total hours of leisure associated with each option are also shown. This calculation assumes that for each of 230 working days per annum, a full-time worker has 5 hours of leisure per day, a part-time worker 10 hours, and a non-working person 15 hours per day. Hours of leisure might be expected to bear an inverse relationship to the income stream and this is broadly confirmed by Table 6.6. The exception is option 4, delayed retirement, whereby the pension streams come on-line 5 years later than usual. Even though a premium equivalent to 7.45% of the state pension for each year of delayed retirement is added to the pension when received, this appears insufficient compensation.

Both options 2 and 3, concerning part-time working from age 65 until death or age 70 respectively, yield higher present value incomes than delayed retirement. It is clear, however, that in all other cases the optimal retirement decision is indeterminate in the absence of some implicit valuation of leisure time in terms of money. To further the usefulness of the model some framework of individual preferences must be superimposed on the objective analysis of income flows thus far obtained.

Table 6.6 Lifetime Labour Supply Options of a 50-year-old

	Caricature	Decision path (See Fig. 6.9)	Present value of net income (PVY) in £K	Leisure hours (undiscounted)
1	Workaholic	(3, 3, 3, 3+6+8)	99.1	27,600
2	Part-time working after 65	(3, 3, 5+6+7)	93.9	37,950
3	Part-time working (65–70)	(3, 3, 5+6+7, 6+7)	89.7	42,550
4	Delayed retirement (to 70)	(3, 3, 3, 6+8)	89.3	36,800
5	Standard	(3, 3, 6+7, 6+7)	87.3	48,300
6	Retire at 60	(3, 2+6, 6+7, 6+7)	83.4	59,600
7	Retire at 55	(3/ 2+6, 2+6, 6+7, 6+7)	80.3	71,300
8	Loafer	(1, 2, 2, 2)	74.6	82,800

The Leisure Valuation Function

The concept of leisure discounting and the valuation of leisure time in general raise complex behavioural issues. We present four arguments below which are believed to affect the valuation of leisure. The first two of these relate to the *quantity* of leisure and the later two to the *quality* of leisure.

As far as the amount of leisure is concerned, the first insight is that leisure becomes progressively more valuable towards the end of life. The effort of working a given number of hours per day absorbs an increasing proportion of a reducing supply of physical and mental effort as an individual ages. This argument does not invoke a peculiar deterioration of health, merely the normal ageing process. The sheer disutility of work increases with age and therefore leisure, in the sense of idleness, becomes increasingly valuable.

The second argument, an extension of the first, is that, regardless of an individual's precise age, the shorter is his or her future life expectancy. the greater will be the disutility of work. Conceivably, some people would prefer to carry on working to the last in order to bequeath wealth to spouses and children, but we assume that such people are in a minority. The majority are expected to choose to increase their leisure to reflect its perceived scarcity value.

The dimension of quality is extremely important to the consideration of the desirability or value of leisure. Our first premise is that, beyond some critical age-range, say 45–50, leisure becomes less enjoyable. The apparent contradiction with the very first argument is removed in the following way. As the body's total supply of effort diminishes towards senility, an increased *amount* of leisure is necessary. However, the *quality* of this leisure is lower than in the prime of life. These leisure hours are typically less productive and hence should be devalued before adding them to leisure hours enjoyed at an earlier age.

Finally, it must be recognized that leisure without income is a fairly worthless commodity. As a generalization, the long-term unemployed on Supplementary Benefit do not enjoy leisure as much as the working man or the retirer. To reflect the observation that this factor is probably most important for the very poor whilst many individuals in the middle of the income distribution

216

may have similar perceptions of the value of leisure, a square root function of relative income is employed.

There is no escaping from the fact that the composite leisure value function given below is a highly subjective attempt to embody the four arguments above. The arguments themselves are in any case based on generalizations of human behaviour. However, without some means of valuing leisure, it is impossible to tackle the retirement decision problem. We have used the following function in the analysis of Section IV:

$$L_t = HL_t \left(\frac{100 - D_A^*}{D_A^* - t + 1} \right) \left(\exp\{-[(t-50)^2/2\sigma^2]\} \right) \sqrt{\frac{Y_t}{Y_{50}}} \; ; t \geqslant 50 \quad (7)$$

where HL_t is the number of hours of leisure in year t of life conditional on employment status, D_A^* is expected age at death in years, t is current age in years, and σ is the health deterioration factor (of which a high value implies a slow rate of deterioration of health after age 50, whilst a low value implies a rapid rate). Y_t is net income from work in year t whilst Y_{50} represents net income from work in the year following the 50th birthday.

IV
Dynamic Budget Lines

In the preceding section, the concept of a dynamic budget line was introduced and some illustrations of the discounted income consequences of various work/part-time work/leisure preferences were presented in Table 6.6. In this section our objective is to consider the evolution of an individual's budget line at annual intervals over his or her remaining years of life. To aid exposition, we shall restrict the analysis to the consideration of two states only: full-time working and full-time leisure. Furthermore, we shall assume that the retirement decision is irrevocable.

The Standard Case

In Table 6.7 we record the characteristics of the 'standard' married man, where all money values are at constant end-1982 prices. In the course of this section the sensitivity of the dynamic

Table 6.7   Characteristics of the Standard Married Man Used in the Dynamic Budget Line Analysis.

Age: 50

Dependent children: none

Conditional life expectancy: 75

Earnings Profile: LEP(2)

Peak earnings per annum: £12,200 (from age 52)

Weekly housing costs: £25

Occupational pension scheme:

- contribution rate: 6% of gross earnings
- type: final salary scheme
- reckonable years' service: current age minus 25 or 40 whichever is the less
- benefit rate: one-eightieth of final salary year of reckonable service
- benefit payable on retirement or at age 70, whichever is the sooner.

Full National Insurance contribution record.

Contracted out of SERPS.

State pension deferred if retirement is between 65 and 70.

Health limitation parameter: average ($\sigma = 50$)

Real rate of time of preference: 5% per annum

Weight on income in Cobb–Douglas utility function: 0.5

---

budget line to each assumption will be examined in turn. First of all, we observe the dynamic budget line for standard men at successive 5-year intervals between age 50 and age 70. These budget lines are pictured in Fig. 6.12. The most dramatic feature of these lines is the kink at age 70 (last year worked being 69) which is caused partly by the decision to defer the receipt of state and occupational pensions until retirement. At age 70 all pension benefits are paid regardless of employment status. The dynamic replacement ratios for the five standard men rise from 0.465 for the 50-year-old to 0.584 for the 65-year-old, falling to 0.51 for the 70-year-old. In other words, the decision to retire immediately at age 65 would result in a level of net discounted income equal to

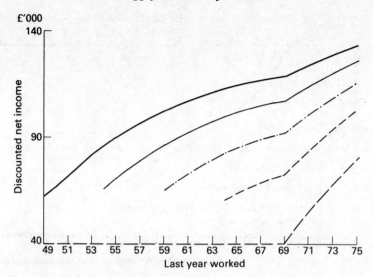

Fig. 6.12 Dynamic budget lines for standard men of ages 50, 55, 60, 65 and 70 with common life expectancy of 75 years

58.4% of that received if the individual worked until death.

The marginal gain from working an extra year for the case of the 50-year-old standard man is given in Fig. 6.13. The increase in the gain for the first year shown is attributable to the shape of the earnings profile. Real earnings reach their plateau at age 52. This means that individuals retiring on their 54th birthday are the first not to receive a boost from the annual increment to their previous year's earnings. The next hiccup in the schedule occurs when long-term Supplementary Benefit becomes payable at age 60, for those unemployed throughout the previous year. (As far as the state is concerned, retirement before age 60 is treated as unemployment.) This has the result of reducing the gain from work whilst aged 60 relative to that during the previous year.

A similar blip arises at age 65, the state retirement age. Provided that the individual's National Insurance contribution record is complete, rent and rate rebates may be payable in addition to the pension. Thus the gain from work falls more rapidly whilst aged 65. Finally, the benefit from working whilst aged 70 is an enormous improvement on that from working the previous year, for reasons already given.

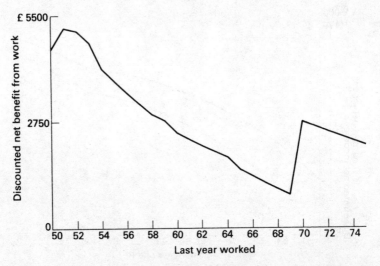

Fig. 6.13 Discounted net benefit from working an extra year for the standard man aged 50

The Life Expectancy Dimension

In Fig. 6.14 dynamic budget lines are presented for (otherwise) standard men with varying life expectancies. Table 6.8 summarizes the relationship between the seven cases.

The discounted value of state and occupational pension benefits ranges from £18,500 for a 50-year-old with a life expectancy of 55 to just over four times as much for one with life expectancy of 85. The marginal gain from an extra 5 years of life tends to decline due to the lower discounted values of the more distant income flows. However, up until age 70 the benefit and pension system becomes more generous and this mitigates the discounting effect. Dynamic replacement ratios lie in a narrow range for all seven cases. The peak replacement ratio is 0.488 for an age at death of 70.

Income Sensitivity

Dynamic budget lines for a selection of multiples of the earnings attributed to the standard man are shown in Fig. 6.15. To discover the redistribution characteristics of the tax and benefit system it is

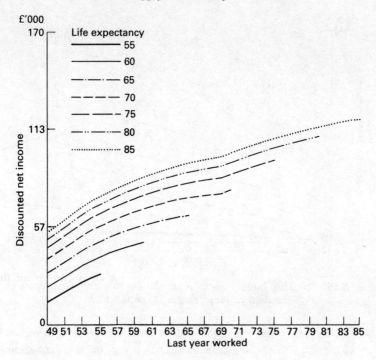

Fig. 6.14 Dynamic budget lines for men aged 50 with life expectancies ranging from 55 to 85

Table 6.8 Analysis of Marginal Payoffs in the Case of Variable Life Expectancy

Age at death	Payoff to 'retire now' option (£K)	Marginal discounted gain from an extra 5 years life (£K)	Dynamic replacement ratio
55	18.5	—	0.453
60	30.6	12.1	0.456
65	42.0	11.4	0.475
70	53.3	11.3	0.488
75	62.2	8.9	0.465
80	69.2	7.0	0.452
85	74.6	5.5	0.447

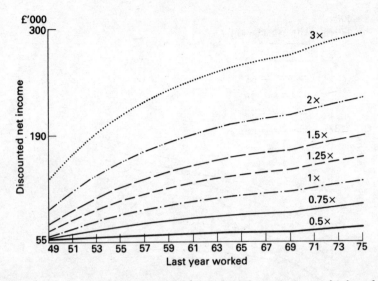

Fig. 6.15 Dynamic budget lines for standard men earning multiples of standard earnings ranging from 0.5 to 3

helpful to index the dynamic budget lines for each multiple of gross earnings to the dynamic budget line for the standard case. These indices are illustrated in Fig. 6.16 for the six variants of earnings. The progressivity of the income tax structure together with the safety net benefit system produces the expected result that the net discounted income differentials are smaller than the gross income differentials for earnings multiples greater than one, and vice versa for earnings multiples below one. This result is most pronounced for the immediate retirement case. Here, the discounted net income of a man earning half that of the standard man is 89% of the discounted net income of the standard man. At double standard earnings, a net income differential of 1.62 is observed.

When the dynamic budget lines are compared at later retirement dates, there is a much closer correspondence between gross and discounted net income multiples. State benefits and flat-rate pensions do not contain an earnings related element, and hence it is the increased occupational pension entitlement that is the principal cause of the convergence of gross and discounted net incomes as the age of retirement increases. The behaviour of

222

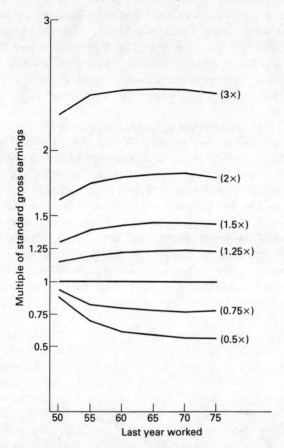

Fig. 6.16 Multiples of discounted net income for selected retirement ages corresponding to the dynamic budget lines in Fig. 6.15

the system when the individual does not belong to a superannuation scheme is not likely to be very different since the State Earnings Related Pensions scheme embodies similar provisions. The precise details are deferred until later in the section.

Housing Costs

For the purpose of the Supplementary Benefit calculations it is not necessary to specify whether housing costs are constituted as mortgage repayments and local authority rates or as rent and rates. The same cannot be said for the calculation of rent and rate rebates. The sensitivity analysis that follows assumes that the accommodation is rented. If wholly owned or owner-occupied accommodation is considered, some small deductions to the incomes will result, to the extent that there is no entitlement to rent rebates.

Figure 6.17 contains the dynamic budget lines for the standard case using housing costs of £0, £10, £20, £30, £40 and £50 per week. The significance of this experiment lies only in the discovery that housing cost variations matter little if the retirement age is above 60. The difference between the lines at ages 50 and at 55 (last year worked) are indicative only of the workings of the Supplementary Benefit system. Clearly the recipients of the larger amounts are only 'better off' in the sense that they are able to enjoy a better quality of housing. The discounted income differences do not imply differences in discretionary spending.

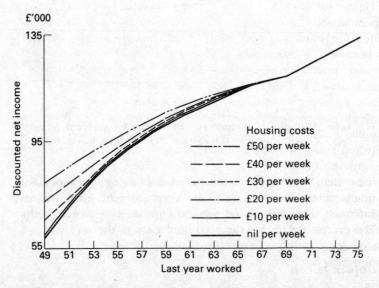

Fig. 6.17 Dynamic budget lines for standard men with housing costs varying from nil to £50 per week

The Non-Superannuable Case

The implications of the non-superannuable case are twofold. First, the employee pays full-rate National Insurance contributions instead of paying both contracted-out rate contributions and superannuation fund contributions. Second, on retirement, the State Earnings Related Pension is received instead of an occupational pension. Under normal circumstances, the non-superannuable employee is likely to receive a lower pension income relative to the superannuable employee, for three reasons.

First, his total rate of contribution is lower than that of a member of an occupational pension scheme. Secondly, the earnings-related part of the state pension allows for a maximum fraction of $20/80$ whereas occupational pension schemes work on the basis of maxima of either $40/80$ or $40/60$. Finally, whereas most occupational pension schemes are final salary schemes, SERPS uses the best 20 years' revalued earnings. Hence an employee whose earnings have risen steadily throughout his life would be penalized to the extent that former, less rewarding years, have to be included.

Figure 6.18 shows that the discounted net benefit in the superannuable case is higher for all retirement ages. The gap is widest for retirement ages 55 to 64. The margin closes after age 64 because SERPS becomes payable. As more of the best 20 years become 'plateau-earnings' years, so SERPS approximates 25% of final salary. For a retiring age of 70 or more the gap is at its smallest and is constant.

Until now we have assumed that the occupational pension is payable on retirement at whatever age, after 50. It may be objected that to compare this entitlement to SERPS is unfair on the grounds that SERPS can only be claimed at age 65. Figure 6.19 reveals that, to deprive the occupational pensioner of his entitlement before state pensionable age (65) results in a significant loss of discounted net income (about 4% at age 60). However, this loss is not large enough to re-order the results of the superannuable and non-superannuable cases from the previous comparison until a retirement age of 69 is considered.

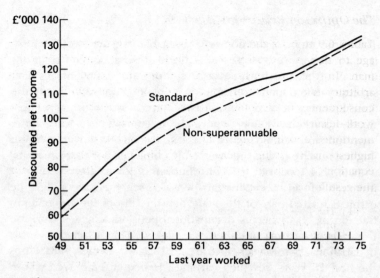

Fig. 6.18 Dynamic budget lines for the standard and non-superannuable cases

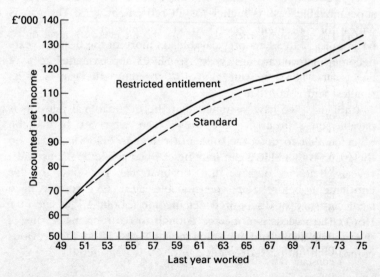

Fig. 6.19 Dynamic budget lines for the standard and restricted entitlement cases

The Optimum Retirement Age (ORA)

Tables 6.9 to 6.15 give the sensitivity of the optimum retirement age to the various assumptions made for our standard married man. In the previous section we described and defined an arbitrary functional form for the value of leisure and here the consequences of combining the income and leisure aspects of the work–leisure decision are analysed. For each simulation, the tables mentioned above record simply the age of retirement with the highest utility value, using the Cobb–Douglas expression at equation (4) on page 197. On the basis of this retirement model, the results may be summarized as follows:

(1) The fewer are the remaining years of life, the smaller is the proportion of those years which will be spent working (Table 6.9).

(2) The optimum retirement age increases with rising life expectancy, but the rate of increase is smaller for life expectancies of 75 and over (Table 6.10).

(3) The level of earnings is critically important for the retirement decision. For earnings as low as £6,000 per annum (at constant end-1982 prices), immediate retirement is advocated as the optimum. Even at £9,000 per annum (a multiple of 0.75), a significant reduction in retirement age is indicated. (Table 6.11.)

(4) For very high earners, the relative income effect enhances the quality of leisure, making work, though lucrative, less attractive than it would otherwise be. For this reason high earnings have an ambiguous effect on the optimum retirement age. (Table 6.11.)

(5) Housing costs are likely to have a comparatively minor effect on retirement age. Any attempt to take advantage of high housing costs by retiring early would most likely be recognized as such by the DHSS. (Table 6.12.)

(6) A severe health limitation, such as a disability, would be likely to bring forward the retirement age by several years. Extraordinarily good health would not, in general, lead to a later retirement date of itself. In conjunction with high income or high life expectancy it may well do so. (Table 6.13.)

(7) The valuation of income flows which arrive at successive points in time is problematic since the individual's rate of time preference may increase with age. On the assumption of a constant rate, however, neither a very low (1% per annum) nor a very high (25% per annum) one yield drastically different optimum retirement ages. This does not appear to be a parameter of great significance. (Table 6.14.)

(8) Having accounted for all other elements of a choice of retirement date, this last may easily outweigh them all. The extreme values for α are likely to be chosen very rarely, but even in the range 0.3 to 0.7, a sizeable variation in retirement dates emerges. Subjective attitudes to work must remain a major ingredient of the personal retirement decision. (Table. 6.15.)

Table 6.9 Sensitivity of ORA to Current Age

	Current Age	ORA
(Standard)	50	64
	55	65
	60	65
	65	66
	70	—

Table 6.10 Sensitivity of ORA to Life Expectancy

	Life Expectancy	ORA
	55	54
	60	59
	65	59
	70	61
(Standard)	75	64
	80	65
	85	66

Table 6.11 Sensitivity of ORA to Earnings Level

	Multiple of earnings of standard man	ORA
	0.5	50
	0.75	60
(Standard)	1	64
	1.25	65
	1.5	65
	2	65
	3	64

Table 6.12   Sensitivity of ORA to Housing Costs

	Housing costs (£ per week)	ORA
	0	64
	10	64
	20	64
(Standard)	25	64
	30	63
	40	62
	50	61

Table 6.13   Sensitivity of ORA to Health Limitation Parameter

	Health limitation parameter (σ)	ORA
	10	59
	20	62
	30	63
	40	64
(Standard)	50	64
	75	64
	100	64

Table 6.14   Sensitivity of ORA to the Real Rate of Time Preference

	Discount rate (% per annum)	ORA
	1	65
	3	65
(Standard)	5	64
	10	62
	25	60

229

Table 6.15 Sensitivity of ORA to Income–Leisure Preference
Parameter

Income–leisure preference parameter (α)	*ORA*
0.1	55
0.3	60
(Standard) 0.5	64
0.7	66
0.9	75

Endogenous Life Expectancy

In the preceding analysis the ORA calculations depend upon an
exogenous assumption for total life expectancy. The sensitivity of
the ORA to varying assumptions about total life expectancy was
reported in Table 6.10. The purpose of this section is to explore
the consequences of endogenizing mean life expectancy in the
ORA analysis.

The English Life Tables provide estimates of the mean future
life expectancy of males (and females) of all ages. The content of
the tables reveals that for every year a person survives, his or her
future life expectancy decreases by less than a year. Thus a 50-
year-old man might have a future life expectancy of 23 years,
whilst a 60-year-old man, one of 15 years. As a result, any
optimizing decision conditional on a current age of 50 will select
an ORA between 50 and 73. When that ORA is reached, the age at
death conditional on that age will most probably be higher than
73. This gives rise to the possibility of a new ORA, larger than the
first. To take account of this new dimension, it is necessary to
iterate using the retirement decision model to find a convergent
ORA, if one exists.

Two cases will be considered. In the first we simulate an
otherwise standard man with poorer-than-average health and in
the second, the (healthy) standard man. In Table 6.16 the results
are shown for the poor health case. The ORA climbs from age 62
on the first iteration to 66 on the fourth when convergence is
achieved. In other words, when the man is 65 his optimum

[2]**Table 6.16** Optimum Retirement Ages for an Otherwise Standard Man with Poor Health Given Endogenous Life Expectancy

		$\sigma = 20$	
Iteration	*Current age*	*Expected Age at death*	*ORA*
1	50	73	62
2	62	76	65
3	65	77	66
4	66	77	66

Convergence at age 66 after 4 iterations.

[2]**Table 6.17** Optimum Retirement Ages for the Standard Man Given Endogenous Life Expectancy

		$\sigma = 50, \ \alpha = 0.5$	
Iteration	*Current age*	*Expected age at death*	*ORA*
1	50	73	63
2	63	76	66
3	66	77	67,73*
4	73	81	77
5	77	84	82
	(Non-convergent)		
		$\sigma = 50, \ \alpha = 0.4$	
2a	63	76	65
3a	65	77	65

Convergence at age 65 after 3 iterations.

* A local optimum occurs at 67, but the global optimum is at 73.

retirement age is 66 and when he is a year older, the optimum remains at 66.

The results for the healthy man, given in Table 6.17, are a little more complicated. If it is assumed that work–leisure preferences are lifelong attributes of individuals, and therefore exogenous to age, then the model implies that the man would probably never retire through choice. Whatever expected life-span lay ahead of him, if he still enjoyed his work relative to his leisure to the same degree, he would continue to allocate a part of this life-span to work. Hence it is probable that he would die before having retired. The point of departure of the case of the healthy man from that of the ailing man occurs at or around age 65. The healthy man still has a great deal of quality-adjusted leisure to look forward to, but the ailing man much less so. The tax-breaks that are available for the over-70s are sufficiently important for the healthy man to consider prolonging his career, whilst for the ailing man they are not.

Finally if, as suggested by Zabalza, Pissarides and Barton (1980), the healthy man has a change of heart about the relative attractiveness of work when he enters his seventh decade of life, then even a small change might be sufficient to persuade him into retirement. This is illustrated in the lower part of Table 6.17 where iterations 2a and 3a refer to the case where $\alpha = 0.4$ after age 60. The man, though healthy, has become less income-oriented and retires at 65.

Appendix 6.1

i: Age-group variable which takes the values
  1 for males aged 45–54
  2 for males aged 55–59
  3 for males aged 60–64
  4 for males aged 65 and above
  5 for females aged 45–54
  6 for females aged 55–59
  7 for females aged 60–64
  8 for females aged 65 and above.

AR_i: The ratio of economically active to total members of the population in Great Britain for age-group i.

      Source: For $i = 1$ to 4 the data have been interpolated between the census years of 1966 and 1971. For $i = 5$ to 8 the data for 1966–70 are derived from the Department of Employment Gazette, October 1971, p. 913. From 1971 to 1983, the data source for all i is 'Great Britain Labour Force Estimates for 1983', *Department of Employment Gazette*, August 1984, pp. 361–6.

AEW_i: The average net weekly earnings in £s of employees in Great Britain in all industries and services excluding those whose pay was affected by absence.

      Source: Between 1966 and 1974, gross weekly earnings for the age-groups were calculated as x_i multiplied by the average for all age-groups of that sex, where the x_is were calculated using the post-1974 data. The values of x_i used were:

i	x_i
1	1.045
2	0.973
3	0.900
4	0.790
5	1.046
6	1.013
7 & 8	0.995

The source for all the average earnings data is the New Earnings Survey.

      Gross earnings were transformed into net earnings using the formula

Net = Weekly value of tax allowance (for $i = 1$ to 4 the married man's allowance, for $i = 5$ to 8, the married woman's allowance)
+ $(1 - \text{tax rate}) \times$
(gross weekly earnings − weekly value of tax allowance)
− National Insurance payment.

      Source of data for tax allowances and rates and for National Insurance contributions is the UK Annual Abstract of Statistics, Tables 16.10, 16.11 and 3.14.

BEN_i: Benefit or state retirement pension payable to persons in age group i.

> *Source:* For $i = 1$ to 3, BEN equals the married man's NI Unemployment Benefit (excluding earnings related supplement). For $i = 4$, BEN equals the married man's retirement pension. For $i = 5$ and 6, BEN is equal to the single person's NI Unemployment Benefit and for $i = 7$ and 8, the single person's retirement pension. All data collected from the DHSS Social Security Statistics Yearbook, Tables 46.06 and 46.09.

UR: The national average unemployment rate for males and females in the UK.

> *Source:* Department of Employment Gazette, Table 2.1.

RCI_i: Days of certified incapacity due to sickness and invalidity per year per member of age-group i, in the UK.

> *Source:* Days of certified incapacity in millions was collected from DHSS Social Security Statistics Table 3.71. Data refer to fiscal years, not calendar years and, as no data are available for 1975/6 the missing values have been interpolated for this year.

> Population numbers for age group i for calendar years were taken from the UK Annual Abstract of Statistics, Table 2.4.

DR_i: Death rate per 1000 population in age group i, in the UK.

> *Source:* UK Annual Abstract of Statistics, Table 2.22. For age-groups 2 and 3 and for groups 6 and 7 the rates were taken to be equal to the respective rates for the combined age-groups, 55–64.

P: Retail Price Index, 1975 = 100.

> *Source:* Economic Trends Annual Supplement (1985 edition) p. 114.

Notes: Chapter 6

1 Amounts prevailing in December 1982.
2 The retirement decision model is a discrete time model with units of 1 year. Hence the reason that life expectancy does not appear to increase between current ages 65 and 66, is because in both cases the fractional parts of the 78th year are ignored by the program. However when the optimization takes place, both the end of 77th year and the end of the 78th year are considered.

7

The New Social Security System

Michael Beenstock and Michael Parker

Background

In June 1985 the government published a major Green Paper on the *Reform of Social Security*. This followed an unprecedented consultation process in the areas of pensions, Housing Benefit, Child Benefits and Supplementary Benefits. As an experiment in 'open government' the entire exercise was unique. The Green Paper itself was prompted by the numerous criticisms of the existing tax-benefit system that has been described at length in Chapters 1 to 3. However, it appears that the series of reviews that led up to the Green Paper was to some extent unplanned. In 1983 the DHSS set up an enquiry into pensions that focused initially on the 'early leavers' problem that afflicted members of occupational pension schemes. Initially, this enquiry embraced pensions more generally and the government eventually announced its intention in the Green Paper to abolish the State Earnings Related Pension Scheme (SERPS), despite the fact that it had previously declared that SERPS was inviolate.

In 1984 a review of Housing Benefit was set up following the fiasco of the unified Housing Benefit system, which integrated the Housing Benefit schemes operated by the DHSS, on the one hand, and the local authorities on the other. It seems that more or less off the cuff, the government decided to instigate its 'mini-

Beveridge' in the summer of 1984; it was a case of in for a penny, in for a pound.

Right from the start, however, the DHSS did not seek the involvement of the Inland Revenue or the Treasury; there was no attempt to integrate the tax and benefits systems, although the Green Paper mentioned this as a possibility as taxation and benefits are computerized in the 1990s.

The main tasks that the DHSS set for itself in the Green Paper were as follows:

(1) to make the benefits system simpler,
(2) to target benefits more accurately upon those in greatest need,
(3) to remove the worst features of the poverty and unemployment traps.

In December 1985 the Green Paper was followed by a White Paper (Cmnd 9691) which broadly adhered to the original proposals. However, instead of abolishing SERPS, the government plans to reduce pension benefits for those retiring after 2001. In this chapter, we describe the budget-line implications of the new Social Security system proposed in the White Paper. Our presentation parallels that of Chapters 1 and 2. We begin by describing the theoretical mechanisms that are implicit in the new system. This is followed by an empirical analysis based on the National Insurance system effective from October 1985, and rates of benefit published in the White Paper Technical Annex.

Principles of Design

We do not discuss here the White Paper's implications for pensions. Instead, we limit the discussion to the implications of the White Paper for budget lines and associated labour supply incentives.

In summary, the White Paper distinguishes between individuals with and without children. Everybody will be entitled to Income Support (IS) up to 24 hours of work per week. IS will be reduced pound for pound as after-tax earnings increase. Thus IS is essentially the same as SB which it replaces, except levels of IS will depend upon age, with people under 25 receiving less than those over 25 and those under 18 receiving less than those over

18. Also, whereas SB could be received for up to 30 hours of work per week, IS is cut off at 24 hours.

Housing Benefit is to be limited to rent plus 80% of rates (instead of the previous 100%). It is to be tapered away at a constant rate as net income rises above the IS level, irrespective of whether the individual is receiving IS, or not. Because HB is to be based on net rather than gross income, it cannot induce marginal tax rates that exceed 100%, as is presently the case.

After 23 hours of work per week, those without children lose their IS, and can only receive HB. Those with children will be entitled to Family Credit (FC), which will reflect the number of children that the recipient has. The amount of FC will be such that the recipient's net income will exceed the IS level, so that working cannot make people worse off and will improve their net incomes. Thus FC, like FIS, is a form of income 'top-up' and like FIS, it is to be tapered away at a constant rate (70%). This means that additional gross earnings must always raise net disposable income, which in turn implies that the poverty trap has been abolished, except for those on very low rates of pay.

Thus for families and single people without children, the tax-benefit system is broadly unchanged, in the sense that the unemployment trap has not been eradicated, since, as demonstrated below, it is possible to be better off out of work than in work. In contrast, for families with children, Family Credit virtually eradicates the unemployment trap, as well as the poverty trap.

We have voiced our criticisms of the Green Paper elsewhere, (Beenstock and Parker, 1985). In summary these are:

(1) The poverty and unemployment traps should also be abolished for families without children.

(2) The concept of tax credits, upon which Family Credit is based, should be generalized into a negative income tax system. To achieve this, taxes and benefits will have to be integrated under a unified administrative system.

(3) Housing Benefit should not be a separate benefit, just as there is no separate food benefit or transport benefit. Housing Benefit should therefore be absorbed into the Income Support and Family Credit benefits.

(4) For those receiving Housing Benefit and Family Credit, the marginal rate of tax will be 94%. Such 'super-tax' rates are too high. Instead, the maximum marginal tax rate should be 60%, which is in line with present maximum rates of income tax.

On the whole, the proposals step in the right direction, but it is a relatively short and faltering step.

Households without Children

We illustrate the basic principles upon which the new system is designed in Fig. 7.1. This diagram draws upon the budget-line theory proposed in Chapter 1. On the diagram, hours worked by the individual are measured leftwards from *a*, while income and benefits are measured on the vertical axis. From the *am* schedule we read off the gross earnings the individual receives for different hours of work. The shape of *am* therefore reflects a constant hourly wage rate, the lower the wage rate, the flatter is its shape. Since the Social Security proposals wisely relate to net rather than gross income, we can safely abstract from taxation to illustrate the mechanics of the proposals.

If the individual does no work at all, and has no other income, he receives Income Support (IS) of *ab*, depending on age, and so on. He will also receive Housing Benefit (HB), which will be 80% of his rates plus his rent. Thus, if he does no work at all, his benefits are *ac*. The first £5 of his earnings do not affect his benefits and he works *af* hours to earn this amount. Thus, *cd* has the same slope over this range as *am*. As he earns additional

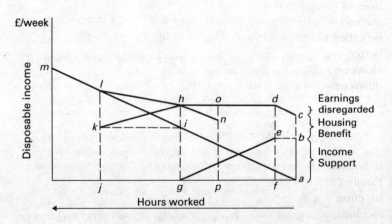

Fig. 7.1 Budget line for the childless

238

money, his IS is reduced pound for pound. After *ag* hours of work, his earnings (*gi*) equal IS plus the disregard, in which case, he comes off IS at this point. The Income Support benefits may be read off the schedule *beg*.

At *g* hours, he continues to receive full HB but this is withdrawn in line with the 0.8 taper, if he works further hours. After *j* hours, his HB has tapered off completely. Thus HB starts at *ih* (=*bc*) at *g* hours, and tapers off to zero at *k*. After *j* hours, he receives no benefits at all. Thus his budget line (the relationship between net income plus benefits, and work) is *acdhlm*. Along *dh*, the marginal tax rate is 100% as under the present system, along *hl* it is 80% and along *lm* it will reflect tax and National Insurance contribution rates.

Income Support cannot be received by those working 24 hours, or more, per week. If *ag* is greater than 23 hours, the analysis in the previous paragraphs is valid. Suppose, however, that *ap* is 24 hours. At *p* hours, IS ceases, in which case *on* of IS is suddenly withdrawn. HB is not affected, therefore the budget line becomes *acdonhlm*. The marginal tax rate exceeds 100% at 24 hours. Depending on the relativity between rates of benefit and rates of pay it is still possible for people to be better off out of work than in work, that is, if 40 hours lies between *p* and *g*.

In summary, and as we illustrate in a later part of this chapter, the new system that has been proposed is not so greatly different from the present system, as far as the general shape of the budget lines of households with no children are concerned. There is still the sort of SB plateau measured in Chapter 2 (except it must now be called the Income Support plateau) and it is still possible to be better off on Income Support than in full-time employment. However, the situation for households with children is rather different.

Households with Children

If households have children, they may be eligible to apply for Family Credit, which, as already mentioned, is explicitly designed to ensure that people cannot be better off unemployed. The mechanisms implied by the interaction of Family Credit (FC) and Housing Benefit (HB) are illustrated in Fig. 7.2, where we discuss

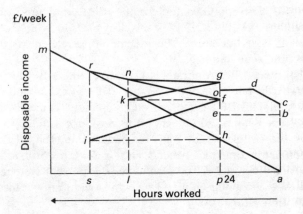

Fig. 7.2 Budget lines for parents

the theoretical construction of budget lines for households with children.

On the diagram, the schedule *am* and *acdo* are comparable to their counterparts in Fig. 7.1. Since *ap* = 24 hours, individuals with children are entitled to Family Credit (FC), if they work beyond *p*. At *p* hours, the individual was earning *ph*, receiving *he* of IS and *eo* (=*bc*) of HB.

Family Credit is designed to include a premium over Income Support. Since IS plus disregards equals *pe*, we assume the premium is equal to *ef*. Thus he receives *hf* of Family Credit when his earnings are *ph* so that his net income before Housing Benefit is *pf*. His HB will be lower because Family Credit is counted as assessable income for HB purposes. The assessable income at 24 hours is *ef* higher than the Income Support level upon which HB is based. So he loses 0.8*ef* of HB. The amount of HB that he gets is *fg* (=*bc* − 0.8*ef*). Therefore, his total income at 24 hours is *pg*, which must exceed *po*, since the loss of HB must be smaller than the FC premium. Accordingly, there is a discrete jump in the budget line, as indicated.

As he works more than 24 hours, his Family Credit tapers off along the *fi* schedule so that at *s* hours, FC is zero. His net income, excluding HB, is read off the *fr* schedule. FC counts as assessable income for HB which tapers off according to the *gk* schedule. At *l* hours, HB is zero. The overall budget line is therefore *acdognrm*.

240

Along *do*, the marginal tax rate is 100%, along *gn* it is 94% (assuming that the FC taper is 0.7), along *nr* it is 70% and along *rm* it reflects tax and National Insurance rates.

It should be stressed that the amount of Family Credit (*hf*) is added to his earnings (*ph*), in which case, there can be no guarantee that as he comes off Income Support and goes on to Family Credit he will become better off. That is, *go* could be negative rather than positive, as in Fig. 7.2. This perverse case will arise if earnings are very low so that when even the maximum amount of Family Credit is added to his earnings it comes to less than the Income Support level. We illustrate such cases below.

If this happens, Family Credit will contain a discount rather than the intended premium over Income Support and it will once more become possible for people to be better off out of work than in work. Therefore we cannot say that Family Credit abolishes the poverty trap or the unemployment trap for people on such low rates of pay that Income Support happens to exceed Family Credit plus earnings. This seems to be an unfortunate, as well as unnecessary design fault in the new architecture. The basic cause of it is that while Income Support is set in absolute terms, Family Credit is simply a supplement to earnings. Accordingly, like FIS, it does not guarantee an absolute minimum income.

Differences between the Old and New Systems

A major aim of the reforms is to alleviate the worst effects of the poverty trap. Hence we turn our attention primarily towards the features of the new system, which are intended to achieve this objective. Three fundamental means-tested benefits are to be restructured. Supplementary Benefit will be rationalized and renamed 'Income Support', Family Income Supplement will be replaced by 'Family Credit' and Housing Benefit will be modified, so that the present six income tapers are reduced to one rent and one rates taper, for incomes above the Income Support level.

Under the new Income Support scheme, the number of 'basic scale-rates' will be reduced and distinctions based upon house-holder status and duration of the unemployment spell removed. Instead, there will be a small number of personal allowances, to which entitlement will depend upon marital status and age. Premiums will be added to reflect the additional needs of families with children, lone parents, pensioners, and the sick and disabled.

The 'capital cut-off' point will be increased from £3,000 to £6,000 and a tariff income system reintroduced. If capital exceeds £3,000, the Income Support entitlement will be reduced by £1.00 for every £250 of the excess. The amounts of 'disregarded income' are also to be adjusted. At present, £4 of net earnings is ignored, both for the claimant and partner, with an additional amount for lone parents (half of earnings between £4 and £20). The new disregards will be £15 for the disabled, lone parents, and couples unemployed for 2 years or more. (If both partners work, the couple will be treated as a unit and the disregard will apply to them jointly.) For pensioners, couples unemployed for less than 2 years and single unemployed people, the basic disregard will be £5. However, the current practice of allowing travel-to-work costs against net earnings will not be continued.

Allowances for additional heating and residual housing costs will cease,[1] and it seems likely that additions in respect of mortgage interest payments will also be discontinued, at least for the short-term unemployed. In the first two cases, the intention is to compensate when setting the Income Support levels, but in the latter, the aim is to shift the onus of payment from the state to the individual. It seems that the hope is either to encourage building societies to allow deferred payments, or to encourage personal insurance provision to cover mortgage payments in the event of unemployment. The White Paper mentions the possibility of continuing to make some allowance for mortgage interest, but only during the early stages of a claim.

The full-time work 'exclusion point' will be adjusted from 30 to 24 hours per week, but under the new scheme, Income Support will not be payable if either partner works more than 23 hours. At present, Supplementary Benefit may continue in payment if the claimant's spouse works more than 30 hours per week, providing that total family income including earnings does not exceed the SB entitlement. In common with the present system, Income Support payments will establish entitlement to free school meals and free welfare foods, for those with children. However, unlike FIS, Family Credit will not carry this automatic 'passporting' feature. Instead the children's credits within the scheme will

242

include an amount to reflect the average charge made by local authorities for free school meals. Lastly, people in full-time education will not be permitted to claim Income Support, as is the case with Supplementary Benefit.

A common net income test is to be introduced for Income Support, Housing Benefit and Family Credit, and this is a welcome innovation. It does much to alleviate irregularities under the current system arising from calculations based upon net income for Supplementary Benefit purposes and gross income for Housing Benefit and FIS.

For Housing Benefit, the treatment of wages is slightly different. The disregard for a couple with only one working partner will be £10, rather than the £5 applicable under Income Support. However, those eligible for the £15 Income Support disregard will be allowed the same amount for Housing Benefit. One parent benefit will be disregarded for lone parents, and the Income Support capital rules will be applied in the calculation of HB. Maximum Housing Benefit will comprise full weekly rent, plus 80% of weekly rates. The rent and rates tapers of 60% and 20%, respectively, will come into operation when income rises above the basic Income Support entitlement. Hence, the allowable rent and rates will be reduced by the excess of income over the IS levels, multiplied by the relevant tapers.

Family Credit is very similar in operation to Family Income Supplement which it replaces, except that the definition of full-time employment is changed from 30 to 24 hours per week, to correspond with the Income Support scheme. The basic entitle-ment will be calculated from an adult credit plus age-related credits for children. The illustrative amounts in the White Paper Technical Annex are £29.85 for adults (the same amount applies to couples and lone parents) and the following children's rates: £5.30 for those under 11, £10.30 for 11–15-year-olds, £13.40 for the 16–17 age-group and £19.20 for those aged 18 and over. When taken together with Child Benefit, these credits exceed the children's allowances within Income Support by amounts which are meant to compensate for the discontinuation of free school meals payments. The suggested taper is 70%, and the threshold is set at £48, which equals the Income Support level for couples. Again, one parent benefit is disregarded, and the Income Support earnings disregards and capital rules apply. At 24 hours, total income (less the relevant disregards) is compared with the threshold, and if it is below, the full amount of Family Credit is payable. Once income rises above £48, FC tapers away at the rate of 70% of the excess. Family Credit counts as assessable income for Housing Benefit purposes.

Some Illustrative Simulations

In the rest of the chapter, we put empirical flesh on to the skeletons presented in Figs. 7.1 and 7.2. In particular, we apply the suggested benefit rates to illustrate the budget lines (and their associated incentive effects for labour supply decisions) implied by the new system. All couples aged 18 or over are allowed a basic Income Support of £48 per week. Single people aged 25 or above and lone parents aged 18 and over are allowed £30.60. It is not exactly clear what will happen for couples under 18, but presumably they will be allowed twice the rate for single people under 18. Similarly, there is little information relating to single parents under 18. One can only assume that they also are to be allowed the standard 16–17-year-olds' rate of £18.20. Single people aged 18–24 are allowed £24, which is exactly half the rate for couples. Finally, as with the present system, additions for children within Income Support are £10.10, £15.10 and £18.20, respectively, for those under 11, 11–15 and 16–17. The new family premium has been set at £5.75 and 'lone parents' with a child in full-time non-advanced education, who is treated as dependent, receive an additional £3.45 'lone parents premium'. Rent, rates and wages details relate to East Anglia, but the choice is purely arbitrary and serves only to illustrate the mechanisms of the new scheme. It should also be noted that for most of the simulations, an hours range of 0–50 has been adopted. This is somewhat greater than the length of an average working week, but serves our purposes better by allowing us more opportunity of depicting the expiry points as well as commencements for the various benefits.

'Structural' Implications of the New System

1 Childless Claimants

The first diagram (Fig. 7.3) relates to a married couple with no children. They rent a one-bedroomed local authority flat in East Anglia and pay £11.94 rent and £5.24 per week in rates.[2] They are not entitled to Unemployment Benefit and have no income other than the male's wages (assuming that he is the primary earner), and Income Support. The employer has not contracted out of the State National Insurance system and does not participate in a superannuation scheme.

We have chosen three wage rates to illustrate a range of potential outcomes for this couple.[3] The upper profile results from adoption of the average hourly wage rate for East Anglia (£3.50).[4] In this case, Income Support ceases at 17 hours and Housing Benefit starts to fall at 18 hours. Housing Benefit is payable over the hours range zero to 27, after which net earnings

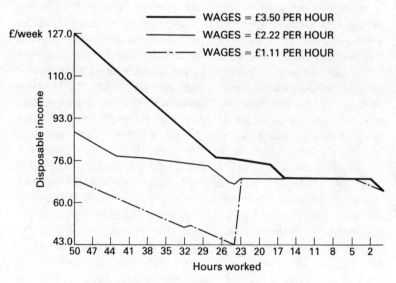

Fig. 7.3 Budget lines for a childless couple

retention is 100%. With this wage rate, Income Support ceases before the end of the plateau, and thereafter, income rises for each additional hour of work. However, with lower wages a very different picture emerges.

The intermediate and lower profiles were produced by wage rates of £2.22 and £1.11, respectively. These rates are exceptionally low, but according to the 1984 New Earnings Survey, 3.8% of 'all males' had wages below £2 per hour. In both cases, total disposable income falls at 24 hours, when Income Support ends. In the former, the reduction is quite small, but in the latter, very pronounced. With wages of £2.22 per hour, Housing Benefit falls to zero at 43 hours, but with the lower wage rate, full payment continues across the whole hours range. The 'kink' at 32 hours on the lower profile results from the commencement of National Insurance contribution payments, and similarly, the slight depression at 41 hours on the centre budget line arises when the percentage contribution rate increases from 7% to 9%. Clearly, the chance of income loss after 24 hours of work is not inconsiderable for those earning low wages, and the gap between the bottom two profiles provides an indication of its magnitude, as wages fall from £2.22 to £1.11.

Figure 7.4 confirms that the same problem may arise for single people. The simulations relate to a 29-year-old person, paying the same rent and rates as in the previous example, and receiving wages of either £2.22 or £1.11. Because the Income Support level for single claimants is lower than for couples, the probability of Income Support entitlement being 'used up' before 24 hours is increased. This occurrence is illustrated by the upper budget line, where payments cease at 17 hours, given wages of £2.22 per hour. Housing Benefit ceases at 31 hours and income then increases progressively by the net wages increment. Again, the kink at 41 hours is caused by the 7% to 9% National Insurance contributions trigger. With the lower wage rate, Income Support ceases at 24 hours and the 'income gap' described in the first example again occurs. By 31 hours, income has almost risen to the Income Support level again, when the commencement of NI contributions creates a further depression. Housing Benefit begins to fall at 34 hours, and continues to taper along the remainder of the profile. Finally, a second 'National Insurance hurdle' occurs at 50 hours as the 7% rate comes into effect.

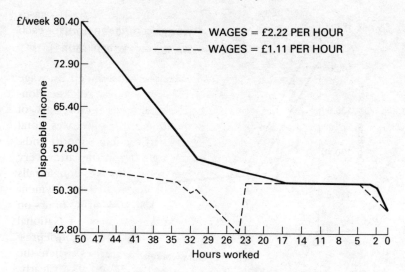

Fig. 7.4 Budget lines for a single person

So, for single people and couples without children earning low wages, it is likely that the poverty and unemployment traps will remain. Furthermore, the new system may intensify these problems, by reducing the extent of 'benefit coverage' for the low paid, as the benefit 'cut-off' point is reduced from 30 to 24 hours.

2   Claimants with Children

Figure 7.5 depicts the budget lines for a married couple with 3 children, aged 4, 8, and 12. The upper profile was produced by a wage rate of £3.70 and the lower by again adopting the average manual worker's wage rate for East Anglia (£3.50 per hour). The family is assumed to pay weekly rent and rates of £17.48 and £5.24, respectively, for a three-bedroomed local authority house. Their only income, in addition to wages, is Child Benefit, and as before, the employer has not 'contracted-out' of the state National Insurance system and does not participate in a superannuation scheme.

At 24 hours, the family is entitled to Family Credit and this effectively increases total disposable income above the Income Support plateau. With the lower wage rate, the new system

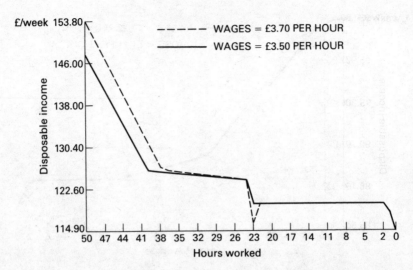

Fig. 7.5 Budget lines for a married couple with 3 children

produces a relatively smooth income profile with a discernible 'step' at 24 hours. Family Credit and Housing Benefit both fall to zero at 40 hours. The upper profile reveals an undesirable feature of the new scheme. Given a wage rate which is twenty pence higher (£3.70), Income Support ceases at 23 hours, and consequently free school meals (and other passported benefits) also cease. As a result, an 'income-gap' appears at 23 hours. In this case, Family Credit is payable over hours 24 to 37 and Housing Benefit, similarly, until 37.

In most cases, the Family Credit scheme will probably ensure that (whilst it is payable) claimants with children do not suffer reductions in their total disposable income by working more than 24 hours. Nevertheless, the high implicit marginal tax rates suggest that they cannot enjoy much of an increase either. Furthermore, the possibility of incomes falling below the plateau remains for families with very low wages. This point is recognized in the White Paper:

> only a very few families where the head is working at least 24 hours a week will have net earnings below the threshold (Para 3.70).

This is effectively an admission that the new scheme will do

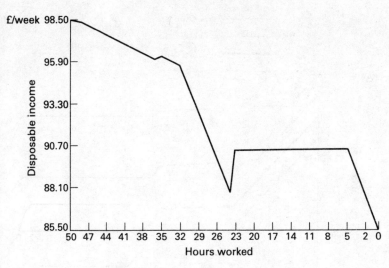

Fig. 7.6 Family Credit and low wages

little to improve incentives for the poorest of the poor. Figure 7.6 illustrates this point specifically. It relates to a married couple with one 4-year-old child, who have identical circumstances to the family described in the previous example, except that wages are set at the extremely low rate of £1 per hour. Despite the payment of Family Credit (which continues along the rest of the profile, from 24 hours, and only begins to taper at 49 hours), total income falls at the end of the Income Support plateau. The steep segment over hours 24–31 reflects the growth in income by the full £1 per hour increase in wages. At 32 hours, Housing Benefit starts to decline, changing the slope of the profile, and at 36 hours National Insurance contributions begin, creating a second 'trap'. In this example, the family are better off when the breadwinner is in full-time employment (i.e. 40 hours) than they would be if he were out of work. The family would only be worse off if he worked less than 27 hours per week. These calculations indicate that the system could allow a recurrence of the unemployment trap. Depending upon the relativities between Income Support, Family Credit and wage rates, it is still clearly possible for families to be worse off in full-time employment. In this sense, the unemployment trap has not been entirely abolished and on some

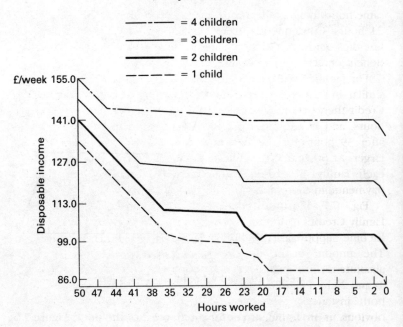

Fig. 7.7 The effect of Family Credit in relation to the number of children

future occasion, it could become a major disincentive to labour supply once more.

Figure 7.7 illustrates the effect of Family Credit, as the number of children increases from 1 to 4. In all cases, the wage rate is set at £3.50[4] and all other family circumstances are identical, except that Child Benefit payments and free school meals allowances rise with the number of children.[5] Rent and rates are again set at £17.48 and £5.24 per week, respectively.

For a family with one 4-year-old child, wages of £3.50 per hour establish entitlement to Family Credit over the hours range 24–35. Income Support for this family ceases after 19 hours and Housing Benefit after 32. The slight levelling out of the profile over hours 22–23 is caused by the Housing Benefit taper, which begins to operate at 22 hours. At the other end of the plateau, a modest incline is noticeable between hours 33 and 35; in other words, after Housing Benefit ceases and until Family Credit ends. With 2 children aged 4 and 8, Family Credit is payable over the

250

same hours range, but in this case, Income Support falls to zero at 21 hours. Consequently, free school meals cease and the budget line dips below the Income Support plateau at that point. Housing Benefit ceases in this instance at 37 hours.

For families with 3 and 4 children, the budget lines are very similar in shape. Income Support ceases at 24 hours and Family Credit then becomes payable. In the former case, it ceases at 40 hours, and in the latter, at 46. Housing Benefit payments cease after 39 hours for the smaller family and after 44 hours for the larger. At 50 hours, the difference in total disposable income for each family is caused by successively higher Child Benefit payments, in increments of £7.

Fig. 7.7 illustrates that with this particular wage rate, Family Credit ensures an increase in total disposable income, over Income Support, as the number of hours worked rises above 24. The amount of Family Credit increases with family size (in absolute terms), and covers a wider range of hours (except for the 1- and 2-child families, where the hours range covered is 24–35 in both instances). However, what is perhaps not immediately obvious, is that the percentage increase in income (above the Income Support plateau) as a result of FC is declining with the number of children. This is evidenced by the progressively smaller 'step' at 24 hours, as we move from the lowest to the uppermost profile. It is caused by the operation of the Family Credit and Housing Benefit tapers.

For example, if we consider a group of families with identical circumstances except for the number of children, the difference in their incomes (excluding means-tested benefits) will simply reflect the additional Child Benefit as the number of children increases. If we also assume that their net earnings place them on the Family Credit threshold, then Family Credit will increase by the premium for an additional child, less 70% of the Child Benefit for that child. Similarly, Housing Benefit will change by 80% of the difference between the Income Support allowance for the child and the additional Child Benefit plus extra Family Credit. Clearly, the size of the step at 24 hours depends upon the number of children and their ages. In this example it declines with an increasing number of children.

The effect of the 94% marginal tax rate, whilst Family Credit and Housing Benefit are payable together, can be seen on the parallel budget line segments after 24 hours, particularly along the top three profiles. Since larger families usually attract higher benefit payments, and many of the unemployed tend to be unskilled and low paid when employed, the outcome of the new scheme does not seem to be very attractive. The 4-child family would need to earn relatively higher wages to be better off in employment. Hence such families face more of a poverty trap, but under the new system they receive less help than smaller families to overcome it. The size of the step is smaller, and when coupled with the flat shape of the budget line after 24 hours, the relative gain from work is particularly unspectacular. The poverty trap may technically have been removed, but it is clear that, in practice, especially for families with many children, the marginal tax rates are extremely high. For them, the poverty trap will apply in practice if not in principle.

A Comparison between the Old and New Systems

Figure 7.8 provides a comparison of budget lines under both systems, for the married couple with 3 children (aged 4, 8, and 12), described in Fig. 7.5. A wage rate of £3.50 per hour was adopted for the two simulations shown here. The most noticeable feature of the budget line under the current system is the 'hump' effect created by Family Income Supplement over hours 30 to 34 and the consequent marginal tax rates in excess of 100% over this range. Turning to the Supplementary Benefit plateau, a number of 'steps' are discernible. These occur when travel-to-work costs are incremented after each completed 8 hours of work.

In this example, Supplementary Benefit ceases at 23 hours and the family then switch to rent and rate rebates, with which they are ostensibly 'better off'. However, local authorities are not legally required to provide free school meals for low-income families, unless they are receiving Supplementary Benefit, or FIS, and for the purposes of this simulation, it has been assumed that the family reside in an area where the local authority has decided against making some discretionary provision. Hence, income falls below the plateau over hours 23 and 24, because free school meals payments have ended with Supplementary Benefit. A further

252

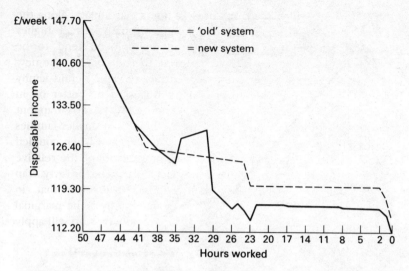

Fig. 7.8 Comparison of budget lines for a married couple with 3 children

income reduction occurs at 26 hours, when 9% National Insurance contributions are triggered. FIS is payable over hours 30 to 34, and thereafter, the rate rebate continues until 38 hours and rent rebate until 41.

Under the new system, Family Credit smooths out the worst of the discontinuities and provides higher incomes over hours 0–29 and 35–38. Payments of FIS generate higher incomes under the old system over hours 30–34 and they are also higher over 39–42. It can be clearly seen that the new scheme creates a flatter profile over hours 24–40. But also incomes are higher over the IS plateau. This reflects the net increase from the changes in disregards, removal of the existing heating addition for a child under 5, and the introduction of the £5.75 family premium. Family Credit and Housing Benefit both eventually cease at 40 hours.

Overall, the new scheme appears to produce a favourable impact, in this case. The example illustrates that, purely on structural grounds, the new system does have potential for improving upon the discontinuities existing under the present scheme, albeit at the price of extremely high marginal tax rates.

The second illustrative case in this section is presented in Fig. 7.9. This relates to the married couple without children,

Work, Welfare and Taxation

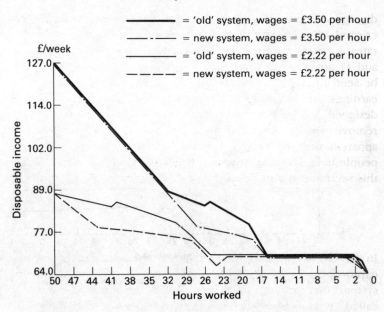

Fig. 7.9 Comparison of budget lines for a childless couple

previously described in Fig. 7.3. Again, they pay rent of £11.94 and rates of £5.24 per week, but the wage rates used in this example were £3.50 and £2.22 per hour. Clearly these wage levels produce similar effects, with the higher rate causing benefit payments to be spread over a narrower range of hours. With earnings of £3.50, Supplementary Benefit falls to zero at 17 hours, and rent/rate rebates cease after 31. Under the new scheme, the Income Support and Housing Benefit 'cut-off' points are 17 and 27 hours respectively. With the lower wage rate, Supplementary Benefit ceases at 26 hours, and the couple then receive rent and rate rebates. The former is still in payment at 50 hours, but the latter ceases after 49. Alternatively, Income Support ends at 23 hours and Housing Benefit at 43, given the proposed system and this lower wage rate.

In general, the old system creates a concave budget line segment (to the origin), whereas the new system produces a convex section. The enclosed areas represent the income loss following introduction of the new scheme, with the magnitude of

254

divergence depending upon the new benefit rates. The problem created by triggering of higher National Insurance contribution rates is clearly visible at 26 hours on the upper budget line pair, and 41 hours on the lower pair. Furthermore, the new system can be seen to create a poverty trap for this childless couple, when earnings are low, which is precisely the effect that a system designed to improve incentives would, presumably, aim to remove. Finally, from the discussion of Figs. 7.3 and 7.4, it is apparent that the budget lines for childless couples and single people have a similar structure, hence the problems described in this section can also be expected to apply to single claimants.

Conclusions

In this chapter we have used a number of specific 'family types' to explore the workings of the government's proposed benefit system. Our primary interest lay with the implications for so-called 'work–leisure' decisions at the level of the individual. Hence we focused more upon structure than on a detailed analysis of gainers and losers, confining our attention to a relatively small number of illustrative cases.

On the basis of this analysis, it appears that the government's stated aim of removing the worst effects of the poverty and unemployment traps could perhaps be achieved by adopting a version of the proposed system. However, there are two significant and interdependent factors which must be considered. The government's initial reluctance to publicize benefit rates in the Green Paper was prompted by a belief that, in the first instance, attention should be directed at the structural features of the proposals. Our discussion of Figs. 7.3 to 7.7 broadly reflected this intention. However, there is a second, equally important aspect, which concerns the comparative impact of the two systems on incomes, and Figs. 7.8 and 7.9 gave an indication of the relative effects.

There can be little argument that the present benefit system is fraught with problems and that irregularities such as the FIS-induced budget line discontinuity are particularly undesirable, if not to say inequitable. However, even if a consensus on structural reform could be secured, the relative income differences under the two systems are likely to provoke the widest criticism. In the final analysis, such differences are the hard facts upon which the system will be judged. On the one hand, it may be argued that replacing an unsatisfactory system with another that alters the mix of people who are relatively worse off, and in the process of doing so, reduces the incomes of some of the poorest members of society, cannot be regarded as an improvement. Alternatively, others may consider that improved incentives and savings on benefits expenditure outweigh any relative income losses.

The approach to reform depends largely upon whether one considers the most important function of the welfare system is to guarantee an adequate level of income maintenance for the low paid and the unemployed, or to reinforce incentives and moderate the cost of benefit payments. Furthermore, the adoption of either viewpoint is closely related to interpretations of the causes of unemployment. If voluntary unemployment is thought to be significant, then smoothing the income profile with the kind of income reduction shown in Fig. 7.9 (wages of £3.50, under the new system) would probably be seen as complementary factors. If on the other hand, unemployment is thought to be largely involuntary, then a smoother income profile, with reduced incomes, cannot do much to improve incentives in an extremely slack job market. In this case, the hardships of those earning very low wages would be increased.

Returning to our assessment of the structural impact of the reforms; the system does appear to have some potential for alleviating the poverty and unemployment traps – but in its present form, this is true only for those with children. For those without, the picture is rather bleak. Once Income Support ceases at 24 hours, there is no equivalent of 'Family Credit' to ensure that incomes increase with additional hours of work. Furthermore, the reduction in the 'full-time work exclusion point' to 24 hours, means that the degree of 'income protection' for the low paid is reduced. For a given wage rate, if there is a negative gap between the benefits plateau and earnings at 30 hours, this will be even greater at 24.

For those who are eligible, Family Credit alleviates the two traps, beyond 24 hours, but as Fig. 7.5 showed, at certain wage rates, Income Support and related 'passported' benefits can cease before this point, causing a fall in income. Also, Fig. 7.6 indicated

256

that even after 24 hours, if wages are extremely low, then total income may fall below the Income Support plateau, despite payments of Family Credit. For the childless, there is nothing to fill the gap at 24 hours and consequently, nothing to stimulate work incentives except desperation created by poverty. On this count, the proposals fail to meet their intended aim. Given that a significant proportion of the unemployed have no children,[6] there is no apparent reason why the incentives problem should be summarily ignored for them. Indeed, it is difficult to imagine why the problem has been left so blatantly without redress. One cynical interpretation could be that incentives are thought to be most effectively improved by adopting different approaches for claimants with children and those without. Single people are more able to withstand hardship than families with children, and so the possibility of an income reduction at 24 hours encourages them to work harder in order to avoid it. Families, on the other hand, have the best interests of their dependants at heart, and so will not chance any income loss from working extra hours. Hence they require some financial inducement. The government initially placed greater emphasis on analysis of the structural aspects of reform, but the adverse structural implications for the childless appear to have been ignored.

There is no apparent reason, other than cost considerations, why a benefit analogous to Family Credit should not be introduced for the childless. The workings of such a benefit are illustrated in Fig. 7.10. The two profiles relate to the married couple with no children, examined above (Fig. 7.3), except that the wage rate has been set at £2.22 per hour. With such low wages, Income Support ceases at 24 hours, under the new proposals, and income falls, as indicated by the lower profile. If a 'credit' was introduced for the childless, the problem could be overcome, within the structural framework of the reforms. This is illustrated by the higher of the two budget lines, over the hours range 24–29. There is no specific Family Credit premium for childless couples and so we have adopted a methodology which allowed us to model the likely effect of FC for these people. The 'credit' in this case was set by adjusting the amount of adult credit so that total income increased at 24 hours by approximately 3%. The 'credit' benefit guarantees a smooth income progression across the unemployment trap area and places the childless in the

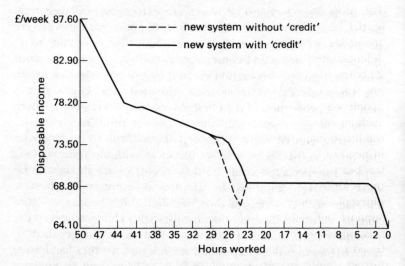

Fig. 7.10 The new system with 'credit' for the childless

same position as Family Credit recipients to benefit from the improved work incentives the new scheme can offer.

Despite the criticisms levelled at the Fowler Green Paper, the proposals should not be rejected out of hand, because certain elements are unsatisfactory. The analysis undertaken above indicates that the new scheme has some potentially good, as well as bad features, and if the former were developed and the latter improved upon, it would (at the least), have *some* chance of success. The greatest difficulty perhaps lies in reconciling the twin aims of improving work incentives, and establishing an adequate level of income maintenance, but also, a careful dovetailing with the National Insurance system is clearly imperative. There is little point in restructuring the benefit system, to alleviate the poverty trap, if the National Insurance system operates to reinforce it. Similarly, the choice of an Income Support 'cut-off' point and the consequent effects upon entitlement to passported benefits, require equally careful treatment, if a poverty trap before 24 hours is to be avoided.

In the final analysis, one is left with the feeling that if the scheme is to work, the architecture requires further development.

The proposals are too narrow in perspective, and only provide partial remedies. Family Credit helps to remove some of the anomalies inherent in the present system, but as we have demonstrated above, other problems arise, both before and after 24 hours of work. Although the number of families with extremely low wages is likely to be small, the fact remains that some of these people will still face the possibility of being worse off in work. Such an anomaly suggests that the aim is to bolster incentives for the broad majority rather than to ensure that those who are most in need of help receive it. Furthermore, a great deal of emphasis has been placed upon simplifying the benefits system, as part of the reforms package. But having said this, we are still left with different income disregards for Housing Benefit and Income Support purposes. In addition, the former will be calculated in relation to Income Support levels, whereas Family Credit will be based upon a fixed threshold. It seems that the opportunity for further simplification and integration of benefits has been missed.

Now that the proposals have passed from Green Paper to White Paper status (despite widespread hostility), it is likely that they will also proceed through Parliament in largely unexpurgated form. So, far from welcoming a programme of general and effective change, we must instead expect a revised system which improves incentives for some, but ignores them for others. Unfortunately, there is little to be gained from such piecemeal change. In solving one set of problems, it creates others and automatically establishes the need for future reform.

Notes

1 Residual housing costs are included in the calculation of Supplementary Benefits requirements, but only if they are additional items of expenditure, not covered by the 'basic scale-rates', for example, ground rent, service charges, or house insurance.
2 Calculated from details published in the Housing Benefit Review (June 1985). Rent and rates are averages of the ranges quoted for 1983/4. These figures were then adjusted by the change in RPI (Economic Trends, April 1985, All Items index) over April to November 1984 plus the adjustment factor used for the 1985 Housing Benefits uprating (5.8%).
3 All earnings details are taken from the 1984 New Earnings Survey and

have been adjusted by the April to November 1984 change in average earnings (whole economy), taken from Economic Trends, April 1985, Table 40, plus the 7% uprating used for most benefits from November 1985.

4   Average hourly earnings, excluding the effects of overtime, for full-time manual males on adult rates, for East Anglia. From the NES, 1984, Table 12 (A66).

5   Providing, in the latter case, that the children are of school age.

6   Numbers for the unemployed as a whole are not readily available, but according to 'Social Security Statistics' (1984), 58% of the unemployed were in receipt of Supplementary Benefit in 1982 (the latest year for which information was published). Of these 55% were classified as 'householders' and 29% of them were without children. The remaining 45% were primarily non-householders and boarders – for whom a breakdown by dependency category was not published. However, it seems highly likely that the majority of this group would be without children.

8

Conclusions and Overview

Michael Beenstock

In this chapter I will not try to summarize all the contributions to this volume. For the most part they have had the limited but informative objective of describing how the taxation and social security systems in the UK interact to influence labour supply incentives. In doing so we have explained the matter at several levels:

in detail for the year 1982/3
over time for families with children
for pensioners
in relation to government proposals for reform.

Our intention has been to describe rather than prescribe.

On the other hand some chapters may have some prescriptive implications as far as policy is concerned. As far as the 1978 and 1981 Family Expenditure Surveys would permit us to investigate the matter, we could find no clear evidence that people's work patterns are influenced by the system of labour supply incentives that is induced by the tax-benefit system. The results reported in Chapters 4 and 5 did not concur with the hypothesis that the unemployed face severe labour supply disincentives or that those who work long hours, or indeed any hours at all, face favourable labour supply incentives. Does this imply that concern over the 'unemployment' and 'poverty traps' is misplaced? Since nobody's behaviour seems to be affected by these traps does this mean that they are not a matter for public concern? The main purpose of this concluding chapter is to answer 'no' to these and related questions. There are several aspects to this response.

Data Deficiencies

As emphasized in Chapters 4 and 5 there is a fundamental problem in measuring the labour supply incentives that face the unemployed. This has nothing to do with the complexities of the tax-benefit system or the argument that it is dangerous to assume that the public understand its implications for labour supply incentives. We acknowledge this to be a problem but this applies to all members of the public, unemployed or otherwise.

The central data problem is that we simply do not know the wage rates the unemployed might have received had they been employed. In contrast the wage rates of the employed are directly observable. Don Egginton has described how we tried to overcome this problem by imputing the hypothesized wage rates of the unemployed according to rates they might have received in past employment or the wages currently being earned in their claimed lines of employment based on the New Earnings Survey. If these imputed wage rates are too high, as we suspect, we will be understating the labour disincentives of the unemployed in a way that could materially influence our statistical findings. Unfortunately, there is no way around this data impasse.

But the data problems do not end here. Since we have used data from the Family Expenditure Survey we need to be sure that these data are reliable. It is well known that for an uncomfortably large proportion of FES households, expenditure behaviour does not properly match income sources. In some cases expenditure seems absurdly low while in other cases households are spending money they claim not to have. A related problem concerns unemployed households in the FES especially in the light of the finding reported in the *Department of Employment Gazette* for October 1985 that almost one million of the unemployed have other sources of income from employment. This begs the question of how reliable unemployed FES respondents are likely to be. In so far as a proportion of them are engaged in the 'black economy' we will have tried in vain to account for their unemployed status.

Therefore data problems may be preventing us from ascertaining the truth. One interpretation of our results is that incentives do not matter. Another is that they do matter but our observations are invalid. Whatever the interpretation it is rather surprising that there is so little evidence, even of an uncertain nature, in favour of the hypothesis that unemployment reflects the disincentive to work.

Micro and Macro Evidence

To our best knowledge our efforts to see whether the unemployed have been influenced by labour supply incentives represent a new departure in microeconometric investigation. This complements the microeconometric investigations into hours of work supplied and female participation by Brown, Greenhalgh and Blundell among others. It also complements the microeconometric work of Nickell into the duration of unemployment spells in the UK. We therefore cannot compare our own microeconometric results with those of other investigators because none exist.

In contrast there have been a number of macroeconometric investigations into the determination of equilibrium unemployment. These tell a different story from our micro results. For example simulations on several macroeconometric models of the UK economy indicate that changes in social security benefits affect the level of unemployment in the expected direction. These effects are summarized in Table 8.1.

According to the model at Liverpool University a 10% real cut in Unemployment Benefit would reduce unemployment by 342,000 after 4 years, which is approximately equal to a fall in the

Table 8.1 The Effects of a 10% Reduction in Unemployment Benefit

Year	London Business[a] School (unemployment 1000s)	Liverpool[a] University (unemployment 1000s)	City University[b] Business School (unemployment rate %)
1	− 56	−174	−0.14
2	−125	−291	−0.28
3	−159	−337	−0.4
4	−172	−342	−0.48

Sources: a Wallis *et al.*, 1984, p. 32
         b Beenstock and Lewington, 1985

rate of unemployment of 1.3%. In the London Business School and City University Business School models the effects are not so great but they are nevertheless quite large.

We can offer no explanation why the macro results are at odds with the micro results. But the fact that the two sets of results lead to different conclusions is further reason for rejecting the conclusion that our findings in Chapters 4 and 5 imply that the tax-benefit system is not a matter for policy concern. At the same time they cast doubt on the macro findings, or at least they indicate that the macro results are perhaps not as self-evident as we might have supposed.

The Future of Social Security in the UK

Major reviews and reforms of the social security system are understandably few and far between. In the last 150 years the milestones have been:

The Poor Law Reform Act 1832
The Royal Commission on the Poor Laws 1909
The Beveridge Report 1942
The Social Security White Paper 1985.

It is therefore likely that, barring political accidents, the White Paper proposals, described in Chapter 7, will underpin the social security system and labour supply incentives until well into the twenty-first century. Between now and then only minor tinkering with the new social security system is likely.

We shall not repeat here our criticisms of the White Paper proposals voiced in the previous chapter. Instead we close this volume by speculating about the tensions that may bear upon the new system in the years to come and about the evolution of the social security system in the next century. In doing so a very broad historical overview is taken dating back to the Elizabethan Poor Laws.

In the long and involved history of the social security system several conflicts have been apparent. First, there has been the conflict concerning 'less eligibility'. The Elizabethan Poor Laws originally intended to prevent destitution by supplying relief in such a way that beneficiaries would not be better off than those who were just above the margins of poverty. Poor Law relief had to be a last resort to avoid starvation and death, hence the harsh conditions under which relief was to be administered. If relief had been an easy option it was feared that too many people would succumb to moral hazard and take advantage of it.

But it was a fine line to draw between death and destitution and life on the Poor Law. Very often self-pride prevented people from submitting to the humiliations of the Poor Law or the destitute slipped through the net. The forces of human compassion tended to soften the harsh edges of the Poor Laws by making the conditions for eligibility less stringent and by making reliefs more generous. Society simply could not live with its own conscience. Thus by 1800 the Poor Law system had evolved into a relatively soft option with index-linked benefits under the Speenhamland system. Labour supply incentives were eroded and the cost of relief grew enormously.

At this point an anti-relief backlash occurred; society had become irritated by its own generosity. The Poor Law Reform Act of 1832 attempted to turn the clock back two centuries by promoting once more the principle of 'less eligibility'. But the same compassionate forces took over once more and the harsh edges began to soften again. There is an irreconcilable conflict between compassion and concern for self-reliance.

The same conflict has befallen the Beveridge system. At first Beveridge wanted to distinguish between the more generous benefits received by those who had paid their contributions and the less generous ones available on National Assistance. But over time the two types of benefits became blurred. This was as true during the interwar years as it was for the postwar period. Society has found it too difficult to live with its conscience, has been easy prey for the poverty lobby but has then objected to its own generosity. And so the merry-go-round goes on and on.

There has also been a separate, but related, 'social insurance' conflict which is a child of the twentieth century. This is because it was not until the Minority Report of the Royal Commission on the Poor Laws (1909) that social insurance was introduced into Britain. Indeed Beveridge was a research assistant to the Webbs while the Minority Report was prepared. Beveridge wanted the social insurance fund to be actuarily sound in the sense that benefits would be properly funded through contributions paid by policy holders. If the risks being insured increased premiums would have to be raised. In practice the strict insurance principles under which the social insurance fund was supposed to operate broke down through political pressure especially in terms of insurance against unemployment. Once the insured unemployed had consumed their benefit entitlement political pressure developed to relax strict actuarial principles so that uncovenanted benefits could be made available instead. In this way Unemployment Benefit became increasingly funded through general taxation rather than through the returns of funded contributions. Indeed National Insurance contributions have long since degenerated into *de facto* taxes and the concept of social insurance has been allowed to wither.

The inherent conflict with social insurance lies in the fact that in times of high risk political pressures undermine the actuarial soundness of the social insurance fund. In this way social insurance tends to self-destruct. The same forces do not apply to private insurance arrangements. If, for example, accident rates increase insurance premiums tend to rise while the policy holder suffers if he is under-insured. The actuarial integrity of private insurance arrangements is inviolate.

In many respects the White Paper tries to resolve both of these conflicts. It resolves the social insurance conflict by abandoning it in essence if not in name. Although National Insurance contributions are to remain they are no more than *de facto* taxes and do not purchase insurance benefits to which there would otherwise be no entitlement. In practice social security benefits will be funded through general taxation. In this sense Beveridge has been abandoned. For the time being it has resolved the 'less eligibility' conflict by reducing benefits to the young unemployed in favour of families with children. But no doubt it is only a matter of time before the compassion–revulsion merry-go-round revolves once more. This conflict is endemic to human nature.

Most probably, as people get richer over time and as the absolute poverty of the worst-off groups diminishes this conflict will decline in importance. The poor in the time of Elizabeth I bear no comparison to the poor in the time of Elizabeth II. Likewise the poor in the reign of William IV will bear little resemblance to their counterparts under William V. Viewed in this broader historical perspective destitution is a passing phenomenon that is bound to be eclipsed in time by the inexorable forces of economic growth. There will therefore be less need for the social security system to prevent mass poverty, as has been the case over the last few centuries. If society contained no absolute poverty there would most probably be no inherent need for social security; without poverty there would have been no Poor Laws.

But there would still be a demand for insurance against contingencies such as sickness, unemployment and longevity. However, these demands could be satisfied privately rather than through social insurance arrangements. Beenstock and Brasse (1986) have proposed a scheme for unemployment insurance in which risks are actuarily priced and are appropriately differentiated. Schemes such as this are radical alternatives to the social insurance principles to which the White Paper proposals pay lip service.

As Britain becomes increasingly opulent the public are likely to demand better insurance arrangements for themselves as the spectre of mass poverty becomes a relic of the past. If the social security system will not deliver these arrangements private markets will begin to mushroom instead. My own expectation is that the social security reforms of the 1980s will go down in history as the last in a line of reforms that stretch back to the Poor Laws of 1601. The watershed will now have to wait until the next round of reforms in the twenty-first century. With a bit of imagination this revolution could have occurred in the 1980s.

References

Adler, M. and Du Feu, D. (1973), 'Welfare benefits project final report' (University of Edinburgh: Department of Social Administration), November.

Adler, M. and Du Feu, D. (1977), 'Technical solutions to social problems?: some implications of a computer-based welfare benefits information system', *Journal of Social Policy*, vol. 6, no. 4, pp. 431–47.

Amemiya, T. (1981), 'Qualitative response models: a survey', *Journal of Economic Literature*, December, pp. 1483–536.

Ashworth, J. S. and Ulph, D. T. (1981), 'Estimating labour supply with piecewise linear budget constraints' in C. V. Brown (ed.) *Taxation and Labour Supply* (London: Allen & Unwin), pp. 53–68.

Atkinson, A. B. (1975), *The Economics of Inequality* (Oxford: Clarendon Press).

Atkinson, A. B. (1984), 'Review of the UK social security system', evidence to the National Consumer Council, March.

Atkinson, A. B., Gomulka, J., Micklewright, J. and Rau, N. (1984), 'Unemployment benefit, duration and incentives in Britain', *Journal of Public Economics*, vol. 23, pp. 3–26.

Atkinson, A. B. and Sutherland, H. (1983), 'Hypothetical families in the family expenditure survey 1980', SSRC Programme Research Note 1, (London: London School of Economics).

Atkinson, A. B. and Micklewright, J. (1983), 'On the reliability of income data in the family expenditure survey 1970–77', *Journal of the Royal Statistical Society – A*, vol. 146, pp. 33–61.

Barr, N. (1975), 'Negative income taxation and the redistribution of income', *Oxford Bulletin of Statistics*, vol. 37, no. 1.

Beenstock, M. and Brasse, V. (1986), *Insurance for Unemployment*, (London: Allen & Unwin).

Beenstock, M. and Lewington, P. (1985), 'Macroeconomic policy and aggregate supply', (London: City University Business School), mimeo.

Beenstock, M. and Parker, M. (1985), 'Abolish the poverty trap', *Economic Affairs*, vol. 6, no. 1, October–November.

Bindoff, S. T. (1950), *Tudor England* (Harmondsworth: Penguin).

Blundell, R. W., Meghir, C., Symons, E. and Walker, I. (1984), 'On the reform of the taxation of husband and wife: are incentives important?', *Fiscal Studies*, November.

Bradshaw, J. (1980), *Equity and Family Incomes: An Analysis of Current Tax and Benefit Policy*, Study Commission on the Family, Occasional Paper No. 5 (London), November.

References

Break, G. F. (1957), 'Income taxes and incentives to work: an empirical study', *American Economic Review*, vol. 47, pp. 529–49.

Brenner, M. H. (1979), 'Mortality and the national economy: a review, and the experience of England and Wales 1936–1976', *The Lancet*, vol. 2, pp. 568–73.

Brown, C. V., Levin, E. and Ulph, D. T. (1976), 'Estimates of labour hours supplied by married male workers in Great Britain', *Scottish Journal of Political Economy*, vol. 23, pp. 261–77.

Burtless, G. and Hausman, J. A. (1978), 'The effect of taxation on labor supply – evaluating the Gary negative income tax experiment', *Journal of Political Economy*, vol. 86, pp. 1103–30.

Chapman, A. and Knight, R. (1953), *Wages and Salaries in the United Kingdom 1920–1938* (Cambridge: Cambridge University Press).

Checkland, S. G. and Checkland, E. O. A. (eds.) (1974), *The Poor Law Report of 1834* (Harmondsworth: Penguin).

Child Poverty Action Group (1982), *Submission to the Enquiry by the Sub-Committee into the Structure of Personal Taxation and Income Support*, April.

Creedy, J. (1982), *State Pensions in Britain* (Cambridge: Cambridge University Press for the National Institute of Economic and Social Research).

Cullingworth, J. B. (1979), *Essays on Housing Policy, the British Scene* (London: Allen & Unwin).

Davies, D., Minford, P. and Sprague, A. (1983), 'The IFS position on unemployment benefits', *Fiscal Studies*, vol. 4, no. 1, March, pp. 66–73.

Deacon, A. and Bradshaw, J. (1983), *Reserved for the Poor – The Means Test in British Social Policy* (Oxford: Basil Blackwell and Martin Robertson).

Department of Employment (1971), *British Labour Statistics Historical Abstract 1886–1968* (London: HMSO).

Department of Health and Social Security (1985), 'Reform of social security – programme for change', vol. 2, Cmnd. 9518 (London: HMSO), June.

Department of Health and Social Security (1985), 'Reform of social security – programme for action', Cmnd. 9691 (London: HMSO), December.

Department of Health and Social Security (1985), 'Reform of social security – technical annex' (London: HMSO), December.

Department of Health and Social Security (1985), 'Housing benefit review – report of the review team', Cmnd. 9520 (London: HMSO), June.

Dilnot, A. W., Kay, J. A. and Morris, C. N. (1984), *The Reform of Social Security* (Oxford: Clarendon Press).

Fields, D. B. and Stanbury, W. T. (1971), 'Income taxes and incentives to work: some additional empirical evidence', *American Economic Review*, vol. 61, pp. 435–43.

Goldberger, A. S. (1964), *Econometric Theory* (New York: Wiley).

Greenhalgh, C. (1980), 'Participation and hours of work for married women in Great Britain', *Oxford Economic Papers*, July, pp. 296–318.

Hall, R. E. (1973), 'Wages, income and hours of work in the US', in C. G. Cain and H. W. Watts (eds.) *Income Maintenance and Labor Supply* (Brighton: Markham House Press).

Harrigan, R. H., Neal, D. G. and Race, D. M. (1977), 'A system for the calculation of apparent entitlement to a range of welfare benefits', mimeo, Operational Research Unit (Health and Social Security), Department of Applied Statistics, University of Reading.

HMSO (1972), 'Proposals for a tax-credit system', Cmnd. 5116 (London: HMSO).

Holden, K. and Peel, D. A. (1979), 'The determinants of the unemployment rate: some empirical evidence', *Statistician*, vol. 28, no. 2, pp. 101–7.

Jordan, W. K. (1959), *Philanthropy in England 1480–1660* (London: Greenwood Press).

Kay, J. A., Morris, C. N. and Warren, N. A. (1980), 'Tax, benefits and the incentive to seek work', *Fiscal Studies*, November.

Kemsley, W. F. F., Redpath, R. U. and Holmes, M. (1980), *Family Expenditure Survey Handbook* (London: HMSO).

Layard, P. R. W. (1982), *More Jobs, Less Inflation – The Case for a Counter-Inflation Tax* (London: Grant McIntyre).

Layard, P. R. W. and Nickell, S. J. (1985), 'The causes of British unemployment', *National Institute Economic Review*, February.

Legg, C. and Brion, M. (n.d.), 'The administration of the rent rebate and rent allowance schemes' (Department of the Environment, Welsh Office).

Marshall, J. D. (1968), *The Old Poor Law 1795–1834* (London: Macmillan).

Matthews, K G. P. (1982), 'Unemployment in inter-war Britain: an equilibrium approach', mimeo, Catholic University of Louvain Centre for Economic Studies.

Minford, A. P. L. (1984), 'State expenditure: a study in waste', *Economic Affairs*, vol. 4, no. 3, April–June.

Minford, A. P. L., Davies, D. H., Peel, D. and Sprague, A. (1983), *Unemployment: Cause and Cure* (Oxford: Martin Robertson).

Morris, C., and Dilnot, A. W. (1984), 'Modelling replacement rates', IFS Working Paper, no. 40.

Nevitt, W. A. (1966), *Housing, Taxation and Subsidies*, (London: Nelson).

Nickell, S. J. (1979a), 'Education and lifetime patterns of unemployment', *Journal of Political Economy*, vol. 87, no. 5, pt. 2, pp. S117–31.

Nickell, S. J. (1979b), 'The effects of unemployment and related benefits on the duration of unemployment', *Economic Journal*, 89, pp. 34–49.

Office of Population Censuses and Surveys (1975), *Census 1971: Report on Economic Activity Part III* (London: HMSO).

Office of Population Censuses and Surveys (1984), *Census 1981: Report on Economic Activity* (London: HMSO).

References

O'Higgins, M. (1984), 'Computerizing the social security system: an operational strategy in lieu of a policy strategy', *Public Administration*, vol. 62, no. 2, pp. 201–10.

Parker, H. (1982), 'The moral hazard of social benefits,' Research Monograph 37 (London: Institute of Economic Affairs).

Parker, H. (1984), 'Action on welfare – reform of personal income taxation and social security', The Social Affairs Unit, Research Report 4 (London).

Pindyck, R. S., and Rubinfeld, D. L. (1976), *Econometric Models and Business Forecasts* (New York: McGraw-Hill).

Plant, M. W. (1984), 'An empirical analysis of welfare dependence', *The American Economic Review*, September, pp. 673–84.

Pollard, S. (1969), *The Development of the British Economy 1914–1967*, second edition (London: Edward Arnold).

Quinn, J. F. (1977), 'Microeconomic determinants of early retirement: a cross-sectional view of white married men', *Journal of Human Resources*, vol. 12, pp. 329–46.

Reform of Social Security (1985), Background Papers, vol. 3, Cmnd. 9519, June.

Rose, M. E. (1972), *The Relief of Poverty 1834–1914* (London: Macmillan).

Royal Commission on the Taxation of Profits and Income (1954), *Second Report*, Cmnd. 9105, Appendix 1, (London: HMSO).

Wales, T. J. and Woodland, A. D. (1979), 'Labour supply and progressive taxes', *Review of Economic Studies*, vol. 46, pp. 83–95.

Wallis, K. F. *et al.* (1984), *Models of the UK Economy* (Oxford: Oxford University Press).

Zabalza, A. (1983), 'The CES utility function, non-linear budget constraints and labour supply. Results on female participation and hours', *Economic Journal*, June, pp. 312–30.

Zabalza, A. and Piachaud, D. (1981), 'Social security and the elderly: a simulation of policy changes', *Journal of Public Economics*, vol. 15, pp. 145–69.

Zabalza, A., Pissarides, C. and Barton, M. (1980), 'Social security and the choice between full-time work, part-time work and retirement', *Journal of Public Economics*, vol. 14, pp. 245–76.

271

Index